CIRCULAR WALKS
ALONG THE
PENNINE WAY

CIRCULAR WALKS
ALONG THE
PENNINE WAY

KEVIN DONKIN

FRANCES LINCOLN LIMITED
PUBLISHERS

Frances Lincoln Ltd
4 Torriano Mews
Torriano Avenue
London NW5 2RZ
www.franceslincoln.com

Circular Walks Along the Pennine Way

First Frances Lincoln edition 2006.

A catalogue record for this book is
available from the British Library.

Printed and bound in China
by Leo Paper Products Ltd.

ISBN 10: 0-7112-2665-2
ISBN 13: 978-0-7112-2665-4

2 4 6 8 9 7 5 3 1

CONTENTS

Introduction 6

THE CHEVIOT HILLS 21
*The Border Ridge 26 • The Cheviot 30 • Windy Gyle 36 • Beefstand Hill 41
Upper Coquetdale 45 • Upper Redesdale 50*

NORTH TYNEDALE 56
*The Border Forest 61 • Hareshaw and Thoughend Commons 66
Wark and Shitlington Commons 71 • Wark Forest 77*

SOUTH TYNEDALE 82
*Hadrian's Wall – East Crags 89 • Hadrian's Wall – Central Crags 95
Hadrian's Wall – West Crags 100 • Hartleyburn and Thirlwall
Commons 106 • River South Tyne – Slaggyford 112 • River South Tyne –
Alston 117 River South Tyne – Garrigill 122*

NORTH PENNINES 127
*The High Fells 133 • Cross Fell 139 • Knock Fell 143 • High Cup Nick 148
Maize Beck 153 • Widdybank Fell 158*

TEESDALE 163
*Upper Teesdale 170 • Baldersdale and Lunedale 176 • Cotherstone Moor 182
Bowes Moor 188*

CENTRAL PENNINES 193
*Stonesdale Moor 200 • Upper Swaledale 205 • Great Shunner Fell 210 Upper
Wensleydale 216 • Cam Fell 221 • Upper Ribblesdale 226
Pen-y-ghent 232 • Fountains Fell 238*

AIREDALE 244
*Malhamdale 250 • Upper Airedale 256 • Leeds & Liverpool Canal 262
Elslack Moor 267*

SOUTH PENNINES 273
*Ickornshaw Moor 280 • Withins Height 287 • Upper Calderdale 293
Stoodley Pike 301 • Cragg Vale 306 • Millstone Edge and Blackstone Edge 313*

DARK PEAK 321
*Black Hill – Wessenden Moor 325 • Black Hill – Upper Longdendale 330
Bleaklow – Old Glossop 336 • Black Ashop Moor 343 • Kinder Scout –
Hayfield 347 • Kinder Scout – Edale 353*

Appendix 359
Select Bibliography 362
Index 363

INTRODUCTION

Stop and consider God's wondrous works! (Job 37:14)

Whilst many guidebooks have been written for long-distance walkers planning to walk the Pennine Way, this is the first time the route has been made available to day-walkers. Since most people are unable to complete a long-distance walk of the magnitude of the Pennine Way, the aim is to make Britain's premier National Trail accessible to those of average ability, breaking it down into manageable sections and combining these with the best possible return routes to create enjoyable circular walks.

The walks encompass many important features missed by the official route, so they not only cover the whole of the Pennine Way, but also set the route within its context, providing an in-depth experience of the landscape and heritage of the Pennines. Where the Pennine Way merely passes through areas, this collection offers an opportunity to really get to know them. Moreover, all variations on the route are covered, including some that are no longer officially recognised.

Completing the Pennine Way in one go can mean enduring a lot of miserable weather and missing some of the best views. For example, it is possible to traverse the whole of the border ridge in zero visibility – hardly doing this section of the route justice. In contrast, undertaking the route as a series of circular walks spread over months or even years allows fine weather days to be selected, so even those who have already completed the Pennine Way might appreciate the opportunity to retread sections that were spoiled by poor weather.

Whatever the particular motivation for undertaking the circular walks in this collection, it will give a real sense of purpose to your hiking. You can set about ticking off the fifty walks, sure in the knowledge that by the finish you will not only have covered the whole of the Pennine Way, but you will have gained a deeper appreciation of this wonderful part of the English countryside.

The young River Swale, near Muker.

INTRODUCTION

The walks included in this guidebook were adopted by the Countryside Agency for its 40th anniversary celebration of the Pennine Way, with an event entitled 'Walk the Way in a Day' held on 24 April 2005. Members of the public were invited to register for an individual walk, with the whole route being covered by different groups and individuals. All of the walks have now been brought together in this collection, and are available for everyone to enjoy.

The Pennines

The Pennines are appropriately known as England's 'backbone', taking the form of a broad ridge about 135 miles (217 kilometres) long, running roughly north–south from Haltwhistle in Northumberland to Ashbourne in Derbyshire. They are composed almost entirely of sedimentary rocks of Carboniferous age – limestone, sandstone and shale – laid down in alternating layers. Uplifting and faulting tilted the whole system from west to east, before ice and water fashioned the landscape that is seen today.

Much of the ridge is over 2,000 feet (610 metres) above sea level, although even at its highest point – Cross Fell in the North Pennines – it falls short of the 3,000 feet (914 metres) mark. Moreover, the Pennine fells are not the kind of dramatic peaks found in mountainous areas such as the Lake District. In fact, most are flat-topped, with a stepped profile that is a result of the differential weathering of the various strata of which they are composed.

The Pennines form the main watershed in Northern England, with the principal rivers rising on their flanks and flowing east to the North Sea or west to the Irish Sea. There are several breaches in the ridge, two of which – the Stainmore Pass and the Aire Gap – are synonymous with troughs separating the different fault-blocks that together make up the Pennines (which are thereby conveniently divided into three parts: North Pennines, Central Pennines and South Pennines).

The term 'Pennines' was coined by W.D. Conybeare and W. Phillips (*Outlines of the Geology of England and Wales*, 1822), although the ultimate source is a clever forgery dating from 1747. Charles Bertram, professor of English at Copenhagen University, claimed to have discovered a fourteenth-century work entitled *De*

Statu Britannica, attributed to one Richard of Cirencester, a monk of Westminster Abbey. The subject of the forged manuscript was the geography of Roman Britain, with the country shown as being divided into two halves by the 'Alpes Penina'.

During the early eighteenth century, Daniel Defoe journeyed extensively throughout what was still a wilderness region, recording his adventures for the benefit of his readers. Despite three centuries of progress during which the country's landscape has largely been tamed, the Pennines retain a wild quality, offering a splendid opportunity for the residents of an over-crowded island to escape to a place of great tranquillity.

The Pennine Way

At one time the Pennines were no more than a barrier to east–west communications, an obstacle that generations of engineers sought to overcome with grand projects for the construction of road, canal and rail links. However, they have now gained a recreational role that makes them a destination in their own

The valley of Crowden Great Brook in the Dark Peak.

INTRODUCTION

> The wildest part of the country is full of variety, the most mountainous
> places have their rarities to oblige the curious, and given constant
> employ to the enquiries of a diligent observer, making the passing over
> them more pleasant than the traveller could expect, or than the reader
> perhaps at first sight will think possible.
>
> Daniel Defoe, *A Tour Through the Whole Island of Great Britain*.

right. The Pennine Way was the first of Britain's National Trails. It
was proposed by journalist and rambler Tom Stephenson in a 1935
Daily Herald article, 'Wanted: A Long Green Trail', and was originally to have been known as the 'Jubilee Trail' in commemoration
of King George V's Silver Jubilee.

The route took many years to establish, even after its approval
in 1951, with numerous difficulties encountered in creating the
necessary 70 miles (113 kilometres) of new public rights of way.
Work on the northern section was still not finished when it was
officially opened on 24 April 1965 by F.T. Willey MP, Minister of
Land and Natural Resources, at a gathering of more than two thou-
sand walkers on Malham Moor. However, since then it has become
established as a virtual rite of passage for anyone who is serious
about long-distance walking in the British Isles.

The Pennine Way is probably the most challenging long-distance
footpath in these islands. It involves sustained high-level walking
through remote and potentially inhospitable country, over terrain
that can be difficult or even dangerous. Whilst the route follows
the watershed for much of its length, it is by no means a ridge-walk
in the classic sense. Rather, it weaves about, often running against
the grain of the terrain and encompassing a wide range of different landscape types.

Long-distance walkers normally take two to three weeks to complete the route, which passes through some of England's finest
countryside, including three National Parks (Northumberland,
Yorkshire Dales and Peak District), an Area of Outstanding Natural
Beauty (North Pennines) and a World Heritage Site (Hadrian's Wall).
Only the South Pennines – with the exception of the Peak District
– has no special landscape designation, and this is despite its dis-

tinctive blend of attractive countryside and industrial heritage.

The Pennine Way runs from the village of Edale in the heart of the Derbyshire Peak District to Kirk Yetholm in the Scottish Borders – a total of 268 miles (432 kilometres). In fact, the name is something of a misnomer, since not only does the route ignore the southern tip of the Pennines – the White Peak – but it includes the moors, forests and hills of Northumberland, all the way up to the Scottish border. The Cheviot Hills are thus a key feature of the route, despite being physically disconnected and geologically distinct from the Pennines.

Over the years there have been significant changes to the route, which is now both shorter and easier. As recently as 1989 it was 314 miles (506 kilometres) long, including a number of 'loops'. A survey undertaken at the time showed that a quarter of the route was in urgent need of repair, with the moorland sections having suffered severe erosion. By 1994 most of the damage had been repaired, diversions had been put in place and nearly half of the route was on man-made surfaces.

The improvements are an unfortunate necessity, and reflect the popularity of the route as much as the fragility of the ground over which it passes. Moreover, the methods used recall the stone-flagged pack-horse routes that were once the basis of the trans-portation system in the Pennines, and most of the sandstone flags were themselves reclaimed from abandoned Lancashire cotton mills. After being air-lifted onto the hills by helicopter, the flag-stones are man-handled into position by conservation volunteers.

Improvements such as these have helped make the route more accessible, and on a sunny day it is not uncommon to see families walking along sections that would once have been out-of-bounds to all but the hardiest of hill-walkers. Even those who are not intimidated by the prospect of sinking up to their knees in liquid peat should appreciate the opportunity to focus their attention instead upon the spectacular views. Nevertheless, the route has evolved into something very different to that originally envisaged by Tom Stephenson.

About this Collection

The guide is organised into nine sections, based upon distinct geo-graphical areas, each covered by between four and eight walks:

High Cup Nick in the North Pennines – to many the most spectacular feature on the Pennine Way.

Cheviot Hills (six walks). A remote and unspoiled area of shapely hills separated by deep valleys. Wind-swept ridges offering spectacular views are criss-crossed by old droveways. Much of the area is covered by MoD ranges.

North Tynedale (four walks). A diverse landscape of open moorland, enclosed pasture and sprawling conifer plantations. The remains of the border troubles include numerous fortified structures.

South Tynedale (seven walks). A beautiful valley flanked by open moorland and rugged fells, with small towns and villages strung along the valley floor. Hadrian's Wall snakes along the serrated ridge of the Great Whin Sill.

North Pennines (six walks). A desolate and inhospitable area, cherished as 'England's last wilderness'. The highest of the Pennine fells crown the broad, wind-swept ridge, with a steep western scarp buttressed by conical peaks. Extensive lead-mining remains.

Winter in the North Pennines – the River Tees beneath Falcon Clints.

Teesdale (four walks). Broad moorland ridges flanked by pasture-covered slopes above charming riverside meadows. Spectacular waterfalls marking outcrops of the Great Whin Sill and reservoirs used extensively for recreation.

Central Pennines (eight walks). Steep-sided fells and broad moorland ridges, separating pastoral dales that shelter picturesque villages. Extensive areas of limestone scenery. The area is criss-crossed with green lanes created as Roman roads, monastic ways and pack-horse routes.

Airedale (four walks). A broad valley of gently undulating terrain clad in lush pasture. The valleys of the Aire and the Ribble together form an east–west corridor used by important road, canal and rail routes.

South Pennines (six walks). A Millstone Grit-dominated landscape of moorland plateaux, cut by deep valleys sheltering linear settlements that sprang-up during the industrial revolution. The area features a network of old pack-horse routes.

Hebden Dale in the South Pennines.

Dark Peak (six walks). Rugged moorland plateaux and ridges with steep scarps marked by Millstone Grit outcrops. Extensive areas of blanket bog. A real sense of remoteness, despite the proximity to major conurbations.

This amounts to a total of fifty walks, plus an extra 'bonus' walk in the North Pennines (a return visit to Cross Fell – the highest point in the Pennines – via the dramatic Eden Scarp). These range from 6¾ miles (10¾ kilometres) to 19¼ miles (31 kilometres) and cover a total distance of 662 miles (1,066 kilometres), making for an average length of 13 miles (21 kilometres). More significantly, there is a total of nearly 85,000 feet (26,000 metres) of ascent – equivalent to the world's three highest peaks (Everest, K2 and Kangchenjunga I) stacked one on top of another!

Whilst they are designed to be accessible to people of moderate ability, the walks included in this collection are nonetheless challenging, with some difficult terrain to negotiate. All of the walks are on public rights of way, permissive paths or access land. In some cases there are a number of possible return routes for each section of the Pennine Way. Those presented here have been chosen after a thorough investigation of the alternatives, and should not be abandoned in favour of others that might look better on a map. In fact, where there are good alternatives, these are offered.

The starting point for each walk and the direction in which it should be undertaken have also been carefully selected. As well as identifying locations with parking and other facilities, the aim has been to 'front-load' each walk, getting the harder parts out of the way and, wherever possible, providing a final section that can be

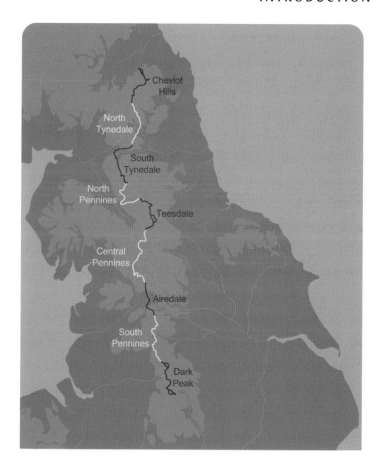

THE PENNINE WAY

 Land over 300 metres

```
0          50          100
|_____|_____|
         km
```

followed in failing daylight. Some of the walks take the form of a figure '8', and so could be split into two shorter routes suitable for winter days or summer afternoons. Others could conceivably be combined to create long, challenging walks for those of advanced ability.

The Pennine Way is traditionally followed north from Edale to Kirk Yetholm. The opposite arrangement is adopted here, although since each walk is self-contained, the sequence in which they are completed is largely irrelevant. Indeed, some will wish to build towards the more challenging walks, saving these for long summer days. Most of the starting points require access to a car, although the need to travel can be minimised by undertaking several walks as part of a holiday, using a single location as a base.

Safety in the Hills

To undertake the walks included in this collection you must be fit, feel reasonably at home in wild country and be able to navigate by compass. In winter conditions some of the routes are suitable only for experienced hill-walkers. A few involve clambering over rocks or

The impressive remains of Milecastle 42 (Cawfields) on Hadrian's Wall.

require a fair head for heights, although this is kept to a minimum.

No estimate is given of the time needed to complete each walk, since this will vary considerably from person to person. Distances are given to the nearest quarter of a mile. Headings are in 'sixteenths' (north, north-north-east, north-east etc.), and are intended only as a general guide. The diagrams are intended to assist in identifying the routes on a proper map, and must not be relied upon for navigation. A system of way-points is employed, linked to the numbered grid references in the route descriptions. To make navigation easier, a highlighter pen can be used to mark each route onto the relevant Ordnance Survey Explorer OL series map.

Once it has been marked-up, the map should be pre-folded and placed in a weather-proof map case or polythene bag. A problem encountered on some of the walks, and one for which there is no adequate solution, is when the route straddles different maps or, worse still, both sides of the same map. Refolding in the field can be difficult in all but the calmest conditions, so it is important to think ahead and make the best use of any shelter. Remember that

Cauldron Snout – an exhilarating scramble on the Pennine Way.

the time to use your map and compass is before you get lost, not after — they will be of little use when you don't know where you are! Also, bear in mind that the countryside is constantly changing, and that maps offer only a snap-shot (this is particularly apparent with regard to conifer plantations).

Before setting out, it is important to check the local weather forecast. However, be aware that general forecasts do not always apply to hilly areas, which tend to generate their own weather. Never press on into bad weather because the forecast suggested it might turn out fine. Instead, try to have an alternative (low-level) walk in reserve. Study the map in advance and be aware of any escape routes. Also, remember to leave details of your starting point, route and anticipated return time with someone reliable.

Each member of the party must be properly equipped. As well as suitable clothing (polyester or other man-made fibres), a waterproof jacket and over-trousers should always be carried. A balaclava and gloves will help to keep you warm in winter, and a sun hat will provide protection during summer. A good pair of boots is

The ruin of an isolated farm building on the moors above South Tynedale.

Required Ordnance Survey Explorer OL (1:25,000) series maps:
Map 1: 'The Peak District – Dark Peak'
Map 2: 'Yorkshire Dales – Southern & Western Areas'
Map 16: 'The Cheviot Hills'
Map 19: 'Howgill Fells & Upper Eden Valley'
Map 21: 'South Pennines'
Map 30: 'Yorkshire Dales – Northern & Central Areas'
Map 31: 'North Pennines, Teesdale & Weardale'
Map 42: 'Kielder Water – Bellingham & Simonside Hills'
Map 43: 'Hadrian's Wall, Haltwhistle & Hexham'

a must, and a spare pair of socks will often come in handy. As well as a map and compass, a whistle and survival bag should be stored away, as should a first-aid kit, emergency food and a good torch. A walking pole can be very useful when climbing steep slopes, crossing rough terrain or fording streams.

Acknowledgments

The invaluable assistance of the following individuals and organisations in the preparation of this guide is gratefully acknowledged:

Heather Scott
Alan Dawson
Richard Bell
Steve Westwood (Countryside Agency)
Mike Baker (Scottish Borders Council)
Captain S. W. Morson (MoD, Otterburn Training Area)
Robert Mayhew (Northumberland National Park Authority)
Tourism Section, Tynedale District Council
Graeme Beresford (Durham County Council)
David Clare (Capita DBS, Cumbria)
Bev Parker (Yorkshire Dales National Park Authority)
Rachel Clifford (Calderdale Metropolitan Borough Council)

And numerous walkers, farmers, villagers and TIC staff who kindly took the time to share their local knowledge.

Disclaimer
No responsibility can be accepted for any injury, loss or damage incurred as a result of following the walks included in this guide.

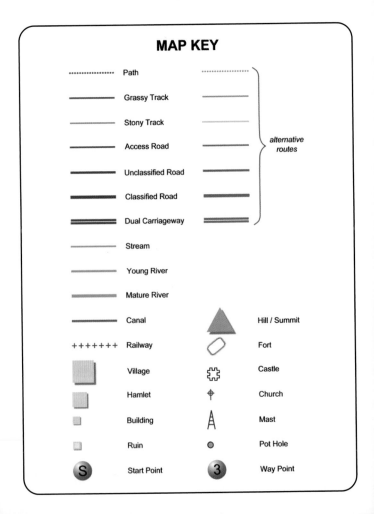

MAP KEY

····················	Path	····················	
————	Grassy Track	————	
————	Stony Track	————	
————	Access Road	————	*alternative routes*
————	Unclassified Road	————	
————	Classified Road	————	
════	Dual Carriageway	════	
————	Stream		
————	Young River		
————	Mature River		
————	Canal		Hill / Summit
++++++	Railway		Fort
	Village		Castle
	Hamlet		Church
	Building		Mast
	Ruin		Pot Hole
S	Start Point	3	Way Point

THE CHEVIOT HILLS

Walk 1: The Border Ridge
Walk 2: The Cheviot
Walk 3: Windy Gyle
Walk 4: Beefstand Hill
Walk 5: Upper Coquetdale
Walk 6: Upper Redesdale

The Hills of the Scottish Border

The Cheviot Hills occupy an area of more than 150 square miles (389 square kilometres) around the Scottish border, stretching from Wooler in the north-east to Newcastleton in the south-west. They are geologically distinct from the Pennines, being a product of volcanic activity during the Devonian period, which deposited a thick layer of andesitic lava. Magma pushed up into the andesite, then cooled below the surface to form the hard granite cores of the highest hills. Around the tops are tors fashioned when the andesite was baked by the magma. The distinctive rounded forms of the hills are a product of their geology, which is resistant to erosion.

The hills are separated by steep-sided, narrow valleys, radiating outward from a central hub around the Cheviot. They are at their most striking towards the end of the year, when patches of golden bracken and drab heather contrast sharply with bleached grass, forming crazy camouflage patterns. To the south of the area is an expanse of rolling moorland – the 'white lands' – where light-coloured grass predominates. Heather is less widespread than in other hilly areas, having fallen victim to over-grazing. The steep hillsides are marked by scree

The Cheviot Hills

The area boasts a half a dozen hills of 2,000 feet (610 metres) or more. As well as the Cheviot (the eponymous head of the group) and Windy Gyle on the border ridge, there is a horseshoe of hills of this size around the Breamish Valley, namely Hedgehope Hill, Comb Fell, Bloodybush Edge and Cushat Law. Others (notably Peel Fell and the Schil) fall a little short of the mark, but by virtue of their prominence are worth a visit.

fields known locally as 'glidders', which traditionally provided material for circular sheepfolds (or 'stells'). Recently there has been some planting of broadleaf species in the sheltered valleys, although most of the tree-cover is provided by conifer plantations.

> The Cheviots rose before me in frowning majesty; not, indeed, with the sublime variety of rock and cliff which characterises mountains of the primary class but huge, round-headed, and clothed with a dark robe of russet, gaining, by their extent and desolate appearance, an influence upon the imagination, as a desert district possessing a character of its own.
> Sir Walter Scott, *Rob Roy*.

People in the Cheviot Hills

The woodland that in prehistoric times covered much of the Cheviot Hills was gradually cleared by human settlers, leaving only scattered remnants. Everywhere there is evidence of hill-top settlements and terraced field systems, such as at the famous Yeavering Bell hill-fort above Kirknewton, recalling a period spanning the Bronze Age and Iron Age when the population of the area was much greater than it is today. Indeed, the population of the Cheviot Hills did not begin to decline until the start of the border troubles.

The ongoing conflict that began with Edward I's invasion of Scotland in 1295 was expressed locally in the feuding of family-clans. During the early years there were set-piece battles involving members of the nobility, triggered by incidents such as illicit hunting and wood gathering in the forests around the border. Later the border troubles degenerated into cross-border raids by small parties of so-called 'moss-troopers'. These were the infamous Border Reivers, who engaged in every kind of villainy imaginable, from the thieving of livestock to kidnapping. In order to establish a degree of order, in 1381 the West, Middle and East Marches were established on either side of the border, each with an appointed Warden. The Union of the Crowns in 1603 heralded the pacification of the area.

The events of the border troubles are recorded in ballads which recall a tradition of story-telling that was later popularised by Sir Walter Scott and others. One of the most famous recounts the story of the Battle of Otterburn (1388), which was fought between

Sir Henry Percy, son of the Duke of Northumberland, and Earl Douglas of Scotland. As peace returned to the area, the practice of driving cattle south from the Tweed Valley to market in England resumed. The border was crossed in several places by important droveways, which avoided the customs posts and turnpikes in the valleys. One of the old crossings is followed by a modern road, with the A68 reaching 1,371 feet (418 metres) as it zigzags over the border at Carter Bar.

Today most of the area is given over to hill-farming, although grouse- and pheasant-shooting are more lucrative activities, recalling the former status of the Cheviot Hills as a hunting chase. The Cheviot sheep no longer have their native hills to themselves, with other breeds having been introduced. There is also cattle-rearing in the sheltered valleys and around the fringes. Herds of black goats roam the hillsides, although these have long been feral. As would be expected, the area is sparsely populated. There are pleasant

Cocklawfoot Farm, where the droveway known as Clennell Street drops into the Bowmont Valley.

THE CHEVIOT HILLS

Cheviot Sheep

'...mo thruaighe ort a thir, tha'n caoraich mhor a' teachd!' ('...woe to thee, oh land, the great sheep is coming!')

The 'great sheep' is the Cheviot breed, which gained infamy as the 'four-footed clansman' when it was used to repopulate the Scottish Highlands in the wake of the clearances. A hardy breed, it is recognised by its white face, lack of horns and Roman snout. It yields a good fleece of short, thick wool which is particularly suitable for the manufacture of clothing – including the superlative Cheviot Tweed. The great sheep can still be seen around its native hills, usually on the relatively sheltered lower slopes (the higher ground being given over to the Scottish Blackface and the more recently introduced Swaledale).

---

villages around the fringes (notably Yetholm, Wooler, Rothbury, Otterburn and Newcastleton), as well as smaller settlements running up the valleys. The upper reaches of the valleys are home only to isolated farmsteads – some of which are now abandoned – while the high ground is entirely devoid of human habitation.

Walking in the Cheviot Hills

This can be an area of exceptional beauty, offering breathtaking views. However, in bad weather it can be a desolate and lonely place, and in winter conditions it is really only suitable for experienced hill-walkers. The Pennine Way starts (or, by tradition, finishes) at the village of Kirk Yetholm in the Scottish Borders, and crosses some difficult terrain during its high-level traverse of the border ridge. Whilst the Cheviot Hills receive only a half the amount of rainfall compared to the Pennines, much of the area is overlain with blanket bog, so any precipitation tends to stand on the surface. Despite the introduction of boardwalk

---

Northumberland National Park

Northumberland National Park was created in 1956, and covers an area of 405 square miles (1,049 square kilometres) between Hadrian's Wall and the Scottish border. It remains one of the least visited – and consequently most unspoiled – of Britain's national parks. Its symbol – the curlew – is a common sight on the moors of Northumberland.

---

and flagstones, the border ridge remains the most gruelling section of the Pennine Way. Unless accommodation can be found in the valleys to north or south – which would itself involve a significant diversion – there is a 26 mile (42 kilometre) non-stop walk from the youth hostel at Byrness to the Border Hotel at Kirk Yetholm.

Otterburn Training Area

Otterburn Training Area was created in 1911. Controversially, it was included in the National Park when this was established in the 1950s. At 89 square miles (230 square kilometres) it is the country's largest military training facility, incorporating the Redesdale, Otterburn and Bellshiels ranges. There are access restrictions on the ranges, although by way of compensation permissive routes have been created between the River Coquet and the Scottish border. There is no live firing in this 'dry' training area, although any suspicious objects should still be avoided. It is common to see squaddies yomping about the hillsides, although it is only the intermittent thump of the big guns on the artillery range that really shatters the calm of this wonderfully remote area. To check firing times, contact Range Control on (01830) 520569 or (0191) 239 4227/4201.

A mountain refuge hut high up on the flanks of the Cheviot.

WALK 1: THE BORDER RIDGE

LENGTH 8½ miles (13¾ kilometres)

ASCENT 1,969 feet (600 metres)

HIGHEST POINT 1,690 feet (515 metres)

MAPS OS Explorer OL Map 16 ('The Cheviot Hills') (East Sheet)

STARTING POINT Kirk Yetholm village centre, Scottish Borders (NT 827 282)

FACILITIES Inn. Public toilets at Town Yetholm.

FEATURES An exhilarating roller-coaster ride along the border ridge, combining alternative high- and low-level Pennine Way routes and offering exceptional views over shapely hills separated by deep valleys.

Kirk Yetholm

Kirk Yetholm and its younger sister, Town Yetholm, are located on either side of Bowmont Water, about 6 miles (10 kilometres) south-east of Kelso. The narrow, winding roads hereabouts are prone to icing, so care is required during winter. There is a lay-by beside the village green, close to the Border Hotel. The latter is famous as the finishing point of the Pennine Way, and serves as a stopover on the St Cuthbert's Way.

The first part of the walk crosses to the valley of Halter Burn before heading up onto the border ridge – a total of 2 miles (3¼ kilometres). Close to the village green, a finger sign shows the Pennine Way heading up a road signed for Halterburn, passing a row of whitewashed cottages that includes the famous Gypsy Palace. The road climbs between lichen-covered walls until, cresting the rise, the view ahead suddenly opens out to reveal a stunning panorama. Heading down into the valley, just over a cattle grid, a finger sign shows the Pennine Way turning left, off the road (1 = NT 839 277).

From here a path is followed south-east, climbing steeply towards the border ridge. Marker posts confirm the route, which initially contours around the bracken-covered slopes of Green Humbleton. This is crowned with an Iron Age hill-fort, the grassy ramparts of which can

Little Egypt

Kirk Yetholm gained the title 'Little Egypt' when the ruling Faa family of Scottish gypsies held court here. As early as 1540, King James V of Scotland signed a treaty with John Faa, the 'lord and earl' of Little Egypt. A cottage known as the Gypsy Palace was the home of the last queen of the Scottish gypsies, Esther Faa Blythe, who died in 1883. Today the gypsies are gone, although a few words from their language are still used by local people.

be seen as height is gained. Parting company with the St Cuthbert's Way, the border ridge is soon reached (2 = NT 853 269).

The Border Ridge

The next part of the walk follows the Pennine Way as it runs along the crest of the ridge for 2¼ miles (3¾ kilometres). A finger sign shows the path turning south, following a drystone wall. Climbing steeply towards a raised col (Whitelaw Nick), the route turns south-east, following a fence towards the top of White Law (3 = NT 857 261).

Although at a modest 1,394 feet (425 metres), the top offers fine views. The prominent hill to the south is the Curr, below which the remains of old settlements can be discerned.

Heading steeply downhill to a saddle, a broad track heads south-south-west, gently climbing a long ridge (Steer Rig) between deep valleys. Returning to a south-east heading, the walk tops out on a short section of made path, with impressive views towards the Cheviot. Over a ladder stile, the Pennine Way diverges from the fence, contouring around the side of Black Hag until arriving at a finger sign marking the point where the alternative high- and low-level routes meet (4 = NT 858 236).

From here the Pennine Way continues along the border ridge towards the Schil (the conical hill in the foreground), although we follow the low-level route back to Kirk Yetholm. On the grassy slopes above is a prominent outcrop known as Corbie Craig ('crow rock'), which is worth visiting before starting the return route. This involves a stiff ascent, although it provides a fine perch upon which to have lunch while admiring the wonderful views.

Halter Burn

Heading west-south-west towards a saddle, a 'there-and-back' visit to the summit of the Curr (1,850 feet/564 metres) might be in order. This involves a significant amount of ascent, but is once again rewarded with fine views. Otherwise, stay on the track as it passes through a gate and starts downhill. The track is cut into the steep, bracken-covered slopes above Curr Burn, heading north-north-west. Arriving at a finger sign beside a gap in a broken wall, switch to a track following the valley of Halter Burn (5 = NT 852 243).

Marker posts confirm the route, which heads north on a track that is generally easy to follow. Arriving at a ruin (Old Halterburnhead), this is flanked by aged sycamore trees and enjoys a beautiful setting in the upper reaches of the remote valley. From here the track swings around to head west-north-west. A finger sign shows the Pennine Way leaving the track and heading down to cross the burn by a foot-bridge (the route having been diverted to avoid Burnhead Farm). Soon a ladder stile leads to a farm access (6 = NT 842 260).

This becomes a tarmac road, which is followed all the way back to Kirk Yetholm. Peniel Revival Centre (a Christian-run retreat, marked on the map as Halterburn) is passed along the way, and bridges provide an opportunity to watch fish darting about in the burn. The road is often frequented by Highland cattle, which stubbornly block the progress of pedestrians and vehicles alike. Passing the point where the road was earlier left (7 = NT 839 277), retrace your steps back to the village.

Old Halterburnhead, the desolate remains of a shepherd's cottage.

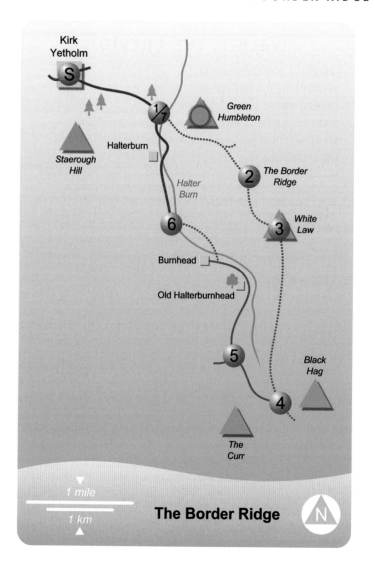

The Border Ridge

Kirk Yetholm
S
1/7
Green Humbleton
Halterburn
Staerough Hill
Halter Burn
The Border Ridge
2
6
White Law
3
Burnhead
Old Halterburnhead
5
Black Hag
4
The Curr

1 mile
1 km

N

WALK 2: THE CHEVIOT

LENGTH 16 miles (26 kilometres)

ASCENT 3,250 feet (990 metres)

HIGHEST POINT 2,674 feet (815 metres)

MAPS OS Explorer OL Map 16 ('The Cheviot Hills') (East Sheet)

STARTING POINT Sourhope Farm, Bowmont Valley (NT 843 201)

FACILITIES None.

FEATURES A challenging hill-walk encompassing both the Schil and the Cheviot, with a dramatic rocky gorge forming the focal point of the wonderful views. Whilst the route crosses some difficult terrain, passage of the notorious Cheviot bog has been improved with flagstones.

Bowmont Valley

The remote starting point is reached by turning off the B6401 at Primsidemill, about 1 mile (1½ kilometres) south of Town Yetholm, then following a narrow road up the Bowmont Valley. After about 6 miles (9¾ kilometres), a short way along a side road signed for Sourhope, a dug-out area provides roadside parking for a few cars.

The first part of the walk follows tracks for 3½ miles (5½ kilometres) up onto the border ridge. Walking past Sourhope Farm, the broad shoulders of the Cheviot can already be seen. Over a bridge, head up a tarmac track towards a fork. Turning left, follow the track as it contours around bracken-covered slopes above

Go sit old Cheviot's crest below,
And pensive mark the lingering snow
In all his scaurs abide,
And slow dissolving from the hill
In many a sightless, soundless rill,
Feed sparkling Bowmont's tide.
    Sir Walter Scott, 'Cheviot'.

Sourhope Farm

Sourhope Farm stands at the head of the Bowmont Valley. There has been a farm here since the fourteenth century, although today it is the location of a research station run by the Macaulay Land Use Research Unit, investigating sustainable hill-farming methods. It also acts as a site for monitoring climate change – part of the Environmental Change Network.

Sourhope Burn, eventually heading north-east. A short way past the access to Auchope Farm, as the track again divides, turn left through a gate (1 = NT 858 215).

Crossing a small stream, the track continues north-east up the valley of Rowhope Burn. Looking up the valley, Black Hag can be identified by the distinctive rock outcrop known as Corbie Craig. As the track passes through a gate in a drystone wall it breaks up, re-emerging as a quad track climbing north-north-west on tussocky grass. As this converges with the Pennine Way at the saddle between Black Hag and the Schil, turn towards the point where a drystone wall is crossed by a ladder stile (2 = NT 861 233).

The Border Ridge

The next part of the walk runs over the Schil before climbing the steep flanks of the Cheviot, a total of 4 miles (6½ kilometres). A finger sign shows the route heading south-east alongside the boundary, crossing boggy ground before climbing steeply. The summit reaches 1,972 feet (601 metres), and is surmounted by a shattered tor of baked andesite offering stunning views (3 = NT 869 223). The path down from the hill follows a fence as it head southeast. As the gradient slackens, the path becomes boggy, so the flagstones are a welcome addition. Arriving at the saddle between the Schil and the Cheviot, to the left is a deep gash in the earth called Red Cribs (4 = NT 874 201).

Continuing east over tussocky grass, the path soon arrives at a mountain refuge hut. A plaque inside the hut records that it was erected in 1988 by volunteers and members of 202 squadron from RAF Boulmer. A short break might be in order, since ahead is one of the most arduous climbs on the Pennine Way, with the route heading east-south-east up beside Hen Hole to Auchope Cairn. At times the path comes quite close to the edge, which in winter is prone to the formation of wind-slab. As the gradient finally starts to slacken, the route zigzags up through a belt of scree to arrive at a groups of cairns. From here a long section of boardwalk provides safe passage of a notorious quagmire as the Pennine Way heads south-east. Crossing a fence stile, a fork is reached (5 = NT 896 194).

Hen Hole

Hen Hole is a dramatic glacial feature on the flanks of the Cheviot. The rocky gorge nestles the headwaters of the College Burn, which tumble down a series of waterfalls known as the Three Sisters. The legendary villain Black Adam was said to have lived in a cave, high up among the crags. Today these are home to peregrine falcons and rare alpine plants — the latter being relics of the last Ice Age.

The Cheviot

A finger sign shows the Pennine Way continuing along the border ridge, and offers the worthwhile option of a 'there-and-back' visit to the summit, 1¼ miles (1¾ kilometres) away. Crossing another fence stile, the path initially heads east-north-east, with flagstones providing safe passage of the treacherous bog. An unflagged section of path leads to Cairn Hill, where a finger sign shows the path heading north-east

The Cheviot

At 2,674 feet (815 metres), the Cheviot stands head-and-shoulders above its neighbours. Its great dome dominates the skyline, and is often shrouded in an ominous bank of cloud. The OS pillar marking the summit sits atop a concrete platform, preventing it from sinking into the ground – as did its two predecessors. Around this is a 50 acre (20 hectare) area of blanket bog, a product of the formation of peat on top of the impermeable granite. This is home to cottongrass, mosses and sedges, while the drier patches show heather, bilberry, crowberry and cloudberry. The rare cloudberry has a distinctive cluster of berries, appearing in late summer and much sought after by grouse. The plateau is flanked by andesite tors and littered with the remains of air crashes.

towards the summit. Passing through a fenced enclosure, the indistinct top is marked by an OS pillar (6 = NT 909 205).

By climbing onto the concrete platform it is possible to espy Lindisfarne and the Farne Islands. There is little opportunity to find a resting place here, so it is re-assuring that this is the half-way point on the walk, and that the remainder is mostly downhill. Ignoring a nearby ladder stile, retrace your steps over Cairn Hill to the Pennine Way. Arriving back at the fork (7 = NT 896 194), the border ridge is rejoined for the next 3 miles (4¾ kilometres).

The path initially heads west-south-west on boardwalk and flagstones. When these fail it becomes necessary to wander from the border fence in search of dry ground. It will be a blessing when this whole section of the route has been flagged, not least since the path gets wider every year. On the way down, look out for an isolated rock outcrop off to the left — the so-called Hanging Stone. Also on the left, beyond a sprawling conifer plantation, are the hills around the head of the Breamish Valley. From Score Head the path runs south-south-west down the broad ridge, passing an OS pillar at King's Seat. The droveway known as Clennell Street is met at the point where it crosses the border ridge between Upper Coquetdale and the Bowmont Valley (8 = NT 871 160).

The Hanging Stone
The Hanging Stone is a 17-feet (6-metre) high needle of rock on the western flanks of the Cheviot. It was supposedly named after an incident in which an unfortunate individual was throttled by the strap of his own backpack when he fell from the rock. At one time the Hanging Stone marked the Scottish border, at the boundary between the Middle and East Marches.

Clennell Street
The Pennine Way continues on towards Windy Gyle, although we follow Clennell Street down Cock Law ridge, 3½ miles (5¾ kilometres) back to the starting point. A finger sign points through a gate, joining a rough track running north-west down a ridge. A sign requests that walkers seek an alternative route during lambing time (April–May), although it is noteworthy that there is a general right of access north of the border. Heading steeply downhill, as the track levels out it passes to the right of one 'bump' on the ridge (The Bank), then to the left of another (White Knowe). Through a gap in a conifer plantation, Cocklawfoot Farm is now just ahead, enjoying the shelter of mature sycamore trees (9 = NT 853 186). Passing through the muddy farmyard, a ford at Kelsocleuch Burn provides an opportunity to clean your boots. From here the starting point is just a short walk along the quiet road.

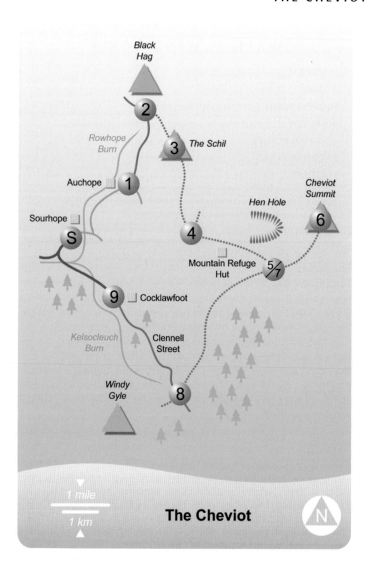

The Cheviot

WALK 3: WINDY GYLE

LENGTH 9¾ miles (15¾ kilometres)

ASCENT 1,686 feet (514 metres)

HIGHEST POINT 2,031 feet (619 metres)

MAPS OS Explorer OL Map 16 ('The Cheviot Hills') (East Sheet)

STARTING POINT Rowhope Burn, Upper Coquetdale (NT 860 114)

FACILITIES Public toilets and inn at Alwinton.

FEATURES An enjoyable hill-walk following droveways and a short section of the border ridge. The views are excellent throughout, but are particularly extensive from the summit of Windy Gyle, which is marked by a Bronze Age burial cairn.

The Street

Turning off the B6341 between Rothbury and Elsdon, follow an unclassified road to Alwinton. The starting point is then 7 miles (11½ kilometres) along a single track road running up the beautiful Coquet Valley. Care is needed on the long, slow drive-in, the road being frequented by sheep and cattle. About 1 mile (1¼ kilometres) past Wedder Leap (Barrowburn) picnic place, at the confluence of Rowhope Burn and the River Coquet, there is a roadside parking area with space for about a dozen cars. During the late eighteenth century this was the remote location of an inn (Slyme Foot) selling illicit whisky.

Alwinton

With a population of just 80, Alwinton (pronounced 'al'inton') is little more than a hamlet, although it does have an inn. This is the Rose & Thistle, where Sir Walter Scott stayed while researching his novel *Rob Roy*. The village hosts the Border Shepherd's Show, held on the second Saturday in October. There are public toilets at the National Park car park, which is a popular starting point for walkers and cyclists heading up Clennell Street.

The first part of the walk follows a droveway for 3¼ miles (5 kilometres) up onto the border ridge. This is The Street, which connects Upper Coquetdale and the Kale Water Valley, and is one of the classic routes in the Cheviot Hills. A finger sign points through a gate to where a quad track heads up the steep, grassy slope at the end of a broad ridge. As the gradient slackens, with the route now heading north-west, a marker post shows a bridleway cutting across the track (1 = NT 850 117).

Continuing straight ahead, the track follows a fence along the crest of the ridge. To the right is the deep valley of Rowhope Burn, to the left that of Carlcroft Burn. Passing to the right of a bump on the ridge (Swineside Law), then dropping to a saddle, the fence is crossed at a kink before the track again heads steeply uphill. The final section, running over Black Braes, is badly rutted. Eventually a finger sign marks the point at which the Pennine Way crosses the track (2 = NT 835 150).

Winter in the Cheviot Hills – Windy Gyle seen from the border ridge.

Windy Gyle

Here we turn off the Street, just short of the crest of the border ridge (the Pennine Way cuts the corner to avoid a mire known as Foul Step). The next part of the walk follows the Pennine Way over Windy Gyle, a total of 2½ miles (4 kilometres). The path initially heads north-east over rough terrain. Crossing a rushy gully at the head of Foulstep Sike, the border fence is met at a star-shaped marker (these identify archaeological remains, and are seen throughout Otterburn Training Area). The gradient stiffens as the route crosses to the Scottish side of the fence, continuing up towards the sprawling cairn that marks the summit (3 = NT 855 152).

> **Windy Gyle**
>
> At 2,031 feet (619 metres), Windy Gyle is over-shadowed by the Cheviot, although it still offers exceptional views. The summit is marked by Russell's Cairn. This is thought to be a Bronze Age burial cairn, although it takes its name from Lord Francis Russell, son-in-law of Sir John Forster, Warden of the Middle March, who was killed near here in 1585 during a Wardens' meeting. Today it is home to an OS pillar and a rough shelter.

This would be a good place to stop for lunch. From the cairn a finger sign shows the Pennine Way heading east-north-east. It is possible to head down on either side of the fence, although the path on the English side is partially flagged (this is joined by following flagstones leading south from the cairn to a stile). On the way down another large cairn is passed, this time surmounted by a star-shaped marker. Eventually the path arrives at the point where Clennell Street crosses the border ridge (4 = NT 871 160).

Clennell Street

It is here that we leave the Pennine Way, following good tracks for 4 miles (6½ kilometres) back to the starting point. Turning onto Clennell Street, this initially heads south-east. Ignoring signed routes running towards the conifer plantation on the left (the first of these being Salter's Road – a droveway and pack-horse route), stay on the track as it swings around to head south. From the head of the valley of Hepden Burn, the track zigzags down the steep,

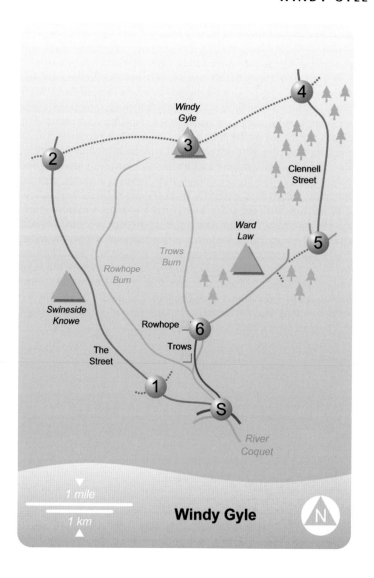

Windy Gyle

bracken-covered slopes of Hazely Law. A finger sign at the bottom shows Clennell Street crossing straight over a hardcore track and continuing on towards Alwinton (5 = NT 875 137).

A short way along the droveway, just before reaching a shed, turn right, joining a track zigzagging down to Hepden Burn. After crossing the stream by a flat bridge (which is sometimes over-washed), a gate leads to a grassy track, heading south-west as it climbs gently out of the gully to arrive at a hardcore track. This is the long access road for Uswayford Farm, and is followed back to the starting point. Ignoring a gate and stile on the left (marking the point at which the Border County Ride leaves our route), stay on the hardcore track as it starts a gradual descent into a long valley.

When the hardcore track swings right to loop around a gully, instead continue straight down the steep slope. Fording a small stream, the track is rejoined. As another track joins from the right, Trows Burn is crossed by a footbridge (6 = NT 855 126). Passing Trows Farm, the track becomes tarmac as it runs beside the busy stream. At Rowhope Farm the stream is crossed by a flat bridge (which again is sometimes over-washed), just before its confluence with Rowhope Burn. From here the access road is followed down the narrow valley back to the starting point.

WALK 4: BEEFSTAND HILL

LENGTH 9¾ miles (15¾ kilometres)

ASCENT 1,499 feet (457 metres)

HIGHEST POINT 1,844 feet (562 metres)

MAPS OS Explorer OL Map 16 ('The Cheviot Hills') (East Sheet)

STARTING POINT Buckham's Bridge car park, Upper Coquetdale (NT 824 107)

FACILITIES Public toilets and inn at Alwinton.

FEATURES The flagged route of the Pennine Way is followed over a series of hills straddling the border ridge (Lamb Hill, Beefstand Hill and Mozie Law), with views that are once again outstanding. Both ascent and descent are by intersecting ridges flanked by deep valleys.

Yearning Law

Buckham's Bridge is 3 miles (5 kilometres) further along the road from the starting point for the previous walk. From the car park, head back down the road a short way until, just before Blindburn Farm, a finger sign on the left marks the start of a bridleway (1 = NT 829 109). This runs 2½ miles (3¾ kilometres) up onto the border ridge, and is one of a number of routes created by the MoD to compensate for the regular closure of paths on its ranges (note that these routes are not marked on the Landranger map).

Passing through a gate, a hardcore track zigzags steeply uphill. This becomes a quad track heading west up the crest of a broad, grassy ridge. Across the deep valley on the right are the steep slopes of Broadside Law. The track swings around to head north-west, climbing less steeply as it crosses tussocky grass, with a few posts providing reassurance. Looking to the north-east, Windy Gyle is prominent. The track skirts the lumpy top of Yearning Law, although this fine promontory would certainly reward a short deviation, providing a viewing platform for the heather-crowned hills that lie ahead.

As the way ahead drops to a broad plain, a confusing plethora of

The steep-sided hills around Blind Burn.

quad tracks criss-cross the area, so keep heading north-north-west. When a marker post indicates a crossroads of routes, continue straight ahead on a track signed for the border ridge. This runs over tussocky grass and passes through the site of an ancient settlement before swinging around to head west. Soon the mountain refuge hut at Yearning Saddle is reached (2 = NT 804 129). This is used as an overnight stopping place by long-distance walkers, and it is worth reading the comments left in the visitors' book. The hut is kindly maintained by the tenants of Blindburn Farm.

The Border Ridge

The next part of the walk follows the Pennine Way for 2½ miles (4¼ kilometres) as it rolls along the border ridge. Initially the path climbs steeply as it heads north-east, following the border fence. The distinctive cairned dome visible to the north of the ridge is the Kip. Soon the OS pillar marking the top of Lamb Hill is reached, and at 1,677 feet (511 metres) the views are unsurprisingly splendid.

From here to Beefstand Hill it is simply a matter of heading north-east alongside the border fence. There is little re-ascent between these bumps on the border ridge. Flagged sections of path provide safe passage of the peaty ground, which is carpeted in heather, bilberry and cottongrass. At 1,844 feet (562 metres), the top of Beefstand Hill is the highest point on the walk, although there is not even a cairn to mark the spot (3 = NT 821 143). Looking to the north, the distinctive form of Hownam Law can be seen, its flat top the site of an Iron Age hill-fort.

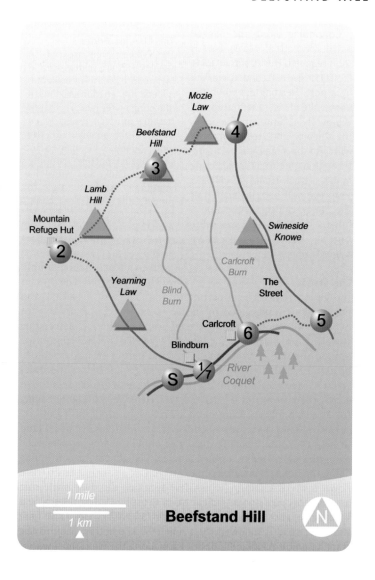

Beefstand Hill

Continuing along the flagged path, the top of Mozie Law is soon reached. This stands at 1,811 feet (552 metres), and is marked by a post. Heading downhill, the view ahead is dominated by Windy Gyle, although the Schil, the Cheviot and Hedgehope Hill will also be recognised. Passing through a gate in an intersecting fence, a track is met (4 = NT 835 150). This will be remembered as The Street, and it is here that a finger sign shows our route turning right, heading down towards Upper Coquetdale.

The Street

The return route retreads part of the previous walk, albeit in the opposite direction. The track heads south-south-east, descending steeply from Black Braes towards a saddle, before contouring around the side of Swineside Law. From here it swings around to head south-east along the broad, grassy ridge. Just before The Street starts its steep descent into Upper Coquetdale, a marker post shows a crossroads of routes (5 = NT 850 117). Here we turn right, leaving the Street to follow a faint path down towards Carlcroft Farm.

This initially runs over tussocky grass, with marker posts confirming the route. Heading steeply downhill towards a waymarked gate, the path hooks around Stogie's Cleugh before continuing along the bracken-covered slope. Arriving at a gate in a fence, turn down towards the farm, which stands beside the river, sheltering among scots pine and broadleaf trees. Crossing Carlcroft Burn by a footbridge, pass to the right of the farm (6 = NT 838 116). From here the quiet road is followed for 1 mile (1½ kilometres) back to the starting point, passing Blindburn Farm along the way. Small waterfalls in the course of the river complete a charming scene.

The Cheviot Adder

The Cheviot Hills are rich in species that are seldom seen in less remote areas. For example, adders are encountered with alarming frequency, often basking on even well-trodden paths. This member of the viper family is recognised by the zigzag pattern running down its back, and whilst its venom is seldom fatal to humans (its usual prey being small mammals), it should nonetheless be given a wide berth. They are most commonly seen when newly awoken from hibernation, when they are still sluggish.

WALK 5: UPPER COQUETDALE

LENGTH 9¼ miles (15 kilometres)

ASCENT 1,148 feet (350 metres)

HIGHEST POINT 1,575 feet (480 metres)

MAPS OS Explorer OL Map 16 ('The Cheviot Hills') (East & West Sheets)

STARTING POINT Chew Green parking area, Upper Coquetdale (NT 794 085)

FACILITIES Public toilets and inn at Alwinton.

FEATURES The course of a Roman road is followed from the marching camp at Chew Green, at the head of Upper Coquetdale. The return route runs down a narrow valley beside a lively stream, then along a quiet road connecting isolated farmsteads.

Dere Street

The starting point is close to the Roman marching camp at Chew Green, at the head of Upper Coquetdale. As an alternative to following the single track road up the valley, a shorter drive-in leaves the A68 in Upper Redesdale and follows MoD roads (Cottonshope Road and Dere Street) over the Redesdale artillery range. However, the availability of this route must be confirmed in advance. Significantly, the starting point is 1,280 feet (390 metres) above sea level, and launches straight onto the border ridge.

The first part of the walk follows the Pennine Way along the border ridge for 4 miles (6½ kilometres). Following a stony track towards the camp, a finger sign shows the route turning right, heading north-west along the course of Dere Street, beside the grassy ramparts (an inspection of the remains might be in order). Soon a marker post shows the route turning east, crossing a gully (Chew Sike) before swinging around to head north along a rough track. As the border fence converges from the left, a finger sign marks the point at which we part company with the Border County Ride (1 = NT 791 096).

At this point a 'there and back' visit to the nearby summit of

Chew Green

Chew Green provided an over-night stopping place for Roman soldiers travelling along Dere Street. There were actually several camps and small forts at this location, built one-on-top of another. This left the confusion of remains seen today, with intersecting ramparts etched into the hillside. It is noteworthy that the site is surrounded by hills – occupying the high ground being evidently less important than factors such as the availability of flat land and a reliable water supply. During the sixteenth century the site was a meeting place for the Wardens of the Middle Marches. By the eighteenth century it was a resting place for drovers, with the section of Dere Street running over the border ridge being employed as a droveway.

Brownhart Law is possible, with a permissive path then a quad track following the border fence. This involves little ascent, and with the summit at 1,667 feet (508 metres) the views are unsurprisingly splendid. Returning to the Pennine Way, continue north along the rough track. A fence stile on the left provides access to the site of a Roman signal station, although the earthworks are lost beneath the heather. Arriving at a gate (2 = NT 788 105), a finger sign shows Dere Street heading down towards Towford in the Kale Water Valley, although we continue along the border ridge.

Dere Street

Dere Street was constructed around AD 80, under the governorship of Gnaeus Julius Agricola, to connect Eburacum (the legionary fortress at York) to Cramond on the Firth of Forth. Locally there were forts at Newstead (Trimontium), Cappuck and High Rochester (Bremenium), with marching camps between. The name of the route is derived from the Anglo-Saxon kingdom of Deira, which together with Bernicia made up Northumbria. This section of Dere Street is known as 'Gamel's Path', after the Old English 'kemylpethe' ('old road').

From here the route takes a broad sweep around to head north-east, diverging from the border fence. Crossing an expanse of grassy moorland, rushy areas warn of boggy ground, although the worst sections are flagged. The view

Brownhart Law Signal Station

The Roman signal station near Brownhart Law was one of a chain that ran across country to the garrison fort at Newstead near Melrose. With the magnificent views of the Scottish Borders, it is easy to forget that in the days of the Roman Empire the northern frontier must have been regarded as 'bandit country' by the men who occupied these isolated outposts.

ahead is now dominated by a procession of hills running along the border ridge, with Lamb Hill foremost. A cairn and a few marker posts provide reassurance of the route, which now heads east (at this point it is necessary to re-fold the map). Passing an old finger sign, the mountain refuge hut at Yearning Saddle is reached (3 = NT 804 129).

Blind Burn

It is here that we leave the Pennine Way, following the valley of Blind Burn for 2½ miles (4 kilometres) down to the road. From the hut, a marker post shows a route heading east. As this divides, take the path running south-east through the site of an old settlement. At another marker post, veer east-south-east on a faint path, heading towards a ruin (4 = NT 817 124). This is Yearning Hall, which is shown on the map as an enclosure surrounding a spring.

Heading down into a gully and crossing a small stream, the narrow path runs around a spur to where Blind Burn is forded. From here the path follows the lively stream down its narrow valley. As the valley broadens-out, veer to the right of a rushy mire. Returning to the stream, a footbridge eventually carries the path to the west bank. Passing to the left of Blindburn Farm

Yearning Hall

Yearning Hall is a ruined croft on the northern slopes of Yearning Law, standing among a few mature conifers and looking rather eerie in this remote location. The fireplace remains, although only sheep and goats reside here now. The name relates to the Anglo-Saxon 'erne' ('soarer'), referring to the eagles that once inhabited this area.

(with its noisy border collies), the Upper Coquetdale road is reached (5 = NT 830 109).

Upper Coquetdale Road

The final part of the return route follows the road for 2¾ miles (4½ kilometres) back to the starting point. The road is quiet, the scenery is beautiful and it is joy to follow the River Coquet towards its source. The river is home to trout and salmon, and an encounter with a heron or even a ring ouzel is common. There are a couple of stiff climbs along the way, although the height gained opens up views of the surrounding hills.

Hill-farming in the Cheviot Hills

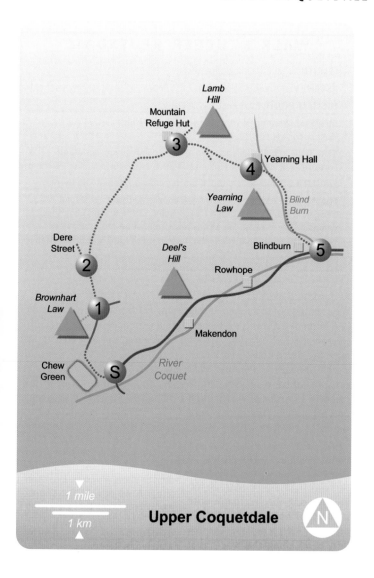

Upper Coquetdale

WALK 6: UPPER REDESDALE

LENGTH 14 miles (22¼ kilometres)

ASCENT 1,972 feet (601 metres)

HIGHEST POINT 1,729 feet (527 metres)

MAPS OS Explorer OL Map 16 ('The Cheviot Hills')
(East & West Sheets)

STARTING POINT Blakehopeburnhaugh picnic place, Redesdale
Forest (NT 785 002)

FACILITIES Public toilets (open during summer). Inn at Old Byrness.

FEATURES A varied walk running through the forests of Upper
Redesdale and along a broad ridge leading to the Roman marching
camp at Chew Green. The return route follows an MoD road over
wind-swept moorland (when the range is not in use) or a forest trail.

Redesdale Forest

The starting point is reached by turning off the A68 about 1½ miles
(2½ kilometres) south of Byrness, joining an access road signed for
the forest drive to Kielder. Heading back along the access road, just
over the River Rede ('red river')
a sign shows the Pennine Way
turning onto a grassy track
running north-west through
norway spruce. The route is here
shared with the Three Kings
forest walk, which takes its
name from a nearby group of
standing stones. Emerging from
the forest, a stony path is followed along the riverbank until
it meets a hardcore track at a
bridge (1 = NT 778 013). Turning
left, head along the track as it
runs back into the forest before

Byrness Chapel
The Holy Trinity Church at Old
Byrness is a quaint little building, standing uncomfortably
beside the busy A68. Looking
around the churchyard, the
names on the gravestones read
like a roll-call of the Border
Reiver clans (Robson, Charlton
etc.). A window in the chapel
commemorates the men who
lost their lives during construction of the nearby
Catcleugh Reservoir.

veering north, crossing the river by a footbridge to arrive at a chapel (2 = NT 771 023).

The tree-shaded lane on the left is used by long-distance walkers to access the youth hostel at Byrness, although the Pennine Way itself runs alongside the A68 for a short way. Crossing the busy road, head up past a few cottages until a finger sign shows the route turning through a gate in a hedge. At the top of a small field another gate leads to a pair of marker posts – that on the right showing the Pennine Way heading north-east up the forested slopes of Byrness Hill on a path that can be very slippery. Forestry roads are crossed during the ascent, with marker posts confirming the route. Emerging from the forest, a short but steep clamber around large boulders leads up onto the ridge (3 = NT 774 033). The top of Byrness Hill is marked by the remains of a fire look-out tower, as well as the first of a string of MoD warning signs.

Ravens Knowe

The next part of the walk runs along the broad ridge for 4¼ miles (6¾ kilometres) to Chew Green. Heading north on a quad track, there are good views across the valleys on either side of the ridge, with Byrness village and Catcleugh Reservoir coming into view. Along the western flanks of the ridge are rock outcrops, beneath which are the upper fringes of the forest. As a fence joins from the left, the Pennine Way veers to the right to avoid a cottongrass mire. Rejoining the fence, a well-defined path is followed north-north-east, with boardwalk providing safe passage of boggy ground. Arriving at the cairned summit of Ravens Knowe, at 1,729 feet (527 metres) this is the highest point on the walk (4 = NT 780 061).

Continuing along a quad track heading north-north-west, the grassy ridge is boggy in places. Crossing the border fence (5 = NT 776 077), a finger sign shows the Pennine Way continuing straight ahead, as well as a faint path turning down towards the headwaters of the River Coquet. Joining a quad track heading east, another finger sign shows the route turning downhill, passing a couple of marker posts before re-crossing the border fence. From

Catcleugh Reservoir

Near the forestry village of Byrness is Catcleugh Reservoir, which was built in 1905 by the Newcastle & Gateshead Water Company to supply the population of Tyneside. It captures the waters of the River Rede, close to their source at Carter Bar. Construction took fifteen years, with the creation of a 15-mile (24-kilometre) narrow gauge railway to carry raw materials and provisions for the 1,000-strong workforce. During the construction, shanty towns grew up on either side of the River Rede, which separated rival groups of workers from Newcastle and Gateshead.

here a path runs beneath the grassy ramparts of Chew Green, above the infant River Coquet. When the Pennine Way turns left, instead continue down towards the road (6 = NT 794 085).

Dere Street

The return route follows access roads for a total of 7 miles (11¼ kilometres). All but the last 1 mile (1½ kilometres) is on MoD roads that are frequently closed for safety reasons, so access must be confirmed in advance with Range Control. Also, it is essential that there is no deviation from the route. Heading steeply uphill, the road soon provides an 'aerial' view of Chew Green. Snow poles accompany the road as it runs south-east, following the course of Dere Street along a moorland ridge, with wide views to right and left. The location of a stone water trough (the curiously named 'Outer Golden Pot') is indicated by a star-shaped marker. For a way the route crosses onto the reverse side of the map, although refolding should be unnecessary. Arriving at a 'T'-junction (7 = NT 792 083), a road sign indicates a right turn.

From here an access road is followed south-west down the remote Cottonshope Valley, which is home to just a couple of isolated farmsteads. A short way before the road enters a conifer plantation, keep an eye open for the entrance to an old Royal Observer Corps bunker on the right. The A68 is met at a point just north of the picnic place at Cottonshopeburnfoot (8 = NT 788 049). Crossing the busy road, follow the grass verge for a short way before turning onto a farm access track. Instead of continuing down towards some cottages, turn left and follow a link running parallel to the A68. This joins the access road that was earlier used to access the starting point.

Alternative Return Route
If the MoD roads are closed, the alternative return route must be followed. This is shorter than the road-walk (at 6 miles/9¾ kilometres), but crosses boggy ground and follows unappealing forestry roads. Retracing your steps along the Pennine Way, this time follow a faint path running alongside the border fence towards the source of the River Coquet. At one time the Pennine Way followed this route – the reason for its diversion becoming apparent as your boots start to fill with water! Upon reaching the place where the

---

Cottonshopeburnfoot
There is some disagreement over whether Cottonshopeburnfoot (nineteen letters) or its neighbour, Blakehopeburnhaugh (eighteen letters), is the longest place name in England. The former is sometimes disqualified on the basis that it was formerly written as two words on Ordnance Survey maps (that is, Cottonshopeburn Foot). Putting the issue into perspective, the longest place name in Wales has fifty-eight letters!

border fence was earlier crossed, rejoin the Pennine Way as it heads south. Ignoring a permissive path signed for Harts Toe, instead turn as a finger sign shows the Border County Ride heading through a gate into the forest (NT 776 073).

Following a hardcore path running south-west through the conifers, a forestry road is soon met. Turning left, follow the track as it heads south-west then south above the valley of Spithope Burn. The route can be tedious, with dense walls of sitka spruce to right and left. Where the trees have been felled, an unsightly tangle of stumps and branches covers the ground. Down in the valley the remote Spithope mountain bothy be seen. When a marker post shows the Border County Ride switching back to head west, instead continue straight ahead on a forestry road running south-east. The standard return route is joined when the track arrives at Cottonshope Road (NT 780 015).

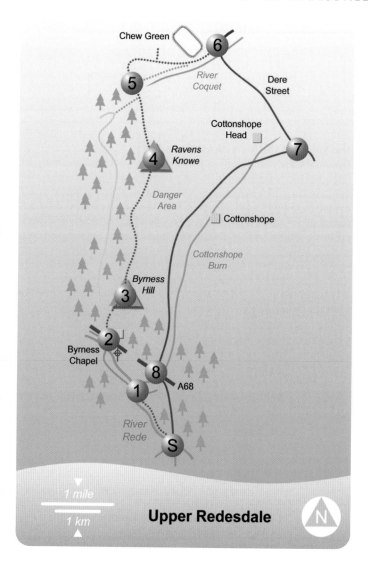

Upper Redesdale

1 mile

1 km

NORTH TYNEDALE

Walk 1: The Border Forest
Walk 2: Hareshaw and Troughend Commons
Walk 3: Wark and Shitlington Commons
Walk 4: Wark Forest

The Valley of the River North Tyne

The landscape of North Tynedale is less spectacular than the Cheviot Hills, and much of the area has been blighted by sprawling conifer plantations. However, the remaining open space exhibits something of its former charm, with an expanse of windswept moorland that was once trodden by the Border Reivers. From its source on Peel Fell, the River North Tyne flows into Kielder Water, before continuing down a broad valley running south-east towards Hexham. Along the way it is joined by the River Rede, with Redesdale being a significant tributary valley.

In terms of its geology, North Tynedale has more in common with the Pennines than with the Cheviot Hills, being underlain by sedimentary rocks of Carboniferous age. The Scremerston Series is dominant, with a repeating sequence of limestone, shale and sandstone strata, as well as thin layers of coal. Above this sequence is boulder clay, deposited during the last Ice Age. After the woodland that once covered the area was cleared by early settlers, the soil degraded to form peat, creating blanket bog on the high ground.

On Kielder-side, the wind blaws wide;
There sounds nae hunting horn
That rings sae sweet as the winds that beat
Round banks where Tyne is born.
    Algernon Charles Swinburne, 'A Jacobite's Exile'.

Peel Towers

Peels were defensive tower houses built by the lesser gentry to provide a refuge for themselves and their vassals. They were three or four storeys high, with walls 8 feet (2½ metres) thick, narrow slits for windows (usually enlarged during subsequent renovation) and a crenellated parapet. Peels were often surrounded by a stockade, offering a place of relative safety into which livestock could be gathered. One type, the parson's peel, would be built close to a church to provide refuge for the priest.

People in North Tynedale

The troubled history of North Tynedale is recorded in the fabric of many of its buildings. Licences to fortify residences were granted from the early fourteenth century, and the signs of the border troubles can still be seen in the remains of peel towers and bastle houses. Even churches were not spared, and the stone slab roof at St Cuthbert's Church in Bellingham was specially constructed to resist being torched by raiders.

As the border area settled down from the beginning of the seventeenth century, there were concerted efforts to increase the amount of land available as pasture. Today the sheltered valleys support cattle rearing and limited arable farming, although the high ground remains untamed, being used only for sheep-grazing and grouse-shooting. The border troubles prevented the formation of large settlements, and much of the population is scattered across the area in small villages and isolated farmsteads. Even the main centres – Bellingham and Wark-on-Tyne – are mere villages. The only significant (civilian) settlements

Bastle Houses

Bastles were fortified farmhouses, built by the more prosperous 'frontier' farmers from the mid-sixteenth century. They were two-storeys high, with a storeroom or livestock shelter on the ground floor, a living area on the first floor and a steeply pitched roof. The stone walls were 4 feet (1¼ metres) thick, with doors of re-enforced oak and narrow slits for windows. The living area was accessed by a ladder – stone steps being added later. As an added deterrent, bastles were generally built within sight of one another.

Black Middens bastle house – a fortified farmhouse in the Tarset Valley.

in Redesdale are Otterburn and Elsdon.

Apart from a few denes, North Tynedale was almost entirely devoid of tree cover until the mid-twentieth century. Today it is home to one of the largest man-made forests in Europe. The Border Forest is made up of endless ranks of sitka spruce (an import from North America) and norway spruce (the traditional

---

The Border Forest

Work began on the creation of the Border Forest in 1926, with most of the planting taking place during the 1950s and 1960s. As well as the core area around Kielder itself, there are several distinct Forestry Commission holdings, namely Redesdale and Wark (Northumberland), Kershope and Spadeadam (Cumbria) and Wauchope and Newcastleton (Scottish Borders). Together these amount to around 250 square miles (650 square kilometres) of densely packed conifers. About 300,000 tons/tonnes of timber is produced annually, most being used for the manufacture of paper and chipboard. Several remote villages were created by the Forestry Commission to house its employees, with a total of 300 terraced houses.

Kielder Water

Kielder Water was created as the largest reservoir in Western Europe to supply the heavy industries of the North East Region. Work began in 1976, but by the time it was completed in 1982, industrial decline meant that the expected demand failed to materialise. Nevertheless, it remains a significant feat of engineering, with a dam 170 feet (52 metres) high and ¾ mile (1¼ kilometres) long. The reservoir has 27 miles (44 kilometres) of shoreline and a surface area of 4 square miles (10 square kilometres). Water is passed down the river to a pumping station at Riding Mill, from where it can be transferred through tunnels to the Wear and the Tees.

Christmas tree), with just a scattering of native species. Whilst its creation has had a devastating impact upon the landscape, it does provide a welcome refuge for the shy red squirrel, roe deer and Cheviot adder, while rare fungi – including species particular to this area – thrive in the arboreal gloom. Also, much has been done to maximise the recreational potential of the Border Forest, focussing particularly upon the area around Kielder Water.

Hareshaw Linn

The Hareshaw Linn Nature Trail at Bellingham offers an enjoyable walk up a dene of oak, ash and wych elm, leading to a 60 feet (18 metre) high waterfall ('linn' being the Gaelic word for a plunge-pool). The route is fairly easy, but seems much longer than its 1½ miles (2¼ kilometres), crossing Hareshaw Burn a number of times as it makes it way towards the head of the dene. At one time the Pennine Way ran up Hareshaw Dene, but there is no longer a link between the two routes.

Walking in North Tynedale

The upper reaches of North Tynedale fall within Northumberland National Park, although this owes more to the area's location – connecting the Cheviot Hills and Hadrian's Wall – than to its distinctive characteristics. The Pennine Way itself treats North Tynedale as an unfortunate necessity, making its way swiftly over moors and through forests, pausing only to seek accommodation at Bellingham and Byrness. The terrain presents few difficulties, and there are no significant climbs. Moreover, the whole area is criss-crossed with quiet lanes and forestry roads, offering easy return routes.

There is a general right of access to Forestry Commission holdings, although there may be localised closures where felling is taking place. Details can be checked in advance with the local office on (01434) 250 209. Visitors must take care to avoid causing fires, and should stay alert for logging lorries, which thunder around the forestry roads. The valley of the River North Tyne offers attractive drive-ins on narrow, winding lanes. An exception is the A68, which is generally straight (it follows the course of Dere Street), but takes the form of a dangerous roller-coaster ride of blind crests and sudden dips.

WALK 1: THE BORDER FOREST

LENGTH 19¼ miles (31 kilometres)

ASCENT 2,231 feet (680 metres)

HIGHEST POINT 1,378 feet (420 metres)

MAPS OS Explorer OL Map 42 ('Kielder Water, Bellingham & Simonside Hills') (East & West Sheets)

STARTING POINT Blakehopeburnhaugh picnic place, Redesdale Forest (NT 785 002)

FACILITIES Public toilets (open during summer). Inn and refreshments at Old Byrness.

FEATURES A long and sometimes gruelling forest walk. Much of the route follows unappealing forestry roads and a moorland path that can be hard going, although there are some significant points of interest along the way, including a prominent beehive cairn and a pair of well-preserved bastles.

Forestry Road

The first part of the walk follows the Pennine Way along a forestry road for 3 miles (5 kilometres). From the picnic place, head along the hardcore track as it crosses Blakehope Burn and passes some cottages and a farmhouse. Ignoring turnings to right and left, follow the track as it runs south-south-east. At a couple of points the literal route follows a parallel course over rough ground, although it is better just to keep to the track. Arriving at a gate (Rookengate), this marks the edge of a private plantation (Gibshiel Estate) (1 = NY 799 956).

Padon Hill

The Pennine Way originally continued straight ahead, but was diverted to follow a moorland path over Padon Hill, a distance of 3¼ miles (5½ kilometres). Whilst the forestry road was certainly monotonous, its hard surface will soon be remembered with fondness. A finger sign shows the route heading south-east along a boggy firebreak (at this point it is necessary to refold the map). Soon the forest gives way to moorland as the path continues alongside a fence, with occasional boundary stones (marked 'GH' for 'Gabriel Hall'). Arriving at Brownrigg Head (2 = NY 816 943), the path turns south-west to follow a drystone wall.

As the path converges with the edge of the forest it heads steeply downhill. The ground can be slippery, and the path is often overgrown with bracken,

> **Padon Hill**
> The 15 feet (4½ metre) high bee-hive cairn on Padon Hill stands 1,243 feet (379 metres) above sea level. It was built by the Morrison-Bell family of nearby Otterburn Hall during the 1920s, using material from an earlier construction. Alexander Peden (c.1626–86), the Scottish Covenanter, is said to have held meetings on Padon Hill, those attending bringing stones with them to mark the place with a simple cairn.

so take care. Leaving the forest behind, flagstones provide safe passage of a mire. Crossing a drystone wall by a ladder stile, the path heads south-south-east up the heather-clad slopes of Padon Hill. As the way ahead levels out, there is the option of visiting the prominent beehive cairn marking the summit (this would make a good spot for lunch). There is no public right of way, but the cairn is often visited by walkers, and a section of fence has been left un-barbed. The views are wonderful, with the Cheviot dominating the northern horizon. In the foreground is the broad valley of the River Rede. Continuing along the path, this soon arrives at an unclassified road (3 = NY 824 917).

Gatehouse

Here a finger sign shows the Pennine Way continuing straight ahead, although we turn right, following the quiet road for 2¾ miles (4½ kilometres) to Gatehouse. Ignoring the turn for Sundaysight, veer left at the next junction, taking the route signed for Greenhaugh (note the overgrown lime kiln). The road runs gently downhill as it heads south-west, passing Highgreen Manor (where it is again necessary to refold the map). The landscape becomes tamer as moorland gives way to pasture. Arriving at a crossroads (Lane End), continue straight ahead. Passing through

Gatehouse

Gatehouse (formerly 'Yethouse') is a remote settlement in the once lawless Tarset Valley. It is the site of a pair of well-preserved bastle houses dating from the mid-sixteenth century, standing like gatehouses on either side of the road. Today they are used as farm buildings, but retain much of their original character. In some respects they are superior to the famous Black Middens bastle, which is located further up the valley.

the hamlet, a short way further along the road, take the second of a pair of gates on the right (4 = NY 786 891). Following a rough track over pasture towards Heathery Hall Farm, pass to the right of the farmhouse and turn left onto an access road (5 = NY 790 895).

Border County Ride

From here the remainder of the return route follows the Border County Ride, a total of 9¼ miles (14¾ kilometres). The tarmac track runs past an imposing group of lime kilns, before arriving at a footbridge across a peat-laden stream (Black Burn) (6 = NY 780 918). Here the Border County Ride enters the forest. In failing daylight this can be a fearful place, the tall conifers creaking ominously as they sway in the wind. Worse still are the harvested areas, which look like the aftermath of a natural disaster. Whilst most of the turn-points are way-marked, careful navigation is required.

The forestry road initially heads north-north-west. Passing through an open area, Black Burn is re-crossed by a concrete bridge. Ignoring the turn for Blackburnhead Farm, continue north.

Lime Kilns

The practice of using lime to 'sweeten' acidic moorland soils is recorded in the remains of kilns dotted about the landscape, and in the visual contrast between improved pasture ('in-bye') and rough grazing ('out-bye'). Lime kilns were constructed to a more or less standard design, usually placed at exposed locations to catch the wind. Limestone would normally be quarried locally, and fed in through the top of the 'pot' in layers, with coal or char-coal in-between. After several days of burning, the slaked lime would be removed from the 'eye' at the bottom of the kiln.

Arriving at a T-junction (7 = NY 777 965), turn left and head north-west, swinging around to north-north-west. At the next T-junction (8 = NY 769 978), turn left again, heading south-west before swinging back to north-north-west. Passing a disused quarry near the top of Loaf Hill, another T-junction marks the highest point on the walk (9 = NY 763 985). Ignoring the waymarked route on the left, turn right and join a gloomy track heading north-east (the marker post for the Border County Ride is hard to spot). This snakes about as it heads downhill. Arriving at a T-junction not shown on the map (10 = NY 774 991), take the track on the left. Eventually this rejoins the Pennine Way, just south of Blakehopeburnhaugh.

> Midway upon the journey of our life I found myself within a forest dark, for the straightforward pathway had been lost. Ah me! how hard a thing it is to say what was this forest savage, rough, and stern, which in the very thought renews the fear.
>
> Dante, *The Divine Comedy: Inferno*.

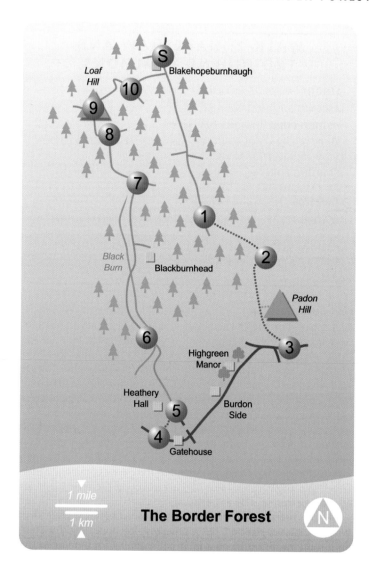

The Border Forest

WALK 2: HARESHAW AND TROUGHEND COMMONS

LENGTH 16 miles (26 kilometres)

ASCENT 1,558 feet (475 metres)

HIGHEST POINT 1,184 feet (361 metres)

MAPS OS Explorer OL Map 42 ('Kielder Water, Bellingham & Simonside Hills') (East Sheet)

STARTING POINT Bellingham village centre, North Tynedale (NY 838 833)

FACILITIES Full range of services.

FEATURES Starting at the historic settlement of Bellingham, the varied route follows the Pennine Way across open moorland before returning on farmland and along the banks of the River North Tyne, using quiet roads where necessary.

Hareshaw Common

Bellingham is on the B6320, about 12 miles (19 kilometres) north of Hexham, and offers plenty of on-street parking. Heading up the front street from the Boer War memorial, turn onto the West Woodburn road, passing the start of the Hareshaw Linn Nature Trail and the site of a medieval castle. Veering left as the road forks, continue past the heritage centre. When the pavement gives out it becomes necessary to walk on the road, although a finger sign soon shows the Pennine Way turning onto a tarmac track leading to Blakelaw Farm. Through the farmyard, head uphill on pasture, with marker posts confirming the route. Passing through a gate, ahead is the rough moorland of Hareshaw Common, with a finger sign showing a choice of ways covering the next 1½ miles (2½ kilometres) (1 = NY 845 854).

The alternative route runs north-north-west beside a boundary. It offers easier navigation, but is otherwise less appealing. The standard route heads north on a faint path, aiming for a point to the right of a belt of Scots pine. Off to the right is a prominent line of

Bellingham – The Capital of North Tynedale

Bellingham (pronounced 'bell-in-jum') is a place steeped in history. For example, St Cuthbert's Church dates from the thirteenth century, and was built upon the spot where the saint's remains were rested. The church is usually open, providing an opportunity to examine the barrel-vaulted, stone slab roof. Next to the churchyard is Cuddy's Well, the waters of which are said to have miraculous healing properties, and which are still used for baptisms. The churchyard itself is home to the infamous 'Lang Pack' grave, which marks the resting place of a would-be thief, killed while attempting to gain access to a nearby hall by hiding in a peddler's pack.

rock outcrops (Callerhues Crag). Crossing a wall by a ladder stile, the route drops into a gully before heading north-west across rough grazing. Over a tarmac track, a couple of ladder stiles lead through a walled paddock beside Hareshaw House Farm, towards the point where the two routes converge (2 = NY 841 875).

Troughend Common

Heading north along an old wagonway, this passes the site of the former Hareshaw Head Colliery before continuing down towards the B6320. Crossing straight over the road, the next part of the walk is on Troughend Common, with another 3 miles (4¾ kilometres) of rough moorland ahead. Initially the path is interrupted by broad drainage channels as it heads north over tussocky grass. As it starts to climb the heather-clad slopes of Lough Shaw, a few marker posts confirm the route. Passing a finger sign, the path heads north-west towards Deer Play – the highest point on the walk, offering fine views over Redesdale (3 = NY 841 903).

From here the path can be hard going as it runs over boggy ground towards Whitley Pike, which is marked by a cairn surmounted by a pole. This might be a good place to stop for lunch, being just a little short of the half-way point. Crossing a fence stile, continue north-west, with flagstones providing safe passage of a cottongrass mire. Arriving at an unclassified road, it is here that we leave the Pennine Way (4 = NY 824 917).

Hareshaw Head Colliery and Hareshaw Iron Company

Hareshaw Head Colliery closed during the 1950s, after operating for 200 years. A wagonway ran from the colliery down to Bellingham, supplying the Hareshaw Iron Company. The ironworks boasted three blast furnaces, twenty kilns and fifty coke ovens, and employed around 500 people. Iron from here was used to construct Robert Stephenson's magnificent High Level Bridge on Tyneside. After the ironworks closed in 1849, the colliery continued to operate, exporting its coal via the Border Counties Railway.

Charlton

Turning left, head along the quiet road, which is followed for 1¼ miles (2 kilometres) to Highgreen Manor, where the second of a pair of finger signs shows a route to Smiddy-Well Rigg. Heading south over tussocky grass, cross a small stream to join a rough track running towards Blackcrag Wood (a pleasant little birch grove beneath rock outcrops). Crossing a footbridge, Tarret Burn is then followed downstream, with a faint path running over meadows towards Smiddy-Well Rigg Farm. From here the route turns east-south-east, following a line of electricity poles towards Sundaysight Farm. Recrossing the burn, head up some fields, initially parallel to a tree-lined clough, before exiting onto an unclassified road beside the farm (5 = NY 817 890).

The next 2 miles (3¼ kilometres) are on quiet roads, heading south to a T-junction (6 = NY 820 880), then south-west towards the edge of the map. Here a gate on the left leads to a hardcore track, running beside a walled plantation (7 = NY 801 869). A marker post soon indicates a turn onto a path heading south-east over tussocky grass. Through a narrow gate, the route crosses the rushy trough of Grassleapot Sike before continuing towards the remote Fieldhead Farm with its wind turbine. Here there are wide views over the valley of the River North Tyne. Another marker post shows the route joining a rough track, hooking around the head of a tree-lined clough above a small waterfall. From here the track runs south-south-east, down towards the hamlet of Charlton, where an unclassified road is met (8 = NY 810 848).

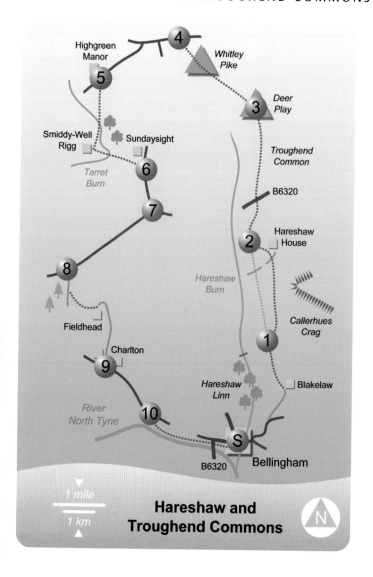

Highgreen Manor

Whitley Pike

Deer Play

Smiddy-Well Rigg

Sundaysight

Troughend Common

Tarret Burn

B6320

Hareshaw House

Hareshaw Burn

Callerhues Crag

Fieldhead

Charlton

Hareshaw Linn

Blakelaw

River North Tyne

Bellingham

B6320

1 mile

1 km

Hareshaw and Troughend Commons

N

The road is followed for ¾ mile (1½ kilometres) as it runs parallel to the tree-lined riverbank. Just before reaching a chevron sign marking a sharp bend, a finger sign on the right points to a fence stile (9 = NY 819 839). From here a riverside path runs 1½ miles (2¼ kilometres) back to Bellingham, providing an opportunity to spot otters along the way. After running along a levy and through a shady grove, the path continues along the beautiful riverbank, passing under a stone bridge. Arriving at the foot of an alleyway, turn left and head up past Cuddy's Well to arrive back at the village centre.

Cuddy's Well, beside St Cuthbert's Church at Bellingham.

WALK 3: WARK AND SHITLINGTON COMMONS

LENGTH 16 miles (25¾ kilometres)

ASCENT 1,657 feet (505 metres)

HIGHEST POINT 804 feet (245 metres)

MAPS OS Explorer OL Maps 42 ('Kielder Water, Bellingham & Simonside Hills') (East Sheet) and 43 ('Hadrian's Wall, Haltwhistle & Hexham') (East & West Sheets)

STARTING POINT Bellingham village centre, North Tynedale (NY 838 833)

FACILITIES Full range of services.

FEATURES An enjoyable walk through the heart of Border Reiver country, passing farm buildings that incorporate the remains of fortified structures. As well as enclosed pasture and rough grazing, the varied route encompasses pleasant denes, forest trails and quiet roads.

Ealingham Rigg

From the Boer War memorial, follow the pavement past the village hall towards the west end of the village. Across the road from St Oswald's RC Church a sign marks the site of the Irishmen's Grave, where around 100 navvies who died of cholera during the construction of Catcleugh Reservoir are buried. Crossing the river by a stone bridge, it is necessary to walk on the main road. Ignoring a turning on the right, continue along the B6320, passing a cemetery and the Forestry Commission offices (1 = NY 837 824).

Here a finger sign marks the start of a permissive path, which thankfully reduces the time spent on the main road. Reaching the top of a wooded slope, turn east, heading towards the point where the Pennine Way used to leave the road. Following a quad track south, then a short section of walled lane, a ladder stile marks the start of a faint path heading south-west over rough grazing. Arriving at a drystone wall, a finger sign marks a right turn, onto

The Bellingham Gingall

Bellingham village hall is the site of a Chinese gingall. This small artillery piece was brought back from the Boxer Uprising of 1900 by Commander (later Admiral Sir) Edward Charlton of HMS *Orlando*. A plaque records that it was captured at North West Fort Taku on 17 June 1900.

a track running towards the Ealingham Rigg transmitter (2 = NY 832 817). This is a bit of an eyesore, being located on the crest of the ridge, but doubtless provides an important service to local people.

Another finger sign shows the route turning over a ladder stile, heading down through the sandstone outcrops of Shitlington Crags. Continuing along the edge of a couple of fields, pass through the farmyard at Shitlington Hall and join a track heading south-west (here it is necessary to switch maps, taking up Sheet 43). A marker post indicates a left turn, crossing a small stream and following a path along the tree-lined banks of Houxty Burn. This in turn is soon crossed by a footbridge (3 = NY 829 798).

Wark Common

Heading uphill on pasture, the route converges with a fence running south-west. Crossing straight over an unclassified road, continue up a pleasant lane along the edge of Wark Common. As the road heads towards a craggy hillock, a finger sign shows the Pennine Way turning onto an access road. Veering left at a fork, head towards Low Stead Farm, which stands above the dene of Blacka Burn. A couple of gates lead around the farm, the thick walls betraying its origin as a bastle house. Exiting by a waymarked stile, head south towards Leadgate Farm. Crossing straight over an unclassified road, a finger sign shows the Pennine Way heading across pasture towards Ash Farm, where it passes beside a barn before continuing over fields. Another finger sign shows the route hooking around Horneystead Farm, which includes the remains of a peel tower dating from around 1600. Heading south-west, a marker post indicates a turn down into the dene of Warks Burn (4 = NY 813 771).

Crossing the gorge by a footbridge, head up through a narrow defile, with a marker post indicating a right turn. Arriving at a ladder stile, a finger sign shows the Pennine Way turning south, heading uphill beside a fence. Cresting the rise, ignore routes to right and left and continue straight ahead, crossing a ladder stile. Dropping down to a rushy area, a quad track is joined as it heads uphill beside a bracken-filled gully (note the attractive little waterfall). The track swings around to head south-west, converging with the edge of a forest. Passing through a gate, the route runs along a firebreak, crossing straight over a hardcore track and an unclassified road, before arriving at another road, close to Ladyhill Farm. Here a finger sign shows the Pennine Way turning right, heading down the road (at this point it is necessary to re-fold the map). Off to the right is Willowbog Farm, which is now a bonsai nursery. As the Pennine Way turns off the road, we begin our return route (5 = NY 798 752).

Stonehaugh

A finger sign points through a gate on the north side of the road, with a bridleway route running north-west beside a drystone wall. Ignoring gates on the right, the faint path runs over the side of a hillock. The fenced area to the right was once a pleasant stand of norway spruce, but is now desolate. Before reaching an unclassified road, pass through a gate on the right and cross some rough ground beside a knot of fir trees to arrive at the road. Turning left, head towards Stonehaugh, where an access road runs between the terraces to arrive at a farmhouse beside a campsite (6 = NY 795 763).

Here a finger sign shows a footpath to Low Roses Bower, heading east then north-east along a firebreak, with marker posts confirming the route (which is shared with a line of electricity poles). Soon it becomes necessary to again refold the map. The path runs above the dene of Warks Burn, at one point following a dark passage through the conifers as it hooks around a gully. At a fork the route turns steeply downhill towards a footbridge.

Stonehaugh Forestry Village

Stonehaugh was built by the Forestry Commission during the 1950s to provide housing for its workers. The village comprises a couple of rows of terraced houses, just thirty-five homes in all, on the edge of Wark Forest. It is known affectionately as 'dodge city' – a reference to the three totem poles that overlook Warksburn picnic place. Wark Forest takes its name from the village of Wark, and refers to an earthwork (Wark-on-Tyne being the site of a Norman motte and bailey).

This is close to the overgrown ruin of Holywell Cottage, which is named for a nearby sulphur spring. Heading uphill on a ramp-like track, the route tips over onto the reverse side of the map for a short way. Close to the ruin of Low Roses Bower, perched above a waterfall, is a privy known as the 'Long Drop'. Here a finger sign marks a right turn, heading over fields towards an unclassified road. Following the road north-west, as it bends sharply to the right, a finger sign marks the start of a bridleway, passing through a gate (7 = NY 801 775).

This is followed north-east over grazing land for 1¾ miles (3 kilometres), crossing Blacka Burn before continuing parallel to the edge of the forest. Arriving at a crossroads of routes, continue straight ahead, with the forest now receding on the left. Heading gently downhill through fields, a hardcore track is joined, leading to an unclassified road. A short way to the right is the location of a standing stone marked with a cross, although we turn left and head north-west up the road, switching maps once again (returning to Sheet 42). A finger sign soon marks a turn onto a hardcore track (8 = NY 817 800).

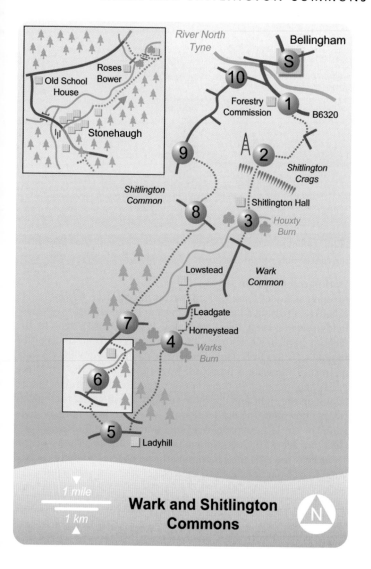

Bellingham

River North Tyne

S

10

1

Forestry
Commission

B6320

Roses
Bower

Old School
House

2

Shitlington
Crags

Stonehaugh

9

Shitlington
Common

8

Shitlington Hall

3

Houxty
Burn

Lowstead

Wark
Common

Leadgate

Horneystead

7

4

Warks
Burn

6

5

Ladyhill

1 mile

1 km

**Wark and Shitlington
Commons**

N

75

The ruin of Holywell Cottage, beside Warks Burn.

Shitlington Common

Arriving at Stone House Farm, a narrow passage runs down the side of a byre. Crossing a ladder stile, head north then north-west over fields towards West Highridge Farm. Passing to the right of the farm, a hardcore track runs through fir trees to an unclassified road (9 = NY 813 812). From here the remaining 2¾ miles (4¼ kilo-metres) of the walk is on roads. Heading uphill, to the left is the grassy moorland of Shitlington Common. Cresting the rise, ignore a lane on the right and continue straight ahead as the road heads steeply downhill. The Border County Ride soon joins our route via a lane on the left. Arriving at a T-junction opposite Dunterley Farm (10 = NY 826 831), turn right and head along an avenue of tall sycamores towards the junction with the B6320. Carefully retrace your steps from here back to the village.

WALK 4: WARK FOREST

LENGTH 16½ miles (26½ kilometres)

ASCENT 1,214 feet (370 metres)

HIGHEST POINT 1,034 feet (315 metres)

MAPS OS Explorer OL Map 43 ('Hadrian's Wall, Haltwhistle & Hexham') (West Sheet)

STARTING POINT Warksburn picnic place, Stonehaugh (NY 789 762)

FACILITIES Public toilets (open during summer).

FEATURES Whilst much of the route follows forestry roads, and there is some difficult terrain to negotiate as it crosses open moorland, this is not the worst of forest walks, and there are promising views over Greenlee Lough towards Hadrian's Wall.

Haughton Common

Stonehaugh does not appear on all road maps, but is signed from the B6320 south of Wark-on-Tyne, following a single track road west for 5½ miles (9 kilometres). From the picnic place, head back along the road to a point south-east of the village where, just past a knot of fir-trees and before a recently harvested area, a finger sign marks the start of a bridleway (this place will be remembered from the previous walk). Passing through a gate, head south-east over rough grazing, following a fence and then a drystone wall until arriving at an unclassified road (1 = NY 798 752).

A finger sign on the south side of the road shows the Pennine Way heading uphill beside a broken wall. As the path levels out it runs along the edge of the forest, which is here softened with birch trees. Finger signs confirm the route as it crosses forestry roads, heading south up a firebreak until it emerges onto the open moorland of Haughton Common (2 = NY 797 736). Hereabouts are the remains of Comyn's Cross, named for a local chieftain from the time of King Arthur. Heading south-west towards an old sheep shelter enclosing a few windswept trees, a quad track is soon joined. This crosses a stream before continuing towards the edge of the forest (which here follows an ancient boundary known as Black Dike) (3 = NY 785 727).

From here the Pennine Way runs through the forest for another 1½ miles (2¼ kilometres), and whilst the waymarking assumes that everyone is heading north, there are no real navigational difficulties. Following a firebreak south-west, the route eventually joins a forestry road heading south. Harvesting on the left has opened up views of the King's and Queen's Crags (the reference being to Arthur and Guinevere). The Great Whin Sill rolls away to the west, with Hadrian's Wall running along its crest. Leaving the forest behind, a finger sign shows the Pennine Way turning off the track, although we continue straight ahead (4 = NY 780 707).

Swallow Crags

The first part of the return route crosses rough pasture for around 5½ miles (9 kilometres) before re-entering the forest. The hardcore track continues south-west towards East Stonefolds Farm, with a screen of Scots pine on the left hardly obscuring the view of Greenlee Lough. The track ends at West Stonefolds Farm, where a sign warns of dogs running free. Passing around the farmhouse, continue along a faint track running over grass. Crossing a small stream by a footbridge, head up to a fence stile (5 = NY 770 701).

The totem poles at Warksburn picnic place, Stonehaugh.

Greenlee Lough

Greenlee Lough (a word equivalent to 'loch', and pronounced 'loff') is the largest natural lake in Northumberland – although it is only 5 feet (1½ metres) deep at most. A bird hide on its northern shore offers good views over the lake, which is visited by whooper swans, mute swans and canada geese, as well as goldeneye, tufted and mallard ducks. The reedy banks are home to pike, while small fish and frogs attract heron. The acidic mire at the edge of the lake provides a habitat for insectivorous sundew plants.

Here a finger sign shows a permissive path to Greenlee Lough, although we turn right and follow a rutted track towards Greenlee Farm. Joining a hardcore track heading south-west along the edge of the forest, on the left are views towards the lake and the Great Whin Sill. Passing the entrance to Gibbs Hill Farm, head up a short incline, looking out for a finger sign on the right (6 = NY 748 691). This marks the start of a route to Wealside Farm, heading west across 1 mile (1½ kilometres) of rough terrain. Navigation is fairly easy as the route initially runs parallel to Swallow Crags, with the location of the farm itself indicated by a group of trees (7 = NY 731 690).

A finger sign to the right of the farm marks the start of a path, heading north-east on tussocky grass. Dropping into a rushy trough, a ladder stile is crossed as the route turns north-west, following a drystone wall. Joining an unclassified road, this eventually passes the entrance to Scotchcoultard Farm, the name of which is derived from 'Scots colt herd', recalling the fact that the Border Reivers concealed stolen horses here. The road ends at a gate (8 = NY 722 712), where a finger sign shows a route to Grindon Green.

Grindon Green

The remainder of the return route follows good tracks and quiet roads through the forest, 6½ miles (10¼ kilometres) back to the starting point. Heading north along a hardcore track, the Hopealone radio transmitter is off to the right. Crossing a peat-stained stream by a footbridge, the track turns north-east, heading towards the ruin of Grindon Green Farm (9 = NY 730 736). This is an eerie place of gnarled trees and moss-covered walls, marooned in a sea of conifers.

Continuing straight ahead, the track is shown on the map as an unclassified road, although from here to Coldcotes Farm it retains a hardcore dressing. Emerging from the forest, Warks Burn is crossed by a concrete bridge that can be over-washed in times of severe spate. Just past Coldcotes Farm, a road joins from the right (10 = NY 771 758). Continuing north-east, the road runs past East Whygate Farm before heading back into the forest for a way. Arriving at the Old School House, turn right and follow the road as it runs steeply downhill, back to the starting point.

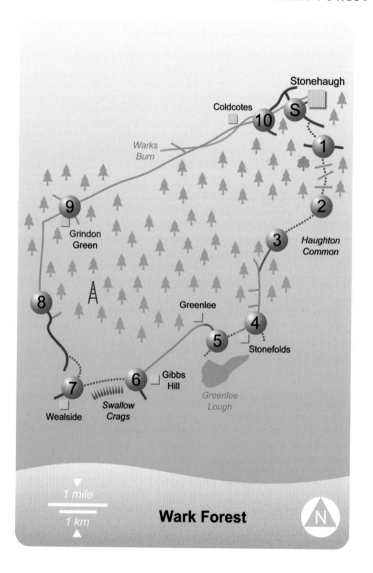

Wark Forest

SOUTH TYNEDALE

Walk 1: Hadrian's Wall – East Crags
Walk 2: Hadrian's Wall – Central Crags
Walk 3: Hadrian's Wall – West Crags
Walk 4: Hartleyburn and Thirlwall Commons
Walk 5: River South Tyne – Slaggyford
Walk 6: River South Tyne – Alston
Walk 7: River South Tyne – Garrigill

The Valley of the River South Tyne

The River South Tyne rises in the North Pennines, on the slopes of Tynehead Fell. It runs swiftly north, passing Alston, then turns east to pass Haltwhistle and Haydon Bridge, being joined by the River Allen along the way. At the village of Warden (near Hexham) it joins with the River North Tyne, their combined waters continuing on towards the North Sea. The northern part of the area falls within Northumberland National Park, and includes the best-preserved section of Hadrian's Wall, running along the crest of the Great Whin Sill. To the south is an expanse of moorland, reaching up towards the most northerly of the Pennine fells. Between the two is the Tyne Gap, an east-west corridor comprising the valleys of the River South Tyne and the River Irthing (a tributary of the River Eden).

The Great Whin Sill

At the end of the Lower Carboniferous period, magma pushing up through fissures formed a thick layer of a dark, basaltic rock called dolerite. This is the Great Whin Sill, which here forms a dramatic serrated ridge – the setting for the 'crags' section of Hadrian's Wall. In fact, outcrops can be traced as far apart as the North Pennines and the Farne Islands. Along the Northumberland coastline, the Great Whin Sill provides the foundations for Norman castles at Bamburgh, Dunstanburgh and Lindisfarne. The term 'whin' refers to the whistling sound made when the hard rock is broken during quarrying – it being prized as a source of roadstone. Its vertically jointed structure is akin to the hexagonal columns of the Giant's Causeway.

Stanegate

Stanegate ('stone street') ran from Corbridge (Coriosopitum) to Carlisle (Luguvalium). It was constructed during Trajan's reign (AD 98–117), after the retreat from Scotland, with forts separated by a day's march (14 Roman miles, equivalent to 13 miles/21 kilometres). The addition of observation towers along the ridge to the north created a basic frontier system. It was originally intended that Hadrian's Wall would be garrisoned from the Stanegate forts. However, during the construction there was a decision to relocate to the Wall itself, building new forts and abandoning the Stanegate forts. Stanegate fell into disrepair after the Romans abandoned the northern frontier, although it was used as a pack-horse route until the first modern road was built through the Tyne Gap in 1753.

People in South Tynedale

South Tynedale is best known for its association with Hadrian's Wall, which is deservedly recognised as a World Heritage Site. The Emperor Hadrian – who was the first to conceive of an end to Roman expansion – visited Britain around AD 122, looking for a suitable place to establish a northern frontier. He appointed Aulus Platorius Nepos governor of Britain to oversee construction of a wall along the entire length of the Tyne-Solway isthmus – the narrowest point south of Caledonia. Hadrian chose the location of his frontier well. It was already the location of a frontier system, with a chain of forts along an east-west route called Stanegate. He must also have been struck by the natural barrier of north-facing cliffs formed by the Great Whin Sill. Whilst Hadrian's Wall consolidated the frontier, it is thought to have acted more as a customs barrier than as a defensive screen. Either way, it would have served as a highly visible reminder of the power of Rome.

The Wall ran 80 Roman miles (equivalent to 73½ miles/118¼ kilometres) from Wallsend-on-Tyne in the east to Bowness-on-Solway in the west. It was planned as a stone wall, 10 feet (3 metres) wide and up to 15 feet (4½ metres) high. The western section was originally constructed with turf – presumably due to the limited number of skilled masons within the legions that undertook the work. The relocation of the Stanegate forts precipitated a narrowing of the Wall,

> And so, having reformed the army in the manner of a ruler, Hadrian set out for Britain, where he corrected many abuses and was the first to build a wall, eighty miles long, to separate the Romans from the barbarians.
>
> Scriptores Historiae Augustae, *Vita Hadriani*.

with stretches just eight or even six feet wide. It is not known whether there was a parapet along the top, and even if there was it was probably not crenellated, since there was never any intention of fighting from the Wall. In front of the Wall there was a V-shaped ditch, 10 feet (3 metres) deep and up to 40 feet (12 metres) wide. Along the Wall itself there were milecastles (that is, fortlets – little more than defended gateways), with a pair of observation turrets at intervals of about a third of a mile between.

The actual construction of the Wall involved two faces of dressed stone, fixed with mortar, with rubble between. Locally quarried sandstone was used throughout. In the west this was red sandstone, which is prone to erosion, partly accounting for a

Housesteads Fort, known to the Romans as Vercovicium, seen from the civilian settlement outside the fort.

The Wall Forts

Fifteen forts were built along the Wall, about half a day's march apart. They varied significantly in size depending upon role and position, but averaged around 5 acres (2 hectares), with a stone-built rampart enclosing a more or less standard layout of buildings. This included the headquarters building, the commanding officer's residence, barracks (each of whch held a 'century' of 80 men), granaries and a hospital. Those forts that housed calvary units also had stables. Whilst they were built by the legions, the forts were manned and maintained by auxiliary cohorts – men recruited in the occupied territories. Those along the crags section were purely infantry forts (Housesteads, Great Chesters, Birdoswald), while those located where north–south roads passed through the Wall held cavalry. The remainder held a combination of infantry and cavalry.

scarcity of remains (although many of the dressed stones found their way into the walls of Lanercost Priory). The legionary units that built the Wall are recorded on 'centurial stones' embedded in the stonework – some of these being still visible. The Wall took about six years to construct, but saw continuous modification

The Antonine Wall

For a twenty year period from the early 140s, under the rule of the Emperor Antoninus Pius, Hadrian's Wall was abandoned for a new frontier system based upon a turf wall along the Forth-Clyde isthmus. This was the Antonine Wall, which is many respects formed a more logical frontier. It was certainly a shorter line – in fact, exactly half the length of Hadrian's Wall. The Antonine Wall brought all of the area of the friendly Brigantes and Votadini under direct Roman control. Even after the new frontier was abandoned in the 160s, control of the area to the north of Hadrian's Wall continued, with a system of forts and roads creating a buffer against the unruly Caledonians.

thereafter. In total, the whole system, including the forts, was manned by a garrison of around 10,000 men.

A barrier known as the 'vallum' ('rampart') was eventually constructed to the south of the Wall. This comprised a ditch 20 feet (6 metres) wide and 10 feet (3 metres) deep, flanked by mounds, with gated causeways providing crossing points at the forts. The addition of the vallum created a secure military zone, making it easier to control the movement of people and goods. During the late second century a new route – the Roman Military Way – was built behind the Wall to make movement between the forts, milecastles and turrets easier. By this time civilian settlements known as 'vici' had developed around many of the forts, providing accommodation for retired veterans and their families, who found work providing services to the army.

As well as the remains of the Roman occupation, the landscape of South Tynedale is littered with fortified structures dating from the border troubles. Some of these were built using dressed stones looted from Hadrian's Wall, and many have been incorporated into the fabric of later buildings. Also benefiting from the availability of materials from the Wall, the Military Road built during the mid-eighteenth century re-established the Tyne Gap as an important transport corridor. The impetus for the its construction was the Jacobite uprising of 1745, which drew attention to the lack of an effective east-west route. The road was conceived by General George Wade (1673–1748), although it was not completed until five years after his death.

In 1839, the Newcastle & Carlisle Railway Company opened a

The Centre of Britain Hotel at Haltwhistle, built around a fifteenth-/sixteenth-century peel tower.

route through the Tyne Gap. The importance of Alston Moor as a centre for lead-mining prompted the creation of a 13¼-mile (21¼-kilometre) branch line from Haltwhistle to Alston, which opened in 1852. Whilst the Tyne Valley line remains open, the branch line closed in 1976. Following an Act of Parliament in 1823, John McAdam oversaw the upgrading of a number of turnpikes around Alston, creating the basis of the modern road system. The main highway through the Tyne Gap is the A69 trunk road, which tops out on Thirlwall Common at a modest 750 feet (229 metres).

Although the area is quite sparsely populated, there is not the sense of remoteness that characterises North Tynedale – the topography having forced settlements closer together. The banks of the River South Tyne and its tributaries are in many places wooded, adding to a pleasant landscape and providing a valuable habitat for species such as red squirrels. The rivers themselves are home to trout and salmon (and therefore otters), while dippers, oystercatchers and sandpipers are fairly common.

Haltwhistle – The Capital of South Tynedale

The historic market town of Haltwhistle makes a plausible claim to being located at the exact centre of Britain. Its name has nothing to do with the railway – it refers to an area of high ground above a confluence (that is, of Haltwhistle Burn and the River South Tyne). King John licensed a market here in 1207. On the south side of the market square is the thirteenth-century Church of the Holy Cross. The town centre also boasts an impressive collection of fortified structures, with five bastle houses and a peel tower on the main street alone. The arrival of the railway in 1837 opened up Haltwhistle as a centre for coal-mining and stone-quarrying, with industry developing along the banks of Haltwhistle Burn (including woollen mills, a grain mill and a brewery). Today the town serves the surrounding villages and acts as a touring base for visitors to Hadrian's Wall.

There is limited arable farming on the valley floor, with walled pasture on the steep valley sides reaching up towards open moorland.

Walking in South Tynedale

Whilst everyone can appreciate the section of the Pennine Way following Hadrian's Wall, the remainder of the route in South Tynedale is often maligned. Poor access to the northern end of the Pennine ridge has consigned the route to the valley floor, with muddy riverside paths, cattle-churned pasture, and endless gates and stiles to negotiate. However, the route as established has its advantages. Whilst the views from the ridge are indeed magnificent, and an absence of other walkers contributes to the sense of an unspoilt wilderness, the terrain is horrendous, with thick heather and tussock grass, interspersed with peat hags and mossy mires. It is therefore unlikely that the Pennine Way will ever be re-routed along the ridge, which will remain the exclusive preserve of grouse-shooters and hill-baggers.

The Pennine Ridge

The northern end of the Pennine ridge – the area above South Tynedale – offers only three hills of over 2,000 feet (610 metres), namely Cold Fell, Grey Nag and Black Fell. These are the highest points on an expanse of moorland that is one of the most remote and inaccessible areas in England.

WALK 1: HADRIAN'S WALL – EAST CRAGS

LENGTH 9¾ miles (16 kilometres)

ASCENT 1,444 feet (440 metres)

HIGHEST POINT 1,066 feet (325 metres)

MAPS OS Explorer OL Map 43 ('Hadrian's Wall, Haltwhistle & Hexham') (West Sheet)

STARTING POINT Steel Rigg car park, Hadrian's Wall (NY 751 677)

FACILITIES Public toilets and refreshments at the National Park Visitor Centre, Once Brewed. Inn at Twice Brewed.

FEATURES An inspiring walk following Hadrian's Wall along a cliff-edge path above the Great Whin Sill. After a detour to Housesteads fort, the route crosses the wilderness area to the north of the Wall before finishing on good tracks and quiet roads, visiting Greenlee Lough along the way.

The Wall

The 'pay and display' car park at Steel Rigg is reached by turning off the B6318 (Military Road) at Once Brewed and heading north along an unclassified road. The first part of the walk follows Hadrian's Wall along the crest of the Great Whin Sill for 3¼ miles (5¼ kilometres). A finger sign shows a link to the Wall, which is then followed east, passing the remains of an un-numbered turret at Peel Gap, built to guard a weak point between turrets 39A and 39B. Heading up a stepped path beside the dramatic cliffs of Peel Crags, there is a significant sense of exposure (indeed, some might prefer to follow the Roman Military Way to Milking Gap, with a parallel track in the lee of the ridge). Reaching the crest, the path continues alongside the Wall. Looking ahead, Crag Lough can be seen pooling at the foot of Highshield Crags. The path crosses a couple of nicks, the first being the site of the well-preserved remains of Milecastle 39, the second being the famous Sycamore Gap.

Switching to the north side of the Wall, the path heads back uphill, before continuing above Highshield Crags. For some way it runs precariously along the edge of the 200 feet (61 metre) high cliffs. The Wall itself appears as an overgrown dyke, surmounted by a drystone wall. Heading into a stand of Scots pine, the path runs gently down-hill towards the Milking Gap, where it continues to the right of the defensive ditch. Crossing straight over a hardcore track, a finger sign points north-east, towards Hotbank Farm and the

The Sycamore Gap

The Sycamore Gap is one of a number of dramatic notches in the 'crags' ridge. It was formed as a glacial melt-water channel, and takes its name from an old sycamore tree at the bottom of the gap. The tree's young heir has taken root in an adjacent stone enclosure. This evocative location was featured in the movie *Robin Hood: Prince of Thieves* – drawing attention to Hollywood's poor grasp of geography!

site of Milecastle 38. As height is gained the Wall reappears to the left, rolling gently along the crest of the ridge above Hotbank Crags. Greenlee Lough, Broomlee Lough and Grindon Lough are all on show. Sewingshields Crags can be seen in the distance, looking like waves petrified in the moment of breaking. Passing the site of Turret 37A, head down into Rapishaw Gap, where a finger sign shows the Pennine Way parting company with the Wall (1 = NY 781 686).

Housesteads Fort

Here it is possible to shorten the walk by 1½ miles (2½ kilometres). However, even if there is insufficient time for a proper visit to Housesteads Fort, a circuit of the perimeter is well worth the effort.

Crag Lough

At the foot of Highshield Crags stands Crag Lough, its reedy banks bounded by willow trees. There are several of these shallow lakes in the area, the others being Greenlee Lough, Broomlee Lough, Grindon Lough, Folly Lake and Halleypike Lough. They were scoured by the passage of ice during the last Ice Age. Unfortunately, they are being progressively in-filled with sedi-ment, and are now about a half the size they were at the time of the Roman occupation. Indeed, old maps of the area also show Caw Lough and Peel Lough, although these have disappeared.

Milecastle 37

Milecastle 37 is one of the best examples on the Wall, with the well-preserved remains of the north gateway and the footprint of the internal buildings visible. The gateway was narrower than at other milecastles, the steep slope to the north making use by carts impractical.

Heading steeply uphill beside Cuddy's Crags, continue along the ridge. Crossing another gap, the path runs above Housesteads Crags, passing Milecastle 37 before entering a sycamore wood straddling the ridge. Arriving at Housesteads fort, head down some steps to join a path running below the north ramparts. Heading down beside the Wall, Knag Burn gateway is soon reached (2 = NY 791 689).

Passing through the gateway, instead of continuing along the route signed for Sewingshields Crags, cross a slab bridge and head up a track towards the east side of the fort. Continuing around the perimeter, the way ahead passes through the remains of the civilian settlement. If you wish to visit the fort itself you will need to pay the admission fee. Otherwise, a permissive path starting at the west gateway follows the Roman Military Way across fields back to Rapishaw Gap. At the bottom of the gap, a finger sign shows the Pennine Way crossing a drystone wall by a ladder stile (3 = NY 781 686).

Housesteads (Vercovicium) Fort

Vercovicium ('place of able fighters') is perhaps the most impressive of the Wall forts. The visible remains generally relate to the third–fourth centuries. Stone ramparts 5 feet (1½ metres) thick enclose an area of five acres (two hectares), and in addition to the four double gateways, many of the internal buildings can be seen. The fort housed a full cohort of up to 1,000 auxiliary infantry. To the south are the remains of a 'vicus' – a civilian settlement – which included shops, a bronze workshop, a tavern and a house where the skeletal remains of a woman and a middle aged man were excavated (the latter with a knife still embedded in his chest). To the east of the fort was a bath-house, fed from Knag Burn. The Armstrong clan of Border Reivers used the semi-ruinous fort as their den, and cattle-thieves were said to inhabit the place as late as the seventeenth century.

Ridley Common

From here the Pennine Way crosses Ridley Common, 1½ miles (2½ kilometres) along the route of a droveway. Pausing to look back, the dramatic cliffs of the Great Whin Sill can now be fully appreciated. Ignoring a path leading to a lime kiln, head north-east over rough grazing to join a rutted track running north. Crossing straight over a hardcore track, the route zigzags downhill before passing through a rushy mire. Here a sign marks a sharp turn, with a faint path heading north-east up the side of a low ridge. Turning north, cross the gully of Haughtongreen Burn, then another low ridge, to arrive at a hardcore track (4 = NY 780 707). Here the Pennine Way heads into Wark Forest, although we turn left.

Greenlee Lough

Following the track south-west, East Stonefolds Farm and West Stonefolds Farm are passed. When a finger sign marks a choice of ways (5 = NY 770 701), this time take the permissive

Knag Burn Gateway

Knag Burn is a rare example of a gateway in the Wall itself, rather than at a fort or milecastle. It was built during the fourth century to provide an alternative to the steep ramp that led up to the north gateway at Housesteads fort. A pair of gates created an 'air-lock', permitting carts to be checked before being allowed through the Wall.

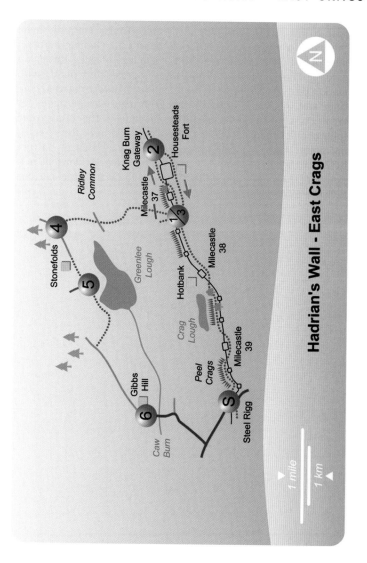

Hadrian's Wall - East Crags

N

Housesteads Fort

Knag Burn Gateway

Ridley Common

2

Milecastle 37

1 3

Stonefolds

4

5

Greenlee Lough

Milecastle 38

Hotbank

Crag Lough

Milecastle 39

Peel Crags

Gibbs Hill

6

S

Steel Rigg

Caw Burn

1 mile

1 km

path to the remote bird hide at Greenlee Lough. From the hide, the path follows a long section of boardwalk running across a mire of tall reeds at the west end of the lake. Passing through a gate, a faint path heads north-west on rough ground, with marker posts confirming the route. Joining a hardcore track, continue past Gibbs Hill Farm, this time ignoring the route signed for Wealside Farm (6 = NY 748 691). The remainder of the return route follows quiet roads, 1½ miles (2½ kilometres) back to the starting point. There are fine views over the wide area of pasture between the Great Whin Sill and Wark Forest. Arriving at a T-junction, turn left and follow the road towards the massive bulwark of Windshields Crags.

WALK 2: HADRIAN'S WALL – CENTRAL CRAGS

LENGTH 10¼ miles (16½ kilometres)

ASCENT 1,444 feet (440 metres)

HIGHEST POINT 1,132 feet (345 metres)

MAPS OS Explorer OL Map 43 ('Hadrian's Wall, Haltwhistle & Hexham') (West Sheet)

STARTING POINT Cawfields picnic place, Hadrian's Wall (NY 712 665)

FACILITIES Public toilets (open during summer). Inn at B6318 junction.

FEATURES Starting at Cawfields, with its dramatic cross-section of the Great Whin Sill and famous milecastle, this is another wonderful roller-coaster ride along Hadrian's Wall. The return route follows a combination of paths, tracks and quiet roads, with an opportunity to visit Vindolanda fort.

The Wall

The starting point is at a reclaimed quarry, 1½ miles (2½ kilometres) north of Haltwhistle, and is signposted from the B6318. The first part of the walk follows Hadrian's Wall for 2¾ miles (4½ kilometres) along the Great Whin Sill. From the car park, a path runs around the north side of the lake, joining a track heading up through a nick in the ridge. This is Hole Gap, where the Wall climbs steeply on both sides (a short 'there-and-back' diversion up the stepped path on the right is well worth the effort, with exceptional views from the head of the quarry face). Passing the remains of Milecastle 42, the path runs alongside the Wall as it follows the crest of the ridge. Looking to the south, beyond the Roman Military Way, the vallum is prominent. Crossing a shallow nick (Bloody Gap), the path continues along the ridge until it eventually starts downhill, passing the remains of Turret 41A to arrive at an unclassified road cutting through Caw Gap (1 = NY 727 669).

This area is known as Shield on the Wall – a reference to a group of shielings that sheltered in the lee of the ridge. Heading up a stepped

Cawfields Quarry

Until quite recently Cawfields was an active quarry, where the Great Whin Sill was plundered for roadstone. This destroyed part of the ridge and a section of Hadrian's Wall. By way of compensation, it revealed a dramatic cross-section of the Great Whin Sill, and led to the formation of an artificial lake. Picnic facilities have been provided beside Caw Burn, together with a car park and public toilets (the latter being closed at present).

path, the crest of the ridge is soon rejoined. Crossing a shallow nick (Bogle Hole Gap), the faint remains of Milecastle 41 are passed. The Wall itself is poorly preserved hereabouts, and for much of the way there is only a drystone wall. Eventually the OS pillar marking the top of Windshields Crags is reached. At 1,132 feet (345 metres), this is the highest point on Hadrian's Wall. The Cheviot can be seen to the north, while to the south are Cross Fell and its neighbours. Far to the west are the hills of the Southern Uplands. Following the ridge gently downhill, the site of Milecastle 40 is passed. Beyond the drystone wall on the left is a long section of the defensive ditch. Crossing an intersecting wall by a step stile, an unclassified road is met (2 = NY 751 676).

Vindolanda Fort

Here we leave Hadrian's Wall (and the Pennine Way), with the next part of the walk following roads for 2¼ miles (3½ kilometres) to

Vindolanda Fort (whilst these are normally quiet, they are prone to spates of tourist traffic). Turning right, head down the road as it passes Peel Bothy, which stands on the site of a peel tower and offers basic accommodation. Arriving at the B6318, cross straight over to join an unclassified road signed for Bardon Mill. This passes the National Park visitor centre, and heads south to Smith's Shield Farm, where there is a turning onto a single track road (3 = NY 755 662).

At this point it is possible to continue straight ahead, cutting 2½ miles (4 kilometres) off the walk. However, even if there is no time for a proper visit to the fort, a circuit of the perimeter is again worthwhile. The road heads east along the course of Stanegate, with the remains of a Roman mile post on the left (this being the only example in Britain still in its original location). Beside the road is an eighteenth-century cottage, Causeway House, which is the only surviving heather-thatched building in Northumberland. Arriving at the car park, if you wish to visit the fort there is a charge. Otherwise, continue along a hardcore track running down a lane towards Chesterholm Farm. Just before crossing a stream, beyond the hawthorn bushes on the left is another mile post. A short way further along the lane, at the entrance to the staff car park, a finger sign marks the start of a footpath to Bardon Mill (4 = NY 773 665).

Following the path along the wooded banks of Chainley Burn, on the far side is an ornamental garden with a reconstruction of a pagan temple. Crossing the stream by a footbridge, those who have

Chesterholm (Vindolanda) Fort

Vindolanda ('bright heath') sits atop a bluff, and was one of a chain of timber forts built around AD 90 to guard Stanegate. It was abandoned when Housesteads was built, but was later rebuilt in stone. The visible remains date from the early fourth century. As well as the stone ramparts, the headquarters building and commanding officer's residence can be seen. To the west is a 10-acre (4-hectare) civilian settlement, with a bath-house and a 'mansio' (a kind of post-inn). Excavation of the site has turned up a wealth of written records giving an insight into life on the northern frontier, as well as the remains of a timber structure that might have been built for Hadrian's visit. The site hosts a speculative reconstruction of a part of Hadrian's Wall, with both stone and turf sections.

visited the fort rejoin the route. Arriving at a fence stile, the path leaves the stream, heading uphill on pasture. Joining a track running towards a farmhouse, cross another fence stile on the right and head north over fields towards High Fogrigg Farm. Turning onto a hardcore track, when this meets another farm access, look for a fence stile to the right. Heading west over pasture, a tree-filled gully is crossed. A hardcore track runs from Layside Farm to the Bardon Mill road, where a sign shows the start of an access road leading to Cranberry Brow Farm (5 = NY 756 658).

The Roman Military Way

Ahead is a straight track, running west-south-west along a broad ridge for 1¼ miles (2¼ kilometres). Initially the surface is tarmac, heading up a hawthorn-lined lane. The views over the valley of the River South Tyne are unfortunately spoiled by a line of electricity pylons. Passing the farm, a rough track continues along the top of some fields until arriving at an unclassified road. Turning right, head along the road for a short way. Soon a gate on the right leads to an access track signed for Hill Top Farm (6 = NY 735 655).

From the farmhouse, cross a ladder stile and head diagonally (west) over a field. The road is rejoined as it heads north to the junction with the B6318. Off to the left is a pair of standing stones, the Mare and Foal. Crossing straight over the main road, a finger sign points to a step stile, with a path heading over rough grazing towards Shield on the Wall Farm. A marker post indicates a turn, with the path leaving the drystone wall on the left to cut across the vallum. Joining the Roman Military Way, the track contours around the back of the ridge to arrive at Caw Gap (7 = NY 727 669).

Crossing straight over the road, a finger sign shows the route to Cawfields, 1 mile (1¼ kilometres) along the Roman Military Way. The pleasant track runs in the lee of the ridge, parallel to the vallum. Approaching Hole Gap, instead of threading through the nick, stay on the track as it swings to the left. Just before reaching the vallum, turn right and follow a narrow path running beside a fence. Arriving at an unclassified road, turn right and head back to the starting point.

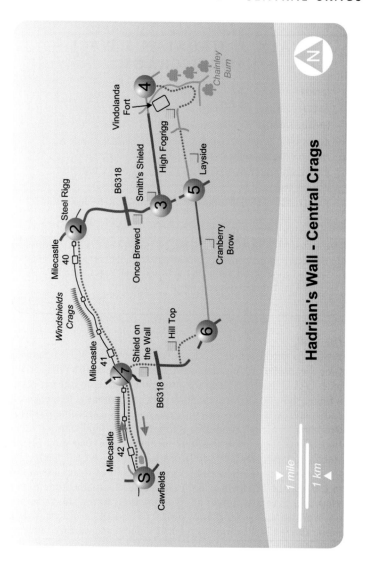

Hadrian's Wall - Central Crags

Vindolanda Fort

Chainley Burn

High Fogrigg

Layside

Steel Rigg

B6318

Smith's Shield

Cranberry Brow

Once Brewed

Milecastle 40

Windshields Crags

Milecastle 41

Shield on the Wall

Hill Top

B6318

Milecastle 42

Cawfields

N

1 mile

1 km

WALK 3: HADRIAN'S WALL – WEST CRAGS

LENGTH 10¾ miles (17¼ kilometres)

ASCENT 886 feet (270 metres)

HIGHEST POINT 948 feet (289 metres)

MAPS OS Explorer OL Map 43 ('Hadrian's Wall, Haltwhistle & Hexham') (West Sheet)

STARTING POINT Walltown picnic place, Hadrian's Wall (NY 668 660)

FACILITIES Public toilets (open during summer). Refreshments at Greenhead.

FEATURES A highly enjoyable walk following Hadrian's Wall over the Nine Nicks of Thirlwall and through the remains of Aesica fort. The return route follows a riverside path through a charming wooded gorge, as well as good tracks and quiet roads, with a chance to visit the historic centre of Haltwhistle.

The Wall

Walltown picnic place is signposted from the B6318, east of Greenhead. The first part of the walk follows Hadrian's Wall for 3½ miles (5¾ kilometres) along the Great Whin Sill. From the car park, a finger sign shows the Pennine Way heading along a tree-covered embankment, with intermittent views across the reclaimed quarry. Dropping to a quiet road, this is followed to a small parking area. Here a finger sign shows the route turning off the road and heading steeply uphill towards the crest of the ridge (1 = NY 675 662).

Cresting the rise, the well-preserved remains of Turret 45A stand at the head of Walltown Crags. This structure actually predates the Wall, and since it was built as an observation tower, the views are unsurprisingly excellent. Looking to the north, a distant tower marks the remote location of the RAF's electronic warfare range at Spadeadam, where the Blue Streak rocket was test-fired during the late 1950s. Heading north-east along the crest of the ridge, the

Walltown Quarry

Walltown Quarry was worked for roadstone from 1871 until the 1970s. As at Cawfields, part of the Great Whin Sill was destroyed, together with a section of Hadrian's Wall. This part of the ridge is known as the Nine Nicks of Thirlwall, although only five of the nicks have survived. Once again, a picnic place has been created around an artificial lake, with a car park, public toilets and an information centre.

crags on the left are home to chives that might have originally been cultivated by the Romans. Close to a northward kink in the ridge are the faint remains of Milecastle 45.

At this point the Pennine Way used to leave the ridge for about 1½ miles (2½ kilometres), following the Roman Military Way along the reverse slope. However, the path beside the Wall has now been established as a public right of way. Continuing along the ridge, the Wall appears as an overgrown dyke among rock outcrops. Arriving at a nick, swing to the right to avoid a steep descent. Crossing a drystone wall by a ladder stile, head steeply uphill, passing Turret 44B. Further along the ridge, the faint remains of Turret 44A are passed. Ahead is another gap – the last of the Nine Nicks, where a turn to the right avoids a drop. Rejoining the ridge, the path begins a gentle descent as it swings around to head east.

Passing the site of Milecastle 44, to the north of the Wall is the defensive ditch. Crossing a drystone wall by a ladder stile, the path runs through a stand of fir trees. Here the Wall is well preserved, despite being overgrown with brambles. Passing Cockmount Hill Farm, continue over fields towards Aesica fort, where the extensive remains are worthy of a thorough inspection. Exiting by a ladder stile beside Great Chesters Farm, the route crosses fields, staying parallel to a drystone wall that marks the course of the Wall. Ahead is the dramatic scar of the quarry face at Cawfields. Crossing a drystone wall by a step stile, an unclassified road is reached (2 = NY 712 665).

Haltwhistle Burn

Heading along the road, the entrance to Cawfields picnic place is passed, offering an opportunity to stop for lunch. A finger sign

Great Chesters (Aesica) Fort

Aesica (after Esus, the name of a Celtic deity) was built on the site of Milecastle 43, and housed a mixed garrison of cavalry and infantry. The west ramparts are well preserved, with the gateway retaining the blocking material used to close it up when it fell into disuse. The headquarters building (complete with vaulted strongroom) and commanding officer's residence have been uncovered, as have the barracks and granaries. A stone altar with a carved jug relief remains *in situ* near the south gateway. The western approach was protected by a system of four ditches, reflecting its perceived vulnerability due to the slope of the terrain. There was a civilian settlement beside the fort, and a bath-house to the south-east – the latter being supplied by a water channel following a winding course for 6 miles (10 kilometres) from the headwaters of Caw Burn.

on the right marks the start of a permissive path following Haltwhistle Burn downstream. This runs along the course of a wagonway that connected Cawfields Quarry and Haltwhistle, and is not marked on the map. Ignoring a flat bridge off to the right, stay on the east side of the stream. When the stream disappears into a culvert, cross a ladder stile and head up the side of an embankment to arrive at the B6318 (3 = NY 712 659).

Heading west along the grass verge, a finger sign on the far side of the road points through a kissing gate. Crossing a footbridge at the bottom of a field, a grassy track is joined. This follows Haltwhistle Burn downstream, passing a group of lime kilns, then a tall chimney and the remains of a colliery engine house. Re-crossing the burn, the way ahead enters a wooded gorge that is home to red squirrels, otters and dippers. Eventually an unclassified road is met, close to Broomshaw Hill Farm (4 = NY 705 650).

At this point there is an opportunity to visit the historic

> ## Haltwhistle Burn
> Haltwhistle Burn begins life as Caw Burn at the outflow from Greenlee Lough, and meanders about to the north of the Great Whin Sill until it finds a way through at Cawfields Quarry. It then follows a wooded gorge down to its confluence with the River South Tyne at Haltwhistle. Close to the quarry is the site of a Roman water mill that served the Wall garrison (the millstones are at Chester's Museum). A short way downstream, atop a bluff, is the site of a small fort dating from Trajan's reign, which seems to have acted as headquarters for soldiers stationed along Stanegate.

centre of Haltwhistle, with a return trip of 1¾ miles (3 kilometres). Turning left, head along the road as it runs down the pleasant dene. Passing a derelict sawmill, follow Willia Road and Aesica Road, with signs indicating the way to the town centre. Upon reaching the main street, the market square is a short way to the left (5 = NY 707 641). After looking around the town centre, retrace your steps back to Broomshaw Hill Farm, following the signs for Burn Gorge (6 = NY 705 650).

Haltwhistle Common

This time stay on the road as it heads up towards Lees Hall Farm, from where a hardcore track runs north over pasture, with views over the wooded gorge on the right, and ahead towards the Great Whin Sill. Crossing straight over the B6318, an unclassified road is joined (7 = NY 707 658). The remainder of the return route is on quiet roads and good tracks, 3 miles (5 kilometres) back to the starting point. As the road bends sharply to the left, ignore a track leading to Aesica Fort. From here the route runs west along the bottom of a broad, trough-like valley, parallel to the vallum. Passing an impressive lime kiln, the fields on the left are dotted with mature broadleaf trees. Continuing along the road as it runs past Walltown Farm, the point at which the Pennine Way turns off for Walltown Crags will be recognised (8 = NY 675 662). Arriving at a T-junction, turn right and head the back to the starting point.

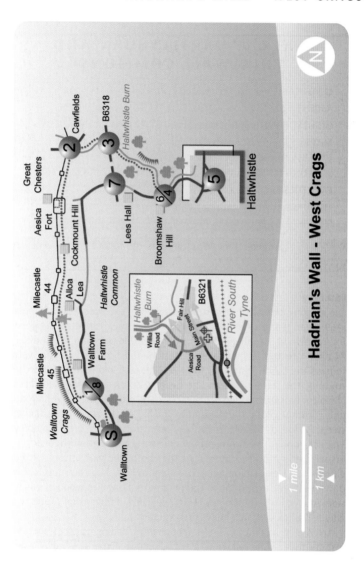

Hadrian's Wall - West Crags

WALK 4: HARTLEYBURN AND THIRLWALL COMMONS

LENGTH 14¼ miles (23 kilometres)

ASCENT 1,821 feet (555 metres)

HIGHEST POINT 948 feet (289 metres)

MAPS OS Explorer OL Map 43 ('Hadrian's Wall, Haltwhistle & Hexham') (West Sheet)

STARTING POINT South Tyne Trail car park, Rowfoot (NY 682 607)

FACILITIES Inn.

FEATURES As well as crossing moorland terrain, the varied route encompasses a railway trail and quiet roads running through lovely countryside. Lambley Viaduct, Thirlwall Castle and Featherstone Castle are just some of the historical points of interest along the way.

Lambley

The starting point is reached by turning off the Haltwhistle bypass (A69) near Bellister Castle and following an unclassified road signed for Coanwood. Arriving at Rowfoot, a side road runs past the Wallace Arms Inn to the former railway station. The first part of the walk follows the South Tyne Trail for 1½ miles (2½ kilometres), with the route of the former branch line heading south-south-west towards Lambley. Passing through another car park, cross straight over a road and continue along the pleasantly shaded track, which runs above steep, wooded slopes. Eventually the track runs onto Lambley Viaduct, which offers breathtaking views – although vertigo-sufferers will be in a hurry to cross. At the end of the viaduct are locked gates – Lambley Station being privately owned – so the route turns down wrought iron steps to follow a path along the wooded valley side. At a crossroads of paths (1 = NY 674 583), a finger sign shows the way to Lambley, which heads up a stepped path.

Arriving at a choice of ways, ignore steps leading up to a gate and instead turn right, following a path running above the valley side. Below is the course of a spur off the branch line, which ran to

Lambley Viaduct

Lambley Viaduct was designed by Sir George Barclay-Bruce as one of nine bridges carrying the Haltwhistle to Alston branch line over the valley of the River South Tyne. Sandstone from quarries at Slaggyford and Bardon Mill was used in the construction of the viaduct, which opened in 1852 and stands 110 feet (34 metres) high, with nine arches of 58 feet (18 metre) span and seven of 20 feet (6 metre) span.

Lambley Colliery until its closure in 1958. Emerging onto a road at the centre of the village, cross over and look for a finger sign pointing to a grassy track between the churchyard and a terrace of stone-built cottages. Passing through a tunnel, a faint path heads west across fields, with the remains of the colliery off to the right. Heading down the side of a row of cottages, an unclassified road is met.

This follows the course of Maiden Way, a Roman route running over the Pennine ridge (the name means 'great ridge way'), and offers a good alternative to the unappealing mix of boggy moorland and cattle-churned pasture that is the next section of the Pennine Way. If the road-walk is preferred, turn right and head north for 2 miles (3 kilometres), before following the Kellah road for 1 mile (1½ kilometres), rejoining the Pennine Way near Batey Shield. Otherwise, turn left and head towards the junction with the A689. Crossing straight over the road, a rough track runs up to meet the Pennine Way as it drops down from Lambley Common (2 = NY 667 585).

Hartleyburn Common

The next 1¼ miles (2¼ kilometres) cover some difficult terrain. Crossing a fence stile, follow a faint path through the heather, with a marker stone confirming the route. Arriving back at the main road, a finger sign shows a path heading north beside a drystone wall, then through a rushy mire. The route becomes indistinct as it runs over tussocky grass towards a ruin (High House). Heading down beside a gully, Hartley Burn is crossed by a footbridge. From here the route runs over pasture towards Batey Shield Farm. Arriving at the farm, a waymarked gate leads to a field, at the bottom of which a small footbridge leads to an unclassified road (where the alternative road-walk joins the Pennine Way) (3 = NY 654 611).

Crossing straight over the road, follow a hardcore track towards Greenriggs Farm, where a ladder stile leads to a field. Over another stile the route runs onto the grassy moorland of Hartleyburn Common. Heading west, follow the crest of a low ridge, keeping to the right of a rushy trough. Arriving at a fence, follow this north, crossing Glencune Burn by a footbridge. Over a ladder stile, a narrow path runs through rushes towards the highest point on the walk, close to an OS pillar. Although at only 948 feet (289 metres), extensive views are coupled with a real sense of remoteness. Continuing north, the A69 comes into view as the faint path runs downhill, passing an old brick building to arrive at a hardcore track. Here a finger sign shows the Pennine Way heading east along a causeway until another track is met (4 = NY 652 644).

Thirlwall Common

Turning left, follow this track down to the busy A69. Carefully crossing the road, at the top of the embankment a finger sign points diagonally across a field (ignore ladder stiles off to the right, which allow golfers to retrieve stray balls). Looking ahead, the Great Whin Sill can be seen, while to the left is the valley of the River Irthing. Over a couple of ladder stiles, the route eventually turns to follow the vallum across the golf course. Crossing the B6138, a path runs in front of a terrace of cottages to arrive at the Tyne Valley railway line. Ignoring a path signed for Greenhead, follow the tree-lined banks of Tipalt Burn towards Thirlwall Castle. Crossing the burn by a footbridge, the route climbs a steep track before following the defensive ditch across pasture. Arriving at an unclassified road, turn right and head past the entrance to Walltown picnic place, where we leave the Pennine way (5 = NY 668 660).

Featherstone

Continuing along the road, the entrance to the Roman Army Museum is on the right. Arriving at the junction with the B6318, cross straight over to where a finger sign points through a gate.

Thirlwall Castle

Thirlwall Castle was built in 1330–50, using stones looted from Hadrian's Wall (the name appropriately means 'gap in the wall'). Although now in a ruinous condition, it was once a substantial hall-house, home to the Thirlwall clan, who despite being charged with protecting the area from raiding Scots were themselves recorded as being inclined to theft. Sir Walter Scott visited in 1797, and it was here that he composed his poem 'To a Lady, with Flowers from the Roman Wall'. Following extensive consolidation work, the castle is now open to the public.

Heading down the side of a field, to the left is a dene with a thick undergrowth of bluebells and garlic. Passing through a gate, follow a stream down to College Farm, where a hardcore track is joined. Just after this crosses Tipalt Burn, a ladder stile on the right leads to the railway line and the A69 (6 = NY 666 645). From here the remainder of the route is on quiet roads, 3¼ miles (5¼ kilometres) back to the starting point. Joining an unclassified road signed for Featherstone, this passes the entrance to Blenkinsopp Castle before starting a long climb as it heads south through pasture. Ignoring turns for Haltwhistle and Lambley, the road runs down a steep wooded bank to Featherstone Bridge (7 = NY 675 619).

This was built in 1778, and is famous for its distinctive hump. On the south side of the bridge there is a choice of ways, with the easiest option being to stay on the road. This follows the wooded banks of the River South Tyne, passing the entrance to Featherstone Castle. A track continuing along the riverside to the former POW camp is worthy of investigation if there is time. Otherwise, follow the road as it zigzags steeply up a wooded slope and continues back to the starting point. For those who are tired of road-walking, a path runs southeast for about 1 mile (1½ kilometres) from the bridge. Straight across the road, a finger sign points to a step stile, from where a path crosses the flood plain. Heading up steps cut into the steep wooded slope, continue over fields punctuated with knots of oak trees. The path runs down the side of a conifer stand before emerging onto the road near the former Featherstone railway station.

Carvoran (Magnis) Fort

Magnis ('rocks') stood at the junction of Stanegate and Maiden Way. The first fort on the site predated Hadrian's Wall, and was rebuilt in 136–7 to house a mixed garrison of cavalry and infantry. Unusually, it is located to the south of the vallum, there being boggy ground beside the Wall. All that remains is the outline of the ramparts, although the site is home to the Roman Army Museum, which includes exhibits of what life was like for troops stationed on the northern frontier.

Featherstone Castle

Featherstone Castle is a mixture of medieval and later construction, with a defensive tower at its heart built by Thomas de Featherstone in 1290. One of his descendants, Sir Albany de Featherstonehaugh, was killed in a feud with the owner of nearby Blenkinsopp Castle in 1530. The estate was forfeited by Sir Timothy Featherstonehaugh when he supported King Charles II during the invasion of 1651. Later it was acquired by the Wallace family. In 1945–8, the grounds were home to 7,000 German POWs.

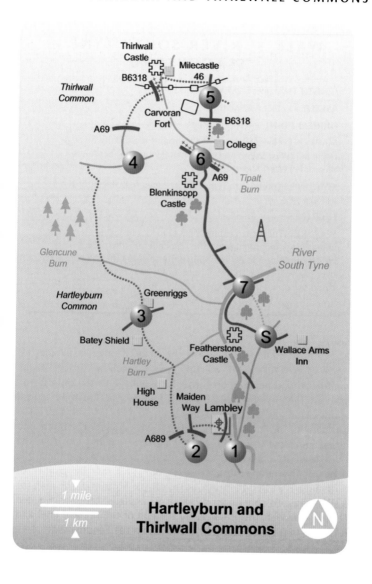

Hartleyburn and
Thirlwall Commons

WALK 5: RIVER SOUTH TYNE – SLAGGYFORD

LENGTH 13¾ miles (22¼ kilometres)

ASCENT 853 feet (260 metres)

HIGHEST POINT 968 feet (295 metres)

MAPS OS Explorer OL Maps 43 ('Hadrian's Wall, Haltwhistle & Hexham') (West Sheet) and 31 ('North Pennines – Teesdale & Weardale') (West Sheet)

STARTING POINT South Tyne Trail parking area, Slaggyford (NY 676 523)

FACILITIES Inn at Knarsdale.

FEATURES Whilst the Pennine Way follows a farmland steeplechase and a boggy moorland path, the remainder of the route is on a railway trail, providing an opportunity to enjoy the splendid views over the valley. The route takes the form of a 'figure 8', and so could be turned into two short strolls.

South Tyne Trail

Slaggyford ('muddy ford') is on the A689, 5 miles (8 kilometres) north-west of Alston. The starting point is reach by turning off the main road and heading up through the village to the old railway station. The first part of the walk follows the South Tyne Trail south-east along the former track-bed, 2¼ miles (3¾ kilometres) to Kirkhaugh. The grassy track is lined with hawthorn, birch and larch, and runs through a belt of pasture reaching up from the river towards open moorland. Crossing a viaduct spanning the dene of Thornhope Burn (1 = NY 687 511), as the hamlet of Kirkhaugh is passed the track drops off the bottom of the map for a short way. Passing under a bridge, Kirkhaugh Station is reached (2 = NY 696 496). This is currently the end of the railway line, and it is here that we turn off the track to join the Pennine Way.

South Tynedale Railway

South Tynedale Railway is England's highest narrow gauge track, and runs along a 2½ mile (4 kilometre) section of the former Haltwhistle to Alston branch line. The stretch heading north out of Alston was opened in 1983, with the link to Gilderdale Halt following in 1986 and the extension to Kirkhaugh in 1999. There are plans to extend the line to Lintley, then Slaggyford – 5 miles (8 kilometres) from Alston (in this event a path will be created alongside the track for the South Tyne Trail). Both steam and diesel trains are run, carrying fare-paying passengers.

Thornhope Burn

Heading up the side of the cutting, double back a short way to cross over the bridge. Joining the Pennine Way at the top of a field, this is followed 2½ miles (4 kilometres) back to Slaggyford. Passing through a gate in a drystone wall, a faint path runs over rough pasture towards the hamlet of Kirkhaugh. Turning onto an access road, a finger sign points through a gate, with the route continuing over fields, parallel to the South Tyne Trail. A finger sign points down into the dene of Thornhope Burn, where the stream is crossed by a footbridge (3 = NY 687 511).

Passing under the viaduct, a faint path runs around the edge of a field before heading down to the riverside. Continuing along the tree-lined riverbank, an unclassified road is eventually met, close to its junction with the A689. From here the Pennine Way follows the main road to Slaggyford (there is no pavement, so take care). Arriving at the village centre, head up the side road used earlier to access the starting point. This time look for a finger sign showing the route turning onto a muddy path beside the former Yew Tree Chapel (4 = NY 677 524).

Maiden Way

Heading north-west along a tree-lined lane, a marker stone shows a path running down into the dene of Knar Burn. Crossing a footbridge beneath a viaduct, turn right and follow the path as it hooks around, passing under the railway embankment by a tunnel. A track runs over fields to Merry Knowe Farm, where a finger sign shows the route passing to the right of the farm buildings. Crossing a step stile next to a shed, the route turns north-east. Arriving at an unclassified road, cross straight over and continue across rough pasture. Dropping down to Thinhope Burn, pass under another viaduct to arrive at a road (5 = NY 675 543).

Following the road as it crosses the burn, a finger sign shows the Pennine Way heading up a track towards Burnstones. This is a former coaching inn, and an inscription on the wall refers to 'Nichols Moor, Dealer in Foreign Spirituous Liquors'. From here a hardcore track heads north onto the moors, with fine views opening up as height is gained. The next part of the walk follows the course of Maiden Way for 3½ miles (5¾ kilometres) to Lambley. Leaving the track as it turns before some old workings, continue straight ahead over rough grazing. Crossing a drystone wall by a ladder stile, a quad track heads north through rushes, with views towards the Great Whin Sill.

Heading down to Glendue Burn, the A689 can be seen converging from the right. Crossing the stream by a footbridge, the pleasant little valley is embellished with birch and fir. Climbing steeply out on a stony path, the way ahead runs beside a drystone wall, with heather moorland to the left. As the path switches to the right-hand side of the boundary, the route tops out at a fairly modest 968 feet (295 metres). The drystone wall is replaced by a fence as the path runs gently downhill, crossing some boggy ground along the way. The second of two stiles on the left bears an acorn marker, and it is here that we leave the Pennine Way (6 = NY 667 585).

Lambley

For the next part of the walk, linking to the South Tyne Trail via Lambley, simply retrace the route followed on the previous walk. Ignoring the stile, follow a rough track down to the A689. From Shanders Houses, follow the route over fields towards the village, where a finger sign marks the start of a path to Lambley Viaduct. This runs behind a row of cottages and above the wooded valley side, before heading down steps to arrive back at the crossroads of paths encountered on the previous walk (7 = NY 674 583).

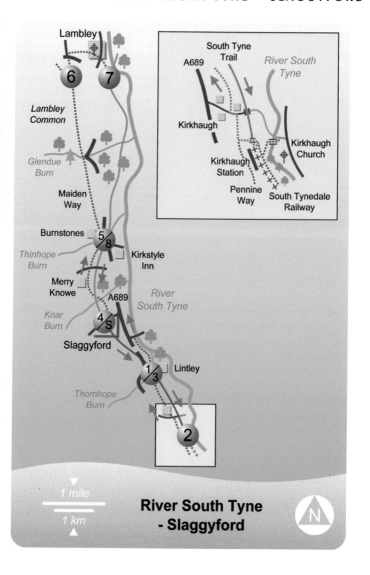

Lambley

6 7

Lambley
Common

Glendue
Burn

Maiden
Way

Burnstones 5/8

Thinhope
Burn

Kirkstyle
Inn

Merry
Knowe

Knar
Burn

A689

River
South Tyne

4
S

Slaggyford

1/3 Lintley

Thornhope
Burn

2

South Tyne
Trail

A689

River South
Tyne

Kirkhaugh

Kirkhaugh
Church

Kirkhaugh
Station

Pennine
Way

South Tynedale
Railway

1 mile

1 km

**River South Tyne
- Slaggyford**

N

Lambley Viaduct, built to carry the Haltwhistle to Alston branch line over the valley of the River South Tyne.

This time take the route signed for the South Tyne Trail (south), which continues down more steps. Heading back uphill, the path passes under the towering viaduct. From the former Lambley Station, the South Tyne Trail is followed south, 4 miles (6½ kilometres) back to the starting point. This is a good quality cycle track, with a smooth surface that provides an opportunity to focus attention upon the lovely scenery. Along the way the route passes through woodland and crosses viaducts spanning the valleys of Glendue Burn and Thinhope Burn – in the latter case, directly above the Pennine Way (8 = NY 675 543).

WALK 6: RIVER SOUTH TYNE – ALSTON

LENGTH 9½ miles (15¼ kilometres)

ASCENT 722 feet (220 metres)

HIGHEST POINT 1,116 feet (340 metres)

MAPS OS Explorer OL Map 31 ('North Pennines – Teesdale & Weardale') (West Sheet)

STARTING POINT Market Cross, Alston town centre (NY 719 464)

FACILITIES Full range of services.

FEATURES Another walk taking the form of a 'figure 8', this time centred upon England's highest market town. Crossing valley side pasture and passing the remains of a Roman fort (Whitley Castle), the return route runs alongside a narrow gauge railway. The paths can be muddy, but the views are lovely.

Nattrass Gill

Alston is located at the crossroads of the A686 (Haydon Bridge to Penrith) and A689 (Brampton to Bishop Auckland) trans-Pennine routes. There is a parking area in the marketplace, although this is often busy with shoppers, so it might be better to park elsewhere (note that the car park at the old railway station is locked at nightfall). The first part of the walk runs south along the valley side for 2 miles (3 kilometres) to join the Pennine Way at Bleagate Farm. Starting at the market cross, head along the cobbled main street (A689). Just before the junction with the B6277, a finger sign marks the start of a path to Nattrass Gill, heading along an alleyway beside St Paul's Mission.

Another finger sign points along a walled lane running past Fairhill Cottage, with the view ahead dominated by Cross Fell. From Annat Walls Farm a path runs along the edge of a field before dropping into a beautiful dene – Nattrass Gill – where the stream is crossed by a footbridge. Heading up a stepped path, a side-stream is crossed by another bridge. Continuing across fields towards High

Alston

At around 950 feet (290 metres) above sea level, Alston ('Alden's town') competes with Buxton in the Peak District for the dubious honour of being England's highest market town. A licensed market has been held here since 1154, serving the mines on Alston Moor. Lead was extensively mined from the early twelfth century, and locally produced silver was sufficient to support a Royal Mint at Carlisle. The cobbled main street is home to a distinctive market cross, donated by Sir William Stephenson of Crosslands Farm, who became Lord Mayor of London in 1764. Charles Dickens visited Alston in 1838 while researching his novel *Nicholas Nickleby*. Today the town is known as the home of Cumberland Mustard and Alston Cheese.

Nest Farm, turn onto an access road signed for Bleagate Farm, where the Pennine Way joins from the left (1 = NY 717 437).

Firs Wood

The next part of the walk follows the Pennine Way back to Alston. Passing through the farmyard, cross a step stile and turn right. Heading north across meadows, the river is off to the left, screened by larch and fir-trees. Re-crossing Nattrass Gill, the path eventually enters Firs Wood, where there is a choice of ways. The Pennine Way continues straight ahead, while another route heads down the valley side to join a riverside path. Passing the youth hostel, the path arrives at the A686 river crossing (2 = NY 716 461).

Whitley Castle

From here the walk follows the Pennine Way north-west to Kirkhaugh. Just over the bridge, close to a war memorial, a finger sign shows the route turning onto a hardcore track. A path runs down the side of a white-washed farmhouse before continuing over pasture towards Harbut Lodge. Passing to the left of the hall, which stands in parkland dotted with horse chestnut trees, a driveway leads to the A689. A short way along the road, a finger sign shows the route crossing a ladder stile, passing to the right of a barn before heading uphill on a rough track. Following a drystone wall to the top corner of a field, ignore a gated lane and instead cross over a step stile. Heading north-west over rushy ground, the path eventually drops into the valley of Gilderdale Burn, which is crossed by a footbridge (3 = NY 698 479).

Continuing north-west over rough pasture, a muddy track is soon joined. The grassy ramparts of Whitley Castle are off to the right as the track swings around to head north-east. Over a drystone wall by a ladder stile, the route continues downhill, to the right of a gully. Dropping down to cross the stream by a footbridge, the path threads through a thicket of birch trees to arrive back at the A689. Re-crossing the road, the route continues over fields, passing to the left of a belt of fir trees, then to the right of

---

Whitley Castle

Whitley Castle is the popular name for the Roman fort of Epiacum, which is connected with that of the Gaulish deity, Epona. It stands on the course of Maiden Way, which crosses over the Pennine ridge, connecting Kirkby Thore (Bravoniacum) and Carvoran (Magnis). The fort was built during Agricola's governorship to an unusual diamond-shaped plan, protected by a system of four ditches on three of its sides. To the west, where it is over-looked by higher ground, there are no less than seven ditches.

Dyke House Farm. Eventually a makeshift sign marks a right turn, down towards Kirkhaugh Station, where we leave the Pennine Way (4 = NY 696 496).

South Tyne Trail

Crossing a hump-back bridge, turn right and head down to the railway terminus, from where there are two routes back to Alston. The first and most straightforward is to follow the South Tyne Trail as it runs alongside the railway, 2½ miles (4¼ kilometres) back to Alston Station. The path is uncomfortably narrow, but the scenery is lovely. Crossing the dene of Gilderdale Burn by a viaduct, a sign marks the boundary between Cumberland and Northumberland (5 = NY 703 486). The River South Tyne is crossed near Harbut Lodge, before the path passes through a picnic place to arrive at the station.

Alternatively, there is the option of a pleasant road-walk back to the starting point. Over a fence stile at the south end of the station, head down towards the river, which is crossed by a footbridge. A hardcore track leads to an unclassified road, which is followed past Kirkhaugh Church, with its slender spire. The wooded valley side is home to red squirrels. Arriving at Randalholm Bridge, the farm is built around a well-preserved peel tower. As the road gains height it veers away from the river. Arriving at the junction with the A686, follow the pavement down towards Alston.

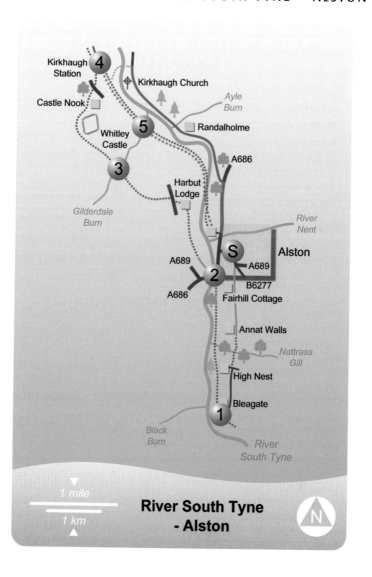

River South Tyne - Alston

WALK 7: RIVER SOUTH TYNE – GARRIGILL

LENGTH 12 miles (19¼ kilometres)

ASCENT 984 feet (300 metres)

HIGHEST POINT 1,542 feet (470 metres)

MAPS OS Explorer OL Map 31 ('North Pennines – Teesdale & Weardale') (West Sheet)

STARTING POINT Garrigill village centre, South Tynedale (NY 745 415)

FACILITIES Public toilets, inn and refreshments.

FEATURES A riverside walk taking the form of a 'figure 8' centred upon the lead-mining village of Garrigill and reaching towards the head of the valley. The meadows are punctuated by numerous gates and stiles, although the scenery is pleasant and there are some fine waterfalls along the way, including Ashgill Force.

Bleagate

Garrigill is signed from the B6277, 4 miles (6½ kilometres) south-east of Alston, and offers roadside parking around the village green. The first part of the walk follows the Pennine Way along a riverside path to Bleagate Farm, 2¾ miles (4¼ kilometres) to the north-west. Heading along Leadgate Road, a finger sign shows the Pennine Way turning onto a hardcore track. Passing the abandoned Redwing Chapel and some old spoil heaps, the path runs above the river, which is flanked with fir trees. Farms can be seen dotted about the valley sides, which are patterned with walled pasture. As the river enters a narrow gorge, the path runs through a grove of birch trees.

Arriving at a footbridge, the Pennine Way crosses the river, although for now we stay on the south bank. The path runs over meadows, and for a while follows the course of an old levy. Heading into another birch grove, it comes close to the water's edge before veering away from the river to cross a side-stream.

Garrigill

Garrigill ('Gerard's gill') is a pleasant village of stone-built cottages, standing beside the River South Tyne. It grew up around the lead-mining industry, and at its peak it boasted 1,600 inhabitants, although this has now dwindled to barely 200. Nevertheless, the village benefits from being located at the crossing point of the Pennine Way and the 'C2C' cycle route, which helps to support an inn – the George & Dragon. At one time there was another pub in the village – the Old Fox – which had a reputation as a rowdy establishment, frequented by lead-miners and poachers.

Soon the river itself is crossed by a footbridge. Heading straight up the valley side, a drystone wall is crossed by a gap stile, before a rough track leads to Bleagate Farm (1 = NY 717 437).

Garrigill Bridge

From here a path runs along the north side of the valley back to Garrigill Bridge. A finger sign shows the route heading south-east across pasture, passing the ruin of Low Sillyhall Farm (which was built around a bastle house). The Pennine Way heads down towards the footbridge that was earlier passed, although we follow a path signed for Garrigill. Crossing a gated gap stile, this runs over pasture dotted with oak and horse chestnut, above the wooded gorge. Passing the imposing buildings of Low Craig Farm, the route continues over meadows, crossing gap stiles identified by tall marker posts. Eventually the path arrives at an unclassified road, next to a tidy cemetery. The road runs past Beldy Chapel, where the landscaped grounds are home to tea rooms. Crossing Low Houses Bridge, the road continues towards Garrigill Bridge, where a finger sign shows a path to Pasture Houses (2 = NY 746 416).

Ashgill Force

The next part of the walk runs south-east for 1½ miles (2¼ kilometres) to Ashgill Force. A path runs above the river gorge before heading up through fields towards some old farm buildings. Crossing a drystone wall by a step stile, head straight over an access road to where a finger sign confirms the route. Passing to the right of a row of cottages (Pasture Houses), a marker post indicates a choice of ways. It is possible to follow a high-level path to Ashgill Force via Ashgillside Farm, although the riverside path – the route of the South Tyne Trail – is more interesting.

Heading down towards a stand of conifers, cross a fence stile and follow a path running steeply downhill. Ignoring a quaint little bridge perched above the constricted gorge, turn onto a path following the river upstream. Crossing boggy meadows, the path turns hard as it meets a busy stream (Ash Gill). Arriving at a crossroads of routes, take the path signed for Ashgill Force, which follows the stream towards the head of the beautiful dene. The path can be very slippery, so take care. Crossing a footbridge and passing the remains of some bays where lead ore was once stored, Ashgill Force suddenly comes into view (3 = NY 759 405).

Tynehead

Retracing your steps a short way, ignore a muddy path heading up the side of the gorge and instead follow a rough track running above the ore bays and up towards Bird's Nest Farm. Passing to the

Ashgill Force

Ashgill Force is a wonderful sight after heavy rainfall. Here the waters of Ash Gill plunge from the head of a rocky amphitheatre into a boulder-choked pool. An elegant road bridge spans the head of the gorge, looking like a petrified rainbow. It is possible to walk behind the waterfall, taking great care on the slippery path and being alert to the possibility of falling rocks. In any event, you can expect to get soaked with spray!

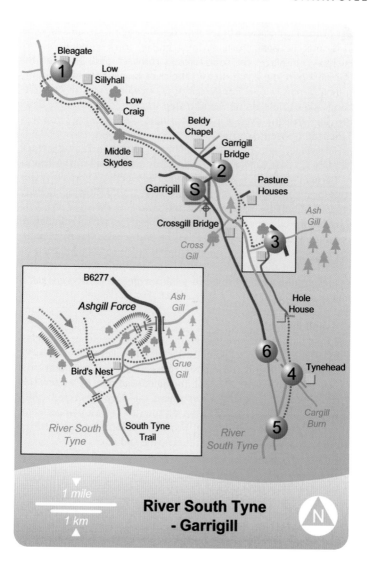

River South Tyne
- Garrigill

left of the farmhouse, a track runs down beside Grue Gill. Arriving at a marker post, turn onto a grassy track running across meadows. In places the route crosses rushy ground, although for the most part the going is easy. The river is again off to the right, tumbling noisily over rocky outcrops. Heading towards the left-hand side of Hole House Farm, a step stile leads to a muddy lane. Crossing straight over, a path continues over meadows towards Tynehead bridge (4 = NY 762 380).

Here finger signs indicate a number of routes, including a track heading up past Tynehead farm towards a waterfall in the course of Cargill Burn, which would certainly be worth a short visit. Our route is a continuation of the South Tyne Trail, following a newly created permissive path towards the source of the river. Crossing Cargill Burn by a footbridge, the route heads up past a ruin before continuing over boggy ground. As the path climbs out of the narrowing valley, the river takes a dramatic tumble down a chute carved out of the bare rock. Marker posts confirm the route as it swings around to head towards a barn, where a hardcore track is met (5 = NY 759 371).

Crossgill Bridge

The final part of the walk follows the track as it becomes an unclassified road, 3 miles (4¾ kilometres) along the valley side to Garrigill. Crossing a cattle grid at the point where an access track joins from Tynehead Farm (6 = NY 757 384), the quiet road runs past a few tidy farms. There are splendid views across the deep, V-shaped valley towards Burnhope Seat, with the ski tows at Yad Moss prominent. The road dips into the dene of Cross Gill before heading into the village, passing a cottage identified as the Old Fox.

NORTH PENNINES

Walk 1: The High Fells
Walk 2: Cross Fell
Walk 3: Knock Fell
Walk 4: High Cup Nick
Walk 5: Maize Beck
Walk 6: Widdybank Fell

The Fells of the North Pennines

The North Pennines extend from the Tyne Gap (A69) to the Stainmore Pass (A66). The area includes the highest of the Pennine fells, and some of England's most dramatic and inhospitable landscapes. The great rivers of the North East Region – the (South) Tyne, the Wear and the Tees – all rise here. In geological terms, the area equates to the Alston Block, which is bounded by the Stublick Fault System to the north and the Lunedale Fault to the south. The ridge was formed by the uplifting and tilting of this block, which dips gently eastward from its steep western scarp – the latter being a feature of the Pennine Fault System. The high fells are capped with a hard, coarse-grained sandstone – the Millstone Grit of the Upper Carboniferous period. This has mostly been eroded away to expose the rocks of the Lower Carboniferous period, which take the form of a repeating sequence of limestone, shale and sandstone strata, underlain by the thick Melmerby Scar Limestone.

Compared with the gently sloping moorland that predominates to the east, the western edge of the Pennine ridge drops dramatically towards the valley of the River Eden. This is the Eden Scarp, which is punctuated by deep glacial valleys, including the great gorge of High Cup. As a consequence of their geology, the high fells of the North Pennines are flat-topped. The only conical peaks are a chain of smaller hills buttressing the Eden Scarp, which are composed of igneous rock of Ordovician age and have more in common the Lakeland Fells. During the period following the last Ice Age, woodland spread across the North Pennines until only the tops of the highest fells remained bare. However, clearance by human set-

The High Fells

The highest of the Pennine fells are all concentrated in the North Pennines. Among a total of twenty-five hills exceeding 2,000 feet (610 metres), a half a dozen stand at more than 2,500 feet (762 metres), namely Cross Fell, Great Dun Fell, Little Dun Fell, Knock Fell, Mickle Fell and Meldon Hill. Cross Fell itself is the highest point in the Pennines, and the highest place in England outside the Lake District. A combination of difficult terrain, restricted access and proximity to the Lake District means that, with the exception of a few of the more accessible hills, the high fells are seldom visited.

tlers left only scattered remnants in the sheltered valleys. Today there is very little tree-cover – conifer plantations being limited in extent and restricted to the lower slopes.

People in the North Pennines

The North Pennines are rich in metalliferous ores such as lead, silver and zinc, as well as mineral deposits, including fluorspar, barytes and witherite. These became the basis of extractive industries that shaped the landscape and the settlement pattern. The area is particularly associated with lead-mining, with lead ore (galena) being found in great quantities. Lead has probably been

Sugar Limestone

In the North Pennines, the Great Whin Sill outcrops dramatically at locations such as Cronkley Scar, Falcon Clints, Cauldron Snout and High Cup Nick. The magma from which the dolerite was formed baked the surrounding rock, forming sugar limestone that in England exists only here – the most extensive outcrops being at Cronkley Fell and Widdybank Fell. Sugar limestone weathers to form sweet, granular soil, providing a habitat for rare flowers, including relic arctic-alpine flora.

mined here since Roman times, but it was during the eighteenth century that the industry took-off, responding to a surge in demand for lead piping from the country's growing industrial centres. At its peak in the mid-nineteenth century, around 6,000 people worked in the North Pennines lead-mining industry.

Mining techniques evolved from simple bell-pits and adits to larger-scale shafts and drifts ('levels'). Hushing was the practice of damming a stream, then releasing the water in a torrent that

Mist filling the great gorge of High Cup.

Nenthead Mines

At 1,437 feet (438 metres) above sea level, Nenthead is England's highest village. The Quaker-owned London Lead Company bought up the mining rights for the area in 1753, then in 1825 established the country's first purpose-built industrial village. This recalled their philanthropic tradition, with a school, a reading room and a wash-house. Nenthead Mines were at one time the most productive in the country, and continued to operate until 1961. The site has recently been re-opened as a visitor attraction. No longer accessible is John Smeeton's Nentforce (Drainage) Level, a tunnel that was navigable by boat as far as Alston.

scoured-away the surface material, exposing the underlying minerals. Lead was mined, separated and smelted in the North Pennines, although with the exception of a shot-tower at Alston, it was not turned into finished products locally. The area was crisscrossed with carriers' ways – pack-horse routes along which trains of up to twenty Galloway ponies carried lead ore from the mines to the smelt mills, then 'pigs' of lead from the mills to Tyneside. The mines were often at highly inaccessible locations, so the workers lived on-site during the week, with so-called 'shops' providing basic lodgings (as well as smiths, stables and stores). At weekends they supplemented their income by maintaining small-holdings – the five-day working week being originally introduced by the London Lead Company.

During the second half of the nineteenth century, the North Pennines produced around a third of the country's lead. The London Lead Company and the W.B. Lead Company (the latter belonging to the local Blackett-Beaumont family) each accounted for about a third of all

Killhope Lead-mining Centre

Park Level Mine at Killhope was operated by the W.B. Lead Company from 1853 to 1910, reopening briefly during the Great War. By the 1870s it was one of the most productive mines in the country, with 150 employees. An overshot waterwheel with a 34 feet (10 metre) diameter was installed in 1877, having originally been built in 1859 for the Blackett Level in Allendale. The site has been fully restored and is open to the public.

Allenheads Heritage Centre

Allenheads Heritage Centre is based around the Armstrong Engine House, which contains the only surviving hydraulic engine built by W. G. (later Lord) Armstrong at his Elswick Works – one of nine commissioned by the W. B. Lead Company in 1852. Others were used for pumping and winding, but the surviving example drove the saw mill, taking its power from reservoirs above the village.

production in the area, with the remainder being the output of smaller enterprises. The price of lead collapsed during the late 1870s, resulting in the closure of mines, population loss and the consolidation of miners' small-holdings into larger farms. Nevertheless, the remains of the lead-mining industry can be seen throughout the area in the form of ruinous structures and pockmarked hillsides.

A lime kiln above Dufton. The North Pennines lead-miners supplemented their income by farming marginal land, which they improved with slaked lime.

The valleys that radiate outwards from the high fells are home to some sizeable towns and villages, notably Alston, Allendale Town, Stanhope and Middleton-in-Teesdale. There are many smaller communities further up the dales, and it is clear that, without the lead-mining industry, such a marginal area could never have supported the population to which the settlement pattern testifies. The only road crossing the main ridge is the A686 (Haydon Bridge to Penrith), which follows a switch-back route over the Hartside Pass. This was one of several roads built by John McAdam during the 1820s to

The North Pennines Area of Outstanding Natural Beauty
The North Pennines AONB – 'England's Last Wilderness' – extends to 940 square miles (2,435 square kilometres) and includes parts of Northumberland, Durham and Cumbria. Due to the extreme sensitivity of the area, it was not designated as a National Park, and so does not receive anything like the number of visitors that each year descend upon the Lake District and Yorkshire Dales. Whilst this is an advantage from the point of view of those seeking a wilderness experience, there is little of the supporting infrastructure that visitors to the National Parks can expect.

serve the lead-mining industry, and tops out at a breezy 1,904 feet (580 metres) at the famous Hartside Café – England's highest diner.

Walking in the North Pennines

The North Pennines is one of the few places in England that can still offer a wilderness experience. The terrain is often difficult and there is a real sense of remoteness. Weather conditions can be unpredictable in summer and near-arctic in winter. Navigation is challenging – especially when the high ground is shrouded in mist – and there are few navigational aids (the proliferation of cairns being rather a source of confusion). Nevertheless, the old miners' tracks and carriers' ways offer good routes. The Pennine Way finds many of its superlatives in the North Pennines, including its highest point (Cross Fell), its most dramatic feature (High Cup) and its most exhilarating scramble (Cauldron Snout).

WALK 1: THE HIGH FELLS

LENGTH 19 miles (30¾ kilometres)

ASCENT 2,707 feet (825 metres)

HIGHEST POINT 2,930 feet (893 metres)

MAPS OS Explorer OL Map 31 ('North Pennines – Teesdale & Weardale') (West Sheet)

STARTING POINT Garrigill village centre, South Tynedale (NY 745 415)

FACILITIES Public toilets, inn and refreshments.

FEATURES A long and challenging hill-walk visiting the highest of the Pennine fells (Cross Fell, Little Dun Fell and Great Dun Fell). Navigation is fairly straightforward and fair weather reveals wonderful views, although in poor conditions the high fells can be hazardous.

The Corpse Road

Garrigill is more than 1,100 feet (335 metres) above sea level, so an ascent of the high fells from this direction offers an easy start. Moreover, the first part of the walk follows an old corpse road up onto the ridge, with 7 miles (11½ kilometres) of gentle ascent. From the Methodist Chapel at the south end of the village, the Pennine Way starts its long climb over the moors, heading south-

The Corpse Road

The dead of Garrigill were carried over the Pennine ridge to Kirkland Church by a 'corpse road' reaching 2,576 feet (785 metres). Whilst there was consecrated ground at Allenheads, it seems that the people of Garrigill had a special affinity for Kirkland. On one occasion – probably in the mid-sixteenth century – a burial party was overtaken by a snowstorm and had to abandon the coffin for a fortnight. After a church was built at Garrigill the track continued to provide access to the lead-mines.

Cashwell Mine

A verse by the 'Pennine poet', W.H. Auden, recalls an encounter with the pumping engine at Cashwell Mine: 'as it groans at each stroke like a heart in trouble, it seems to me something in toil most noble.' Old photographs show a three-storey, whitewashed shop at the mine, although only bare ruins remain. Beware of old mine shafts in this area.

Greg's Hut

Located at 2,297 feet (700 metres) on the northern flanks of Cross Fell (NY 691 354), Greg's Hut provides emergency refuge and a welcome resting place for long distance walkers on the Pennine Way. It was opened by the Mountain Bothy Association in 1972, and is dedicated to John Gregory (1928–68), a member of a local ski club.

west up a walled lane. At one point a faint path – once the official route – cuts the corner, although it is better to stay in the lane. Through a gate, the stony track runs over open moorland, with views across the broad valley of Black Burn towards Cross Fell. Ignoring a track on the right heading towards some old workings, continue towards Cashwell Mine. Here a marker stone shows a bridleway turning left, although the Pennine Way heads up through spoil heaps beside a boulder-choked hush (1 = NY 715 360).

Note the pieces of brightly-coloured fluorspar embedded in the track. Crossing a shallow stream, the route contours around the northern flanks of Cross Fell. A stream on the left can be seen disappearing into a limestone fissure, while further along is a line of shake holes – deep depressions created by water erosion. Passing an old bothy (Greg's Hut), as the track climbs towards the ridge it becomes rutted and boggy. Nearing the watershed, a marker stone beside a stone shelter shows the Pennine Way turning off the track and heading south-east, up towards the plateau (2 = NY 684 352).

Cross Fell, Little Dun Fell and Great Dun Fell

The next part of the walk follows the crest of the ridge for 3¼ miles (5 kilometres). Initially the path is hard going, it being difficult to distinguish between boggy grass and mossy stream. Climbing up through the garland of scree wrapping around the flanks of Cross

Cross Fell

Cross Fell reaches 2,930 feet (893 metres), and was once known as Fiends Fell, recalling its ominous appearance and extreme weather. This in turn is related to the infamous Helm Wind, which wreaths the ridge in an eerie bank of cloud. St Augustine of Canterbury is credited with exorcising Fiends Fell, although it is more likely that the name was changed during the early 1500s when a cross was erected at the summit. During the 1830s, the plateau was the scene of a political rally, complete with brass band.

Fell, a beehive cairn marks the edge of the plateau. Heading south-south-east towards the summit, this is marked by a cross-shaped stone shelter and an OS pillar (3 = NY 687 343). In fair weather this would be a good place to stop for lunch, with fine views across the Upper Eden Valley towards the Lakeland Fells.

Heading east-south-east towards a cone-shaped cairn, Cow Green Reservoir comes into view, although it is to the radar dome on Great Dun Fell that the attention is drawn. From a tall cairn, a rough path picks its way down through the scree belt, following a stream towards the saddle with Little Dun Fell. Passing a marker stone showing a bridleway crossing the route, the area to the left holds the source of the River Tees and is home to the starry saxifrage. Continuing south-east, the flagged path crosses a peaty mire before climbing the steep slopes of Little Dun Fell. Here the summit – standing at 2,763 feet (842 metres) – is marked by a stone shelter (4 = NY 704 330).

Continuing across the flat top, head steeply downhill towards the saddle with Great Dun Fell. There are distant views of the Central Pennines, while the Cheviot Hills can be seen on the northern horizon. The flagged path crosses boggy terrain before heading back uphill, contouring around the side of Great Dun Fell (5 = NY 710 321). Here there is a choice of ways. The easier option is to follow the radar station access road, which is surely the highest stretch of tarmac in the country. However, the literal route cuts across rough terrain, following a path heading south-east towards the head of Dunfell Hush. Crossing the gully, a few small cairns lead to the point where a gated track leaves the access road (6 = NY 716 316).

Great Dun Fell Radar Station
The civilian radar station on Great Dun Fell became operational in 1988, replacing an earlier installation. It stands at 2,782 feet (848 metres), and the 66 feet (20 metre) diameter dome is one of the principal landmarks of the North Pennines. The highest recorded gust of wind in England and Wales occurred here, reaching 133 mph (214 km/h) on 17 January 1993.

Trout Beck
The next part of the walk follows an old miners' track running beside Trout Beck to its confluence with the River Tees, 3½ miles (5½ kilometres) away. The stony track converges with the hush, which is now a deep gash in the ridge. Continuing down the track, ahead are views across a daunting expanse of bleak moorland. Following the beck east then north-east, the track has been washed away in places and it is necessary to take to higher ground. The beck skips over rocky outcrops in its course, and at one point runs in a shallow gorge. An array of instruments show that the track is nearing Moor House. This was once a shooting lodge, but it is now a site for monitoring climate change. Ignoring a bridge leading to the station, stay on the track as it passes the remains of a lead mine at Troutbeck Foot. Arriving at

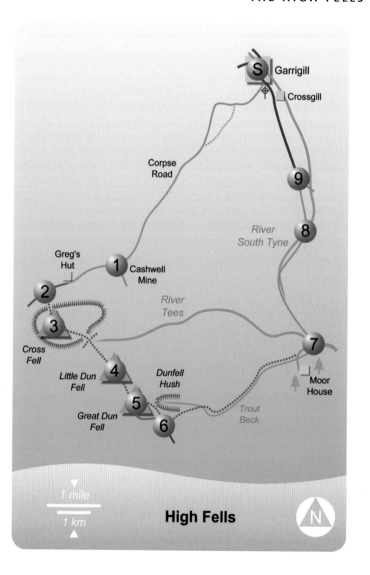

High Fells

the confluence of Trout Beck and the River Tees, the latter is crossed (7 = NY 761 339).

Tyne Head

Continue along the access road as it heads north-west then north. This is followed back to the starting point – still 5¼ miles (8¾ kilometres) away. Tarmac gives way to hardcore, although the surface is still comfortable. Crossing the barely noticeable watershed, a gully on the right holds the source of the River South Tyne, with a sculpture marking the location. From here the access road continues down the deepening valley, with the infant river quickly gathering strength. Ignoring a finger sign indicating a turning for the South Tyne Trail (8 = NY 759 371), stay on the track as it becomes an unclassified road (9 = NY 757 384) heading towards Garrigill.

WALK 2: CROSS FELL

LENGTH 10¾ miles (17½ kilometres)

ASCENT 2,526 feet (770 metres)

HIGHEST POINT 2,930 feet (893 metres)

MAPS OS Explorer OL Map 31 ('North Pennines – Teesdale & Weardale') (West Sheet)

STARTING POINT Blencarn village centre, Upper Eden Valley (NY 639 312)

FACILITIES None.

FEATURES An enjoyable hill-walk climbing Cross Fell via the steep Eden Scarp. The way up onto the ridge involves some tricky navigation, so fair weather is advisable, although the descent follows a good track. This is a 'bonus' walk, offering a return visit to Cross Fell – the highest of the Pennine fells.

The Eden Scarp

The eastern approach to Cross Fell hardly does the hill justice, so this bonus walk offers a return visit via the western scarp of the Pennine ridge. Blencarn is 7 miles (11½ kilometres) north-west of Appleby-in-Westmorland, and can be difficult to locate among the maze of narrow roads criss-crossing the area. It is nevertheless a pleasant little place, with red sandstone cottages clustered around a village green. There is roadside parking near the village hall. The first part of the walk follows a bridleway for 4½ miles (7½ kilometres) up onto the ridge. Passing through a gate at the east end of the village, a finger sign shows a rough track heading north-east over grazing land and through a broom thicket. Tree-lined pasture can be seen running right up to the foot of the scarp, from where steep grassy slopes reach up towards extensive scree fields. Leaving the track as it swings through a gate on the right, continue on towards Wythwaite Farm (1 = NY 654 316).

Passing through a gated sheepfold and fording Littledale Beck, the grassy track continues through an area of bracken before heading steeply up the valley side. Cresting the rise, the radar dome on Great

Dun Fell comes back into view, perched above the unsightly barytes mine at Silver Band. The route now takes a dramatic swipe across the face of Wildboar Scar. Whilst the track is fairly wide, there are steep slopes to the left. Swinging around to head north-east, a small cairn marks the start of a faint path climbing through scree fields. Passing an upright stone, continue across tussocky grass above the deep valley of Crowdundle Beck. A few small cairns provide reassurance of the route, although these are widely spaced and navigation can be tricky in poor visibility (the temptation to leave the path and head straight up the treacherous, scree-covered flanks of the plateau should be resisted). The path eventually levels out before meeting the Pennine Way at an altitude of 2,608 feet (795 metres) (2 = NY 697 339).

The Plateau

The next part of the walk follows the Pennine Way over the plateau, a distance of just 1¼ miles (2 kilometres). Breaching the scree belt to arrive at a tall cairn marking the edge of the plateau, continue west-north-west towards the summit (3 = NY 687 343). Having climbed the dramatic Eden Scarp to get here, Cross Fell seems a very different hill to that encountered on the previous walk — more like a mountain, in fact! From the OS pillar, head north-north-west towards a beehive cairn, then down through the scree belt to join the old corpse road coming up from Garrigill (4 = NY 684 352).

The Corpse Road

The return route follows this down to Kirkland, then a quiet road back to Blencarn, a total of 5 miles (8 kilometres). Following a chain of cairns over the watershed, the views across the Upper Eden Valley are stunning. A derelict shed off to the left is marked on the map as 'bothy'. The rough track heads steeply downhill before crossing a mossy mire. As a stony track joins from the right, the grass verge will be preferred. To the right is the deep valley of Ardale Beck, its slopes marked by scars and scree. At the foot of the valley can be seen a small pike — Lad Slack — around which Maiden Way once climbed.

Passing a cairn, the track starts zigzagging downhill. Diverging from the valley, the way ahead runs beneath a promontory with a scar on its nose (High Cap). To the left is Kirkdale — another deep valley cutting

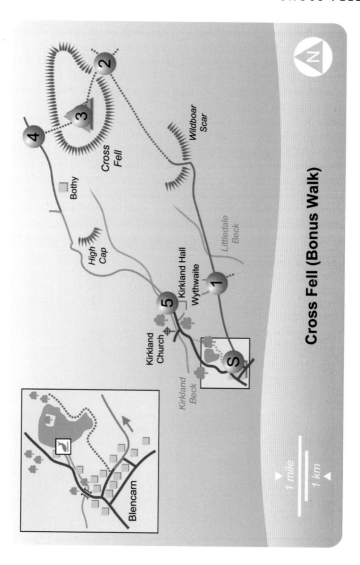

Cross Fell (Bonus Walk)

down through the scarp. The track runs over rough pasture dotted with hawthorn. Kirkland Beck is crossed before the track joins a leafy lane, passing the red sandstone buildings of Kirkland Hall to arrive at the start of an unclassified road (5 = NY 651 326).

A gated track on the left leads to some cultivation terraces known as the Hanging Walls of Mark Anthony, possibly dating from Roman times. However, we follow the quiet road as it runs beside the tree-lined beck. Soon the parish church is passed, with a small footbridge providing access to the churchyard. Arriving at a junction, follow the route signed for Blencarn. Soon a finger sign shows a path running over meadows towards the village, although it is easier to stay on the road. Blencarn Lake is a popular spot for anglers – being stocked with rainbow trout. Dropping into a wooded dell, the road crosses Blencarn Beck before arriving back at the village.

Kirkland Church

The Church of Saint Lawrence the Martyr was built in 1768 on the site of a much older (and larger) building. The church building itself, together with the gravestones and ancient stone cross in the churchyard are fashioned from red sandstone.

WALK 3: KNOCK FELL

LENGTH 12¼ miles (19¾ kilometres)

ASCENT 2,441 feet (744 metres)

HIGHEST POINT 2,605 feet (794 metres)

MAPS OS Explorer OL Maps 19 ('Howgill Fells & Upper Eden Valley') (Upper Eden Valley [North] Sheet) and 31 ('North Pennines – Teesdale & Weardale') (West Sheet)

STARTING POINT Dufton village car park, Upper Eden Valley (NY 689 250)

FACILITIES Public toilets, inn and refreshments.

FEATURES Another enjoyable hill walk, this time starting at the old lead-mining village of Dufton and following steep paths leading up onto Knock Fell. Descending on a radar station access road, the remainder of the return route runs around a pair of shapely peaks (Knock Pike and Dufton Pike).

The Eden Scarp

Dufton is 3 miles (5 kilometres) north of Appleby-in-Westmorland, and is reached by carefully navigating the confusing maze of narrow roads east of the A66. From the car park, turn right and head along the road as it runs past Dufton Hall Farm. Here a finger sign shows the Pennine Way turning off the road, joining a lane. Soon another sign marks a left turn onto a flagged path heading north-west beside a small stream. Eventually an old miners' track (Hurning Lane) is joined, passing through the farmyard at Coatsike Farm before entering a leafy lane. Dropping into the valley of Great Rundale Beck, the stream is crossed by an old clapper bridge (1 = NY 692 273).

Whilst it is only 2¾ miles (4½ kilometres) from here to the summit of Knock Fell, there is a total of 1,850 feet (564 metres) of ascent. The track follows a drystone wall north-east over rough pasture, with views of Knock Pike to the left, its symmetry marred by quarrying. Eventually a finger sign shows the Pennine Way

Dufton

Dufton ('dove farm') is one of a number of red sandstone villages tucked-in beneath the Eden Scarp. It remained a small agricultural community until the arrival of the London Lead Company, which donated the water fountain that stands on the village green. The fountain, which is less fussy than its counterparts at Nenthead and Middleton-in-Teesdale, bears a Latin inscription from Ovid's *Metamorphoses* ('there is a clear pool, whose waters gleam like silver'). Two rows of lime trees on the village green frame the views of the high fells, although it is to the distinctive conical form of Dufton Pike (1,578 feet/481 metres) that the attention is drawn.

leaving the track, joining a path running around a bluff and heading down into the valley of Swindale Beck. The lively stream is crossed by a footbridge that replaced one washed away in 2002 (2 = NY 700 285).

Heading steeply uphill, a sign marks the boundary of the National Nature Reserve. Pausing to look back, there are extensive views over the beautiful Upper Eden Valley. A couple of marker posts confirm the route, which runs up the left-hand side of Knock Hush. Arriving at the head of the hush-stream, an indistinct path heads north-east over tussocky grass. Passing a tall cairn at the plateau's edge (Knock Old Man), the path continues north-east, soon reaching the summit cairn (3 = NY 721 302).

Knock Fell

At 2,605 feet (794 metres), this is the fourth highest point in the Pennines. From the summit, a faint path heads north-north-east, soon swinging around to north-north-west. Scattered about the plateau are numerous cairns (or 'curricks') that were originally raised by shepherds to aid navigation, but which are now a potential source of confusion in poor visibility. Keeping to the right of a scree field, head gently down a broad ridge. Passing a scree-covered mound that is home to a stone shelter, flagstones provide passage of mires and a line of old fence posts act as guides as the path continues down towards the radar station access road (4 = NY 717 314).

The tarmac track is followed for 1½ miles (2½ kilometres), providing an easy descent from the ridge. Initially it heads down between steep, scree-covered slopes, beside a busy little stream (Knock Ore Gill) that quickly gathers strength. Passing the turning for Silver Band mine, as the valley falls away sharply on the right, snow poles are replaced by crash barriers. A distinctive hush and the remains of a conveyor system that once carried lead ore down from Great Dun Fell can still be spotted on the far slopes. Ignore a path signed for Dufton. When the access road turns to the right, a finger sign marks the start of a path to Knock (5 = NY 702 295). At this point there is a choice of ways.

Dufton Pike

The easier option is to stay on the tarmac track as it becomes an unclassified road heading down to Knock then back to Dufton, a total of 4¼ miles (6¾ kilometres) of pleasant lanes, passing the beautiful St Cuthbert's Church along the way. Whilst this option is enjoyable, there is a fine – albeit rather circuitous – route to Dufton, running around Knock Pike and Dufton Pike, following paths and lanes for 5¼ miles (8½ kilometres).

Leaving the access road, head south-west down a beaten path crossing rough pasture. Joining a quad track, this runs to the east of a promontory (Flagdaw) before contouring around the gorse-covered slopes of Knock Pike, above the valley of Swindale Beck. Heading across a field, a sunken lane is joined. Shortly before reaching Knock, a finger sign on the left shows a path to Dufton 'via Back of Pike' (6 = NY 683 273). Following a rough track, cross a fence stile and continue to the right of a drystone wall. Over a step stile, the path zigzags down into the dene of Swindale Beck, which is crossed by stepping stones close to its confluence with Great Rundale Beck. Climbing steeply out of the dene, continue above the latter stream until arriving back at the clapper bridge crossed earlier (7 = NY 683 273).

This time join a grassy track heading east through a deep defile between Brownber Hill and Dufton Pike. Hazel and hawthorn climb the steep slopes on either side of the valley, which was formed as a glacial meltwater channel. To the left are views up a glaciated

Looking towards the radar station on Great Dun Fell from Knock Old Man.

valley holding the headwaters of Great Rundale Beck. Ignoring a step stile on the left, follow the track until it meets a gate (8 = NY 704 268). From here a stony track heads south along the side of Dufton Pike. To the left is the valley of Little Rundale Beck. The track swings around to head south-west, entering a hedge-lined lane before passing Pusgill House. Ignoring the turning for the Pennine Way, retrace your steps back to the starting point.

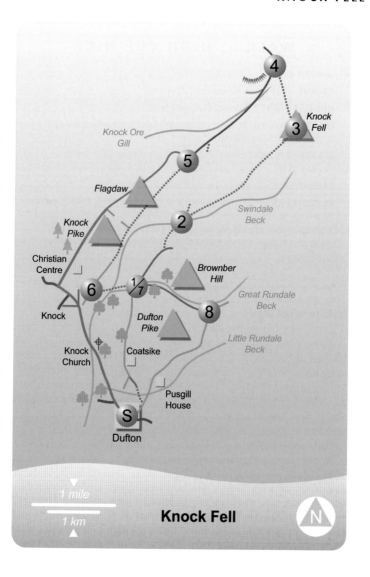

Knock Fell

WALK 4: HIGH CUP NICK

LENGTH 9½ miles (15¼ kilometres)

ASCENT 1,608 feet (490 metres)

HIGHEST POINT 1,936 feet (590 metres)

MAPS OS Explorer OL Map 19 ('Howgill Fells & Upper Eden Valley') (Upper Eden Valley [North] Sheet)

STARTING POINT Dufton village car park, Upper Eden Valley (NY 689 250)

FACILITIES Public toilets, inn and refreshments.

FEATURES After a charming dene and tame farmland, the character of the route changes dramatically as it heads up the great gorge of High Cup before returning via an old miners' track. The difficult climb up through the nick makes the walk unsuitable for adverse conditions.

Dufton Ghyll Wood

A finger sign beside the car park marks the start of a stony track running past a caravan site, down into Dufton Ghyll. At the bottom of the charming dene, just before the track crosses a stone bridge, another finger sign marks a turn over a rickety footbridge, joining a path leading to Redbanks Bridge. This runs south-east along the wooded valley floor, passing overgrown quarries where the St Bees Sandstone is exposed. All too soon the trees thin out and a gate leads to an unclassified road (1 = NY 694 245).

Crossing a road bridge, a finger sign shows a path to Keisley. This joins the access for Greenhow Farm, then continues south-east over fields, keeping to the right of a tree-lined boundary. Eventually another finger sign shows the route turning over a dry-stone wall on the left, heading north-east up the middle of a field then along a hedge-lined track to arrive at an unclassified road (2 = NY 707 238). Ignoring a path signed for High Cup Nick (via Bow Hall), turn right and head along the lane, with the distinctive forms of Murton Pike and Roman Fell dominating the view ahead. A short way after the road crosses Keisley Beck by a stone bridge, a finger sign on the left marks the start of a path to Harbour Flatt Farm (3 = NY 717 234).

High Cup Gill

From here to the head of High Cup Gill is a distance of 2¾ miles (4½ kilometres), with a difficult climb up through the nick. Crossing a fence stile, head south-east over pasture, veering to the left of a tree-crowned hillock. Approaching the farm buildings, turn onto a stony track heading down through a scattering of ash and hazel. Fording a stream, leave the track and head north-east up the broad ridge separating High Cup Gill and Trundale Gill. Veering to the left before Middletongue Crag is reached, the path heads down to the valley floor.

Ahead are stunning views up the great gorge, with a collar of cliffs arrayed on either side of a boulder-choked cleft. Crossing a drystone wall, High Cupgill Beck is followed upstream to the point where it emerges from the ground. Ahead is a boulder field of

High Cup Nick from the gill – a daunting scramble.

dolerite blocks, torn from the Great Whin Sill by the passage of ice. The boulders can be very slippery, so take care. The final section of the climb up through the nick is a daunting scramble, although the boulder field is reasonably stable (the route marked on the map heads up very steep slopes to the left, offering an alternative). High Cup Plain is gained at the point where a mossy stream empties into the cleft (4 = NY 746 262).

High Cup Nick

The great gorge of High Cup is reminiscent of the glacial trenches seen in the Cairngorms, although it looks so out of place in the North Pennines that the splendour of the scene is greatly exaggerated. The dramatic cliffs are an outcropping of the Great Whin Sill, exposed by the passage of ice. The boulders littering the valley floor are relics of the collapsed sill – the underlying limestone being eroded away. One of the pinnacles along the cliff edge, Nichol's Chair (or Nichol's Last), was named for a local cobbler who, for a bet, sat on top while mending a pair of shoes. Occasionally the stream that empties into the cleft can be seen spurting upward. Peregrine falcons also catch the updraft, circling as they hunt for prey.

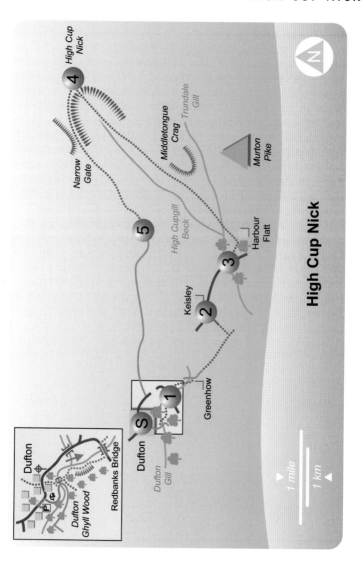

High Cup Nick

The Miners' Track

From here the view is particularly stunning, with the cliffs of High Cup Scar running around the rim of the great gorge like the aisles of a Cyclopean temple. Weather permitting, this would be a good place for lunch. The return route follows the Pennine Way down an old miners' track, 4 miles (6½ kilometres) back to the starting point. Following a chain of marker stones leading around the head of the gorge, the route soon tops out at a respectable 1,936 feet (590 metres). From here a rough track runs south-west along a broad shelf (Narrow Gate), with steep, scree-covered slopes to the right and a sheer drop to the left. Veering to the right as the track comes perilously close to the edge, a short climb leads to a parallel track.

Heading downhill, the view over the gorge is replaced by a panorama encompassing the Lakeland Fells, Howgill Fells and Central Pennines. Dropping into an overgrown quarry, note the lime kiln perched above (5 = NY 722 250). Passing through a walled enclosure, the track runs over rough grazing before entering a lane. To the north is Dufton Pike, its pyramid-like form being particularly striking from this angle. Eventually the track becomes tarmac, running gently downhill under the shade of oak, ash and sycamore. Arriving at an unclassified road, turn right and head back into the village.

WALK 5: MAIZE BECK

LENGTH 14¾ miles (23¾ kilometres)

ASCENT 1,280 feet (390 metres)

HIGHEST POINT 1,936 feet (590 metres)

MAPS OS Explorer OL Maps 19 ('Howgill Fells & Upper Eden Valley') (Upper Eden Valley [North] Sheet) and 31 ('North Pennines – Teesdale & Weardale') (West Sheet)

STARTING POINT Cow Green Reservoir car park, Upper Teesdale (NY 811 309)

FACILITIES Inn and Langdon Beck.

FEATURES The walk combines alternative Pennine Way routes – one following an old miners' track, the other crossing rough moorland terrain. In addition to Cow Green Reservoir, the great gorge of High Cup is once again a highlight. Note that if Maize Beck is in flood, a linear route must be followed.

Widdybank Fell Nature Trail

Cow Green Reservoir is reached by turning off the B6277 at Langdon Beck Hotel, 7 miles (11 kilometres) north-west of Middleton-in-Teesdale, and following an unclassified road for 3 miles (5 kilometres). Given its remoteness, the car park is surprisingly popular. Heading back along the road, a sign points along a gravel path leading to an access road. This is followed south for 1½ miles (2½ kilometres) to the dam. Across the reservoir is the heather-clad dome of Meldon Hill, while Cross Fell and its neighbours form the skyline. Straight ahead is the long ridge of Mickle Fell. Outcrops of sugar limestone can be identified beside the road. A meteorological station was placed here when the reservoir was built, answering fears that such a large body of water would raise temperatures and displace the rare flora.

Passing the concrete dam, the access road heads downhill. The source of the deafening roar coming from the foot of the dam is the River Tees, which here gushes through pipes. At times the reser-

> ### Cow Green Reservoir
> Cow Green Reservoir was built in 1967–71 by the Tees & Cleveland Water Board to meet the needs of industrial Teesside. The dam itself is 1,875 feet (572 metres) long and 82 feet (25 metres) high. The high water mark is 1,603 feet (489 metres) above sea level – only slightly lower than England's highest reservoir (Chew Reservoir in the Dark Peak). Many conservationists opposed the construction of the reservoir, which submerged 770 acres (312 hectares) of rare habitat. By way of compensation, the access road was made available as a nature trail.

voir overflows and water spills over the face of the dam. The Pennine Way joins from the left, just before the river is crossed (1 = NY 815 288). Beneath the bridge the river hurries excitedly towards Cauldron Snout, which although not visible is just a short way downstream. The peaty froth seen floating on the surface of the river recalls the tale of a green-haired mermaid called Peg Powler, who was said to prey upon children who ventured too close to the water. The froth is known locally as 'Peg Powler's Suds'. Here it is necessary to switch maps, taking up Sheet 19.

Birkdale
A short way along a stony track, a sign warns walkers against attempting to ford Maize Beck when in flood. Passing a barn, a short deviation over the rushy grazing on the left leads down towards the confluence of the River Tees and Maize Beck, from where there are stunning views of Cauldron Snout and Falcon Clints. Continuing along the track, a finger sign shows the Pennine Way turning down towards the Birkdale Farm. Despite the presence of a few mature broadleaf trees that have somehow managed to grow here, this is a desperately bleak place (2 = NY 804 279).

From here an old miners' track runs 2½ miles (4 kilometres) to the ford. A finger sign shows the Pennine Way crossing Grain Beck by a footbridge, with a rough track running over boggy ground towards the remains of Moss Shop. MoD warning signs mark the boundary of Warcop Training Area. From here the route heads west-south-west, skirting the edge of the danger area as it crosses bleak moor-

Warcop Training Area

Warcop Training Area was established in 1942 as a tank gunnery range, covering 39 square miles (101 square kilometres). Roman Fell provides the back-drop to the firing ranges, and Little Fell is still littered with shell cases. There are significant access issues, and the numerous warning signs marking the boundary intrude upon what is otherwise a wilderness.

land. Height is slowly gained as the track runs along a stony causeway, then over peaty ground, with occasional cairns confirming the route. Heading down into the trough of Maize Beck, the track continues along the north bank. Side-streams cascade down through channels where the bare limestone has been blackened by peat. A couple of marker stones indicate the point at which Maize Beck is forded (3 = NY 768 268).

High Cup Plain

If the beck is in flood, the north bank must be followed to the bridge at Maize Beck Gorge – in which case this becomes a linear route. Assuming that the beck can be forded, the miners' track is followed for a further 1½ miles (2¼ kilometres). The track gains height slowly as it veers away from the beck, with moss-covered cairns confirming the route. Running onto High Cup Plain, it is not unusual to encounter grazing horses during summer. A marker stone indicates a sharp turn towards High Cup Nick, with the head of the gorge once again providing a good place to stop for lunch (4 = NY 746 262).

Continuing around the head of the gorge, as the Pennine Way heads down towards Dufton we turn north-east along a faint path running beneath the scree-covered scarp of Dufton Fell. Small cairns confirm the route, which runs past a 'rockery' of limestone outcrops. Over a rushy area, the footbridge at Maize Beck Gorge is reached (5 = NY 749 270). Here the beck has cut a deep channel, with walls of peat-blackened limestone that are home to the rare rose-root. Crossing the bridge, the gorge is followed south-east. From here there is 1¼ miles (2¼ kilometres) of difficult terrain to negotiate. As well as crossing boggy ground, one or two side-streams can themselves be quite deep. The miners' track is eventually rejoined at the ford (6 = NY 768 268).

Maize Beck Gorge.

Cow Green Reservoir

From here simply retrace your steps back to the starting point, a total of 5½ miles (9 kilometres). Birkdale Farm is a welcome sight after travelling through such inhospitable country (7 = NY 804 279). Just before re-crossing the River Tees (8 = NY 815 288), it is possible to turn onto a tarmac track heading up to the west end of the dam, from where a walkway runs along the top to rejoin the access road.

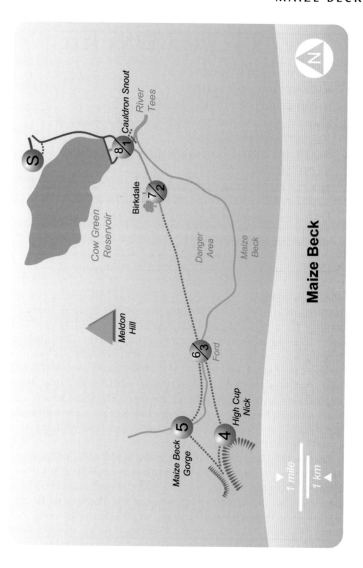

Maize Beck

WALK 6: WIDDYBANK FELL

LENGTH 11 miles (17¾ kilometres)

ASCENT 984 feet (300 metres)

HIGHEST POINT 1,673 feet (510 metres)

MAPS OS Explorer OL Map 31 ('North Pennines – Teesdale & Weardale') (West Sheet)

STARTING POINT Langdon Beck, Upper Teesdale (NY 853 312)

FACILITIES Inn.

FEATURES After crossing the rough pasture of Upper Teesdale, a sustained clamber along the boulder-strewn riverside path beneath Falcon Clints is followed by an exhilarating scramble up the side of Cauldron Snout. Cow Green Reservoir access road provides an easy return route.

Forest-in-Teesdale

Turning off the B6277 at Langdon Beck Hotel, there is roadside parking for a half a dozen cars. Head back to the junction and cross over the main road to where a finger sign points along a tree-lined access road, running above the beck towards Valence Lodge. Crossing a bridge behind the whitewashed farm buildings, pass through a gate and head south-east up the valley side. After negotiating some boggy ground another gate leads to a good track at High Hurth Caves. The bones of a prehistoric man were discovered here in 1887, together with lynx and wolf remains (1 = NY 869 309).

From here there are fine views over the broad valley of the River Tees. Turn onto a track heading south-south-west. This runs down through fields towards Forest-in-Teesdale. Joining an access road, continue past the school, which now has just 15 pupils on its register. Passing through Hanging Shaw car park, turn right and head along the main road to where a finger sign points down a farm access. Over a gap stile to the right of the whitewashed farmhouse, a faint path crosses paddocks before turning down

Widdy Bank Farm

Close to Widdy Bank Farm is an outcrop of Silurian slate that once provided material for pencils known locally as 'widdies'. The farm dates back to 1698, and now serves as a station for the management of the Moor House & Upper Teesdale National Nature Reserve. This is England's largest reserve, extending to 29 square miles (74 square kilometres). It is managed by English Nature, which owns the western half and has management agreements with landowners covering the remainder.

towards a rushy mire. Joining a hardcore track heading towards Cronkley Bridge, a finger sign shows the Pennine Way turning onto a path running along the north bank of the River Tees (2 = NY 862 294).

The River Tees

The stony path narrows as it runs beneath a steep slope. Arriving at the confluence with Harwood Beck, the tributary is followed upstream towards Saur Hill Bridge (3 = NY 855 302), where markings indicate the distances to Kirk Yetholm (121 miles) and Edale (149 miles). Crossing the beck, a hardcore track is joined. Leaving this before it reaches a farmhouse, head up to a step stile and continue west-south-west over rough pasture, with sections of boardwalk providing passage of boggy ground. The dolerite cliffs of Cronkley Scar dominate the scene as the River Tees comes back into view. Dropping to the riverbank, continue towards Widdy Bank Farm (4 = NY 837 298).

From here a grassy track runs beneath the flanks of Widdybank Fell. Passing through a gate, the way ahead suddenly pinches out, with a narrow path weaving through boulders that run right down to the water's edge. As the valley floor broadens and turns boggy, there are sections of boardwalk. However, the route soon degenerates into a horizontal scramble over slippery boulders. Above are the shattered dolerite cliffs of Falcon Clints, which were once home to golden eagles and may still be frequented by kestrels and peregrine falcons. Juniper grows in abundance hereabouts, and only the MoD warning signs on the far side of the valley detract from the scene. Passing the confluence with Maize Beck and continuing around a bluff, Cauldron

> Always my boy of wish returns
> To those peat-stained deserted burns
> That feed the Wear and Tyne and Tees
> And, turning states to strata, sees
> How basalt long oppressed broke out
> In wild revolt at Cauldron Snout.
> W.H. Auden, 'New Year Letter'.

Snout comes suddenly into view. The scramble up the side of the falls necessitates care, with a puzzle of dolerite blocks forming giant steps. Upon reaching the top, a path leads to the reservoir access road (5 = NY 815 288).

Cow Green Reservoir

It is here that we leave the Pennine Way, with the final part of the walk being on tarmac – 4 miles (6¾ kilometres) back to the starting point. Heading up the access road, this is followed north as it runs along the shoreline. Looking across the reservoir, a line of butts can be seen marching up the slopes of Meldon Hill, while the heather moorland of Widdybank Fell is itself thick with grouse. Eventually an unclassified road is joined (6 = NY 817 309).

This runs over pock-marked terrain that reveals the area's lead-mining past. Snow poles provide an indication of the altitude – this being the highest point on the walk. As the road starts downhill, ahead are fine views of Upper Teesdale, with the characteristic whitewashed farms dotted about a landscape of walled pasture suspended

Cauldron Snout

At Cauldron Snout the River Tees cuts through the Great Whin Sill, cascading 200 feet (61 metres) down a series of eight cataracts. The route up the side of the falls is one of the most perilous sections of the Pennine Way, the slippery rock being kept wet with spray. There have been several fatalities, and a ghost called the Singing Lady is supposed to inhabit the area. According to the tale, she was a Victorian farm girl who drowned herself here when an affair with a lead-miner ended.

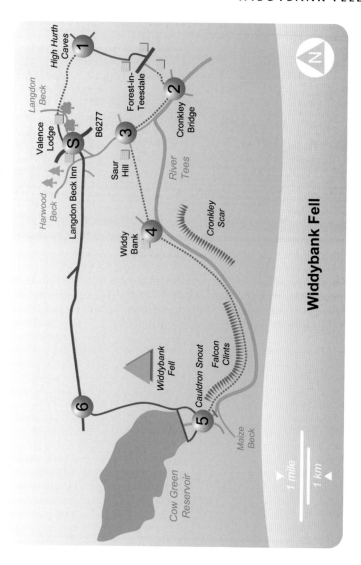

Widdybank Fell

The River Tees overflowing Cow Green Reservoir.

beneath moorland fells. As another road joins from the left, continue gently downhill. Harwood Beck is met at a point where it cuts through glacial moraine. Crossing the beck, follow the road as it runs past farm buildings towards the hotel.

TEESDALE

Walk 1: Upper Teesdale
Walk 2: Baldersdale and Lunedale
Walk 3: Cotherstone Moor
Walk 4: Bowes Moor

The Durham Dales

The rivers Derwent, Wear and Tees rise in the North Pennines and flow east towards the North Sea. They have carved three fine dales, separated by broad ridges that in places reach 2,000 feet (610 metres) above sea level. The ridges are capped in Millstone Grit, which dominates the geology of the eastern part of the area (recalling the tilting of the Alston Block). Further up the dales this has been worn away to expose the rocks of the Lower Carboniferous period. The Great Whin Sill outcrops extensively in Upper Teesdale, creating such dramatic features as Low Force, High Force and Holwick Scars.

Derwentdale is a thickly wooded, incised valley holding a sizeable tributary of the River Tyne, cutting through beautiful heather moorland dotted with lead-mining remains. Upper Weardale is also V-shaped, but is broader and deeper than its northern neighbour. The lower slopes, though steep, serve as meadow and pasture, while the narrow valley floor is occupied by linear settlements that reach up towards the head of the dale. Upper Teesdale is broader-still and 'U'-shaped, recalling the work of glaciation. The valley floor and lower slopes are patterned with walled fields. Some

Teesdale – The Valley of the River Tees

The River Tees is born on Cross Fell. It flows south-east to Barnard Castle, then east through the Tees Lowlands, entering the North Sea on industrial Teesside, where it is scarcely recognisable as the lovely river that graces Teesdale. Low Force, High Force and Cauldron Snout in Upper Teesdale are among the country's finest waterfalls, in each case being formed where the river cascades over outcrops of the Great Whin Sill.

maintain that Teesdale is in fact one of Yorkshire's dales – the area to the south of the River Tees being at one time part of the North Riding of Yorkshire. However, all three dales are now unambiguously part of County Durham.

People in the Durham Dales

The place names found in the Durham Dales reflect the origins of the people who settled here. Whilst those in the northern dales are generally Anglo-Saxon, Upper Teesdale shows Viking influence. Indeed, the tributary valley of Baldersdale is named after one of their deities. Old Norse words appear frequently in connection with landscape features ('beck', 'force' etc.), and it is noteworthy that the terms 'fell' and 'dale' are themselves Viking in origin.

The area to the north of the River Tees fell within the see of the Bishops of Durham. In 1072, William the Conqueror granted special authority to these 'prince bishops', with the intention of making them strong enough to protect his northern border. They ruled over the Palatinate of Durham, had their own army, raised taxes and minted coin. The Forest of Weardale was their private chase, where they hunted game from the early thirteenth century. More recently it was lead-mining that left its mark upon the area, with the North Pennines orefield extending throughout the Durham Dales. Upper Weardale was associated with the extraction of lead and silver from the twelfth century, when Bishop Hugh de Puiset was granted mineral rights by the Crown.

As lead-mining grew in importance during the eighteenth century, so did Methodism. It seems that whenever life is short and work is hard, people turn to the Lord for a sense of purpose. John Wesley himself visited Blanchland in 1747, with the first Methodist preachers arriving in Upper Weardale during the fol-

There are two kings in England, namely the lord king of England wearing a crown in sign of his regality, and the lord bishop of Durham wearing a mitre in place of a crown as symbol of his regality in the Bishopric of Durham.

Master William of Boston, Steward of the Bishopric of Durham (1302).

Low Force in Upper Teesdale.

> O for a thousand tongues to sing my great Redeemer's praise,
> the glories of my God and King, the triumphs of his grace!
> My gracious Master and my God, assist me to proclaim,
> to spread through all the earth abroad the honours of thy name.
> Jesus! the name that charms our fears, that bids our sorrows cease;
> 'tis music in the sinner's ears, 'tis life, and health, and peace.
>   Charles Wesley, 'O For a Thousand Tongues to Sing' (1739).

lowing year, crossing 'quagmires and enormous mountains' in a snowstorm to get there. After touring the dales in 1752, John Wesley returned regularly, often preaching in the open-air to congregations of lead-miners and their families. At Ireshopeburn he preached under a tree known as 'Wesley's thorn'. When the construction of a railway line threatened the tree in 1894, a campaign by local people resulted in its diversion. The popularity of Methodism has waned as the population of the dales has declined, but many of the chapels remain as a testimony to one of the country's great revivals.

Through its association with Hannah Hauxwell, who once single-handedly ran an isolated farm in Baldersdale, the Durham Dales are as synonymous with hill-farming as any other part of the country. Hill-farming continues to dominate the landscape, with isolated farmsteads scattered across the valley sides. Swaledale sheep predominate, with limited cattle rearing where conditions permit. The harsh climate has restricted agricultural intensification, so the meadows and pastures are rich in rare plant species, including

Low Birk Hatt Farm

Low Birk Hatt Farm was home to Hannah Hauxwell, who was featured in the 1973 Yorkshire Television documentary 'Too Long a Winter'. Here she lived alone, without electricity, telephone or running water, often snowed-in for days on end. She has since moved to an easier life at Cotherstone, with the farm becoming a nature reserve managed by Durham Wildlife Trust. Traditional farming methods are maintained. No artificial fertilisers are used and the meadow is left uncut until July, giving wild flowers time to seed and birds an opportunity to nest. In the north-west corner of the meadow is a visitor centre (Hannah's Barn).

> **Raby Estate**
> A distinctive feature of Upper Teesdale is the whitewashed farm build-
> ings of the Raby Estate. The practice evidently originated in the mid-
> eighteenth century when the then Lord Barnard, out for a shoot, needed
> a place to shelter and had no way of knowing which properties belonged
> to his estate. It has since been a requirement of tenants of the Raby
> Estate – the area to the north of the River Tees – that they regularly
> whitewash their properties. The land to the south of the river belongs to
> the Earl of Strathmore's estate, where there is no such obligation.

some (such as adder's tongue fern) that flourish on ground that has never been treated with artificial fertiliser.

Some species, notably the wood anemone, may be relics of the period following the last Ice Age when woodland covered much of the North Pennines. Prior to the spread of this ancient woodland the area was dominated by tundra vegeta-tion. On higher ground are colonies of rare wildflowers that were widespread at this time, and which survived where tree cover was limited. Upper Teesdale is renowned for its unique combination of distinc-tive flora. The most famous is the spring gentian, a fragile little flower with bright blue petals,

Harwood Beck and one of the characteristic whitewashed farmhouses of Upper Teesdale.

Barnard Castle

The capital of Teesdale is Barnard Castle, or 'Barney' as it is known locally. Guy de Baliol was granted the Forest of Teesdale by King William Rufus in 1093. He built a wooden fortress above the site of a Roman crossing point on the River Tees. His nephew, Bernard de Baliol, rebuilt this in stone in 1125 – the imposing fortress becoming the foundation of the town. A market is still held at the town every Wednesday. At the bottom of the main street is an octagonal market cross, which served as town hall and lock-up. Nearby is the charming Bowes Museum, which was completed in 1892 in the style of a French chateau, one of its finest exhibits being a mechanical silver swan.

which in the British Isles grows only here and in western Ireland.

Upper Teesdale is more sparsely populated than it was in the heyday of the lead-mining industry, and even the main centre – Middleton-in-Teesdale – is just a modest-sized village. Together with the market town of Barnard Castle, which stands at the foot of the dale, it serves a scattering of small settlements and isolated farmsteads, the latter extending right up the dale.

The nature reserve at the head of Blackton Reservoir.

Baldersdale and Lunedale – Two Valleys and Five Reservoirs

Whilst the flow of the River Tees is interrupted only at Cow Green, the tributary valleys of Baldersdale and Lunedale are occupied by chains of reservoirs. The waters of the Balder and the Lune are multiplied by numerous moorland streams, making for big spates which the dams help to control. There are three reservoirs in Baldersdale (Balderhead, Blackton and Hury) and two in Lunedale (Selset and Grassholme). As well as meeting the needs of the industrial Teesside, the reservoirs offer recreational opportunities and provide an important habitat for wildfowl.

Walking in Teesdale

Upper Teesdale offers some fine walking country, although most visitors keep to the well-worn paths on the valley floor and the lower slopes. In contrast, the high ground can be hard-going, and is mostly the preserve of grouse-shooters – although the ridge between Weardale and Teesdale is crossed by a number of roads. The Pennine Way follows the River Tees past the spectacular High Force. It also crosses rough moorland terrain, and it is worth noting that the streams are prone to sudden spates, making fording hazardous. However, the waymarking is good, and the stiles are generally well-maintained. Middleton-in-Teesdale provides a welcome opportunity for those on the route to rest and replenish their supplies.

High Roads

The ridges flanking the Durham Dales are crossed by some of the highest public roads in the British Isles. The A689 reaches 2,057 feet (627 metres) at Killhope Cross, between Weardale and Nenthead. An unclassified road between St John's Chapel in Weardale and Langdon Beck in Teesdale tops out at 2,070 feet (631 metres), with fine views of the North Pennines. Only the A93 ('Devil's Elbow') at Glenshee in Scotland is higher, at 2,182 feet (665 metres), although the Bealach na Ba near Applecross (2,054 feet/626 metres) is surely the most spectacular of Britain's high roads.

WALK 1: UPPER TEESDALE

LENGTH 18¾ miles (30¼ kilometres)

ASCENT 1,526 feet (465 metres)

HIGHEST POINT 1,788 feet (545 metres)

MAPS OS Explorer OL Maps 19 ('Howgill Fells & Upper Eden Valley') (Upper Eden Valley [North] Sheet) and 31 ('North Pennines – Teesdale & Weardale') (East Sheet)

STARTING POINT Middleton-in-Teesdale village centre (NY 947 254)

FACILITIES Full range of services.

FEATURES Starting at the lead-mining village of Middleton-in-Teesdale, this long walk follows the River Tees upstream, passing a pair of spectacular waterfalls (Low Force and the superlative High Force) and Cronkley Scar before returning by a droveway and a quiet road.

The River Tees

The first part of the walk follows the Pennine Way along the south bank of the River Tees for 7½ miles (12 kilometres). Heading south out of the village on the B6277, the river is crossed by a stone bridge. Just past the auction mart, a finger sign on the right shows the Pennine Way turning through a gate onto a hardcore track. This ends at a barn, from where a path continues along the edge of fields, crossing drystone walls by step stiles. At times the river comes into view as it meanders about the valley floor. A finger sign shows the route diverging from a drystone wall, heading diagonally across a couple of fields.

The path runs above the steep, tree-covered riverbank before dropping to cross a side stream by a footbridge. Over another stream by stepping stones, the route continues along the riverbank. The character of the narrowing valley starts to change, with birch and rowan replacing sycamore and oak. Ignoring steps leading down to Scoberry Bridge, continue beside the river, passing some overgrown mine entrances. Ahead the river rushes through a gorge of vertically jointed dolerite. An unusual rock promontory beside the river provides a good vantage point (note that the rock

Middleton-in-Teesdale

Middleton-in-Teesdale owes its fortunes to lead-mining. It became the northern headquarters of the London Lead Company in 1880, which provided houses, a school and a reading room. The company was the first to introduce a five day working week, allowing its employees to devote time to other activities, including study and chapel. The water fountain in the village centre was placed here in 1877 as a memorial to the company's retiring superintendent, Robert Bainbridge (there is an identical fountain at Nenthead). The parish church is notable for its detached bell-tower, which dates from 1557. Today the village serves the surrounding population and acts as a base for tourists. There is a car park in the village centre.

can be slippery). Passing the Wynch Bridge, Low Force comes into view (1 = NY 903 279).

Past a grove of birch trees, a stagnant pool has formed where a dolerite wall holds back the river. After the turn for Holwick Head Bridge, head steeply uphill on a made path and continue through an area of juniper bushes. A narrow path heads through the bushes on the right, a short way to the best viewing point for High Force (be wary of the cliff edge). Returning to the path, the top of the waterfall is soon reached (2 = NY 880 284).

Continuing along the riverside path, the landscape is blighted by an active whinstone quarry. Crossing a couple of side streams by footbridges, the view over the river improves, with the outcrops of Dine Holm Scar inhabited by a pleasing mix of scree, heather and juniper. Another stream is crossed by stepping

The Wynch Bridge and Low Force

The Wynch Bridge (or 'Two Inch Bridge') is an elegant suspension footbridge, built in 1830 by the Duke of Cleveland, a short way downstream from Low Force. It replaced an earlier construction of 1704, which was the first suspension bridge in Europe (this collapsed in 1802, killing one of the men crossing at the time). Low Force is more evocatively known as the 'Salmon Leap'. Anywhere else in the country it would be the main feature, but so close to the superlative High Force it is merely a warm-up act. Here the course of the River Tees divides as it cascades over the Great Whin Sill, forming a tree-covered islet called Stable Crag.

High Force

At High Force the River Tees drops 69 feet (21 metres) over the Great Whin Sill to a plunge pool. This is not the highest waterfall in England, but it is certainly the most spectacular. There are actually two falls, separated by a central buttress, although that to the north is often dormant. In 1880, a man was drowned after being stranded in the middle by a sudden surge. Such spates are less common today, with Cow Green Reservoir regulating the flow. The river above the falls is inhabited by sandpipers, redshanks and oystercatchers. The surrounding area is Britain's largest juniper wood. Until the end of the nineteenth century, juniper was cut for firewood and fencing. The berries were used to flavour bread and cakes, as well as gin. When boiled, the steam was inhaled as a treatment for bronchitis.

stones before the path heads uphill on flagstones and continues along a broad ridge. To the right are extensive views over Upper Teesdale, with whitewashed farms dotted about the landscape. Soon a pair of marker stones is reached (3 = NY 861 283).

The stone on the left shows a path connecting to the Green Trod, providing an opportunity to shorten the walk by 5½ miles (9 kilometres). However, the delights of Cronkley Fell should not lightly be foregone. Turning north, continue along the Pennine

Force Garth Quarry

At Force Garth, the Great Whin Sill is plundered for roadstone, desecrating a beautiful part of Upper Teesdale. Whilst the quarries on Hadrian's Wall are now closed, Force Garth is likely to remain active for many years. When blasting takes place it is necessary for walkers on the Pennine Way to pause for a short while (this is indicated by a siren).

Way as it heads gently downhill. Crossing a gated gap stile, the route drops through a nick in a juniper-covered ridge, weaving through a jumble of boulders. Turning through a gate, head up to Cronkley Farm, from where a hardcore track runs down towards Cronkley Bridge. Just before reaching the bridge, turn through a gate on the left (4 = NY 862 294).

Cronkley Scar

Here we leave the Pennine Way, continuing along the south bank of the river for another 2¾ miles (4½ kilometres). Following a rough track towards a byre, pass though a gate and head around the rear of the building to join a riverside path. This runs across a heather-covered plain, with Widdy Bank Farm appearing on the far side of the river. Heading into the valley between Cronkley Fell and Widdybank Fell, scree fingers reach down from the dolerite cliffs of Cronkley Scar, with juniper bushes dotted about the hillside. For a time there is some clambering over boulders – recalling the path beneath Falcon Clints – as well as some boggy ground to negotiate. Crossing a side stream, there is one more difficult section before the riverbank broadens-out and the route switches to the Green Trod (5 = NY 827 282).

The Green Trod

The former droveway is followed east for 5 miles (8 kilometres). Climbing the steep slopes of Cronkley Fell, the name of the route accurately describes its appearance, with a ribbon of lush grass running through the heather. Looking back, there are good views towards Falcon Clints. As the path levels-out, a chain of cairns leads across the plateau. Arriving at a small pool, Fox Earth Gill can be seen rising from beneath a slab of sugar limestone – creating a pleasant spot for a break. Running alongside an erosion control enclosure, the path soon diverges from the fence to head downhill beside a feeder

The Green Trod

The Green Trod is part of a drove-way that ran from Scotland to Yorkshire. For the most part it used Roman roads, with the forts at Bewcastle, Birdoswald and Whitley Castle serving as stances. It then followed the River South Tyne upstream, before crossing the River Tees close to where Moor House now stands. Running around the side of Meldon Hill, Maize Beck was forded near Birkdale. Arriving at Holwick, it turned south across the moors to God's Bridge, continuing on into Yorkshire.

of Skyer Beck. Ahead are good views over Upper Teesdale, with the skyline notched by Coldberry Gutter – a hush cutting through the ridge north of Middleton-in-Teesdale. Off to the right is White Force, which itself can be a significant waterfall after heavy rainfall. Arriving at the bottom of the slope, the 'short-cut' route joins from the left (6 = NY 860 280).

Crossing a couple of broad streams, the route heads up a steep slope towards a cairn before continuing east over heather moorland. As the path founders in a rushy mire, Blea Beck is crossed by stepping stones. This can be difficult when the beck is in spate, and it is worth noting that there is a bridge on a grouse-shooters' track a short way upstream. The path eventually joins the hardcore track at a cairn (7 = NY 880 276). Following the track as it heads down between scree-covered slopes, a marker post indicates a right turn over a stile flanked by carved sheep sculptures. From here a stony track runs down a deep trough, on either side of which are Holwick Scars – another outcrop of the Great Whin Sill. Continuing down towards Holwick, a gate leads to an unclassified road (8 = NY 903 270).

Crossthwaite

The final part of the walk follows the quiet road for 3 miles (5 kilometres) back to the starting point. Holwick was once a resting place for drovers, and still boasts a pub – the Strathmore Arms Inn. The road runs through a pastoral scene of tidy farms and tree-lined fields, offering an enjoyable end to the walk. Passing the abandoned Crossthwaite Quarry, this was an important source of ironstone during the nineteenth century. Arriving at the junction with the B6277, turn left and follow the pavement back to the village.

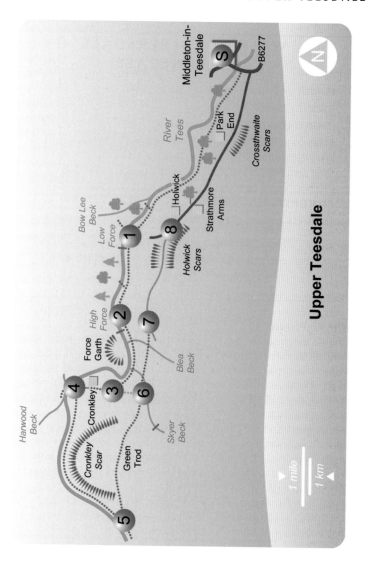

Upper Teesdale

WALK 2: BALDERSDALE AND LUNEDALE

LENGTH 13½ miles (21¾ kilometres)

ASCENT 1,591 feet (485 metres)

HIGHEST POINT 1,427 feet (435 metres)

MAPS OS Explorer OL Map 31 ('North Pennines – Teesdale & Weardale') (East Sheet)

STARTING POINT Hury Reservoir south car park, Baldersdale (NY 967 192)

FACILITIES Public toilets at the north car park.

FEATURES An enjoyable walk running beside the reservoirs of Baldersdale and Lunedale and crossing a series of moorland ridges. The remote farm where Hannah Hauxwell once lived and a Bronze Age tumulus are passed along the way. The return route follows a railway trail and quiet roads.

The Reservoirs

The starting point is reached by turning off the B6277 at the north end of Cotherstone and heading 3 miles (5 kilometres) up the Baldersdale road. From the car park at the south end of the dam, walk ¾ mile (1 kilometre) along the road until, just before Willoughby Hall Farm, iron gates lead to a hardcore track (1 = NY 956 189). Following the track above Hury Reservoir, when it turns onto the dam at the foot of Blackton Reservoir instead join a permissive path running along the south shore. This becomes narrow as it loops around wooded inlets where streams empty into the reservoir. Eventually a farm track is joined as it crosses Hunder Beck by a bridge (2 = NY 933 181).

A short way ahead is Blackton Bridge, which is notable for being the mid-point on the Pennine Way. Crossing the bridge, turn onto a grassy track heading up towards Low Birk Hatt Farm, which was once the home of Hannah Hauxwell. Passing through a gate leading to the farm, an access road runs north through pretty meadows (a

Hury and Little Hury Reservoirs

Hury is the lowest of Baldersdale's reservoirs. It covers an area of 125 acres (51 hectares), including a 'lagoon' at its head known as Little Hury. It was built in 1894, the use of stone and the prevalence of crenellated walling dating it to the era of grand architecture. Like Grassholme Reservoir in Lunedale, it is a popular spot for anglers, being well-stocked with trout. Northumbrian Water permits public access to the reservoirs of Baldersdale and Lunedale, excluding those areas fenced off as nature reserves.

stretch of boardwalk on the left provides access to a visitor centre, which is well worth a look). Arriving at an unclassified road, a finger sign on the far side shows the Pennine Way crossing a dry-stone wall by a step stile (3 = NY 933 190).

From here the route crosses the ridge between Baldersdale and Lunedale, negotiating 1½ miles (2¼ kilometres) of rough terrain (an unclassified road running parallel to the Pennine Way offers an easy alternative). The faint path follows a drystone wall heading north-north-west over grassy moorland, climbing gently towards the water-shed. Cutting across a couple of walls by step stiles, the route turns north as it heads downhill. Ahead are the reservoirs of Lunedale – Grassholme and Selset. Passing to the right of a byre, continue over pasture until an unclassified road is met (4 = NY 930 212).

A finger sign beside How Farm shows the Pennine Way heading through a gate and across a field. Following a line of trees, a step

Blackton and Balderhead Reservoirs

Blackton Reservoir was built by the Stockton & Middlesbrough Water Board in 1896, and covers an area of 66 acres (27 hectares). The reedy area at its head is designated as a nature reserve, with a bird hide providing an opportunity to survey visiting wildfowl (there are some helpful identification boards). Balderhead Reservoir was built in 1965 – the final link in the chain stretching up Baldersdale. It extends to 275 acres (111 hectares) and at its completion was the largest reservoir in the country, with a dam 3,030 feet (924 metres) long and 156 feet (48 metres) high. Below the dam is Baldersdale Youth Hostel, which provides accommodation for long-distance walkers on the Pennine Way.

> **Grassholme and Selset Reservoirs**
> Grassholme Reservoir was built in 1915, and covers and area of 142 acres (58 hectares). Close to the dam is a visitor centre, with refreshments, toilets and a car park. At the head of the reservoir is a nature reserve, complete with bird hide. Selset Reservoir was built in 1960 and extends to 265 acres (108 hectares). After heavy rainfall, a thundering torrent of water pours down the overflow channel at the north end of the turf-faced dam.

stile leads to a rushy area, beyond which another unclassified road is met. Heading down the road, the neck of Grassholme Reservoir is crossed by a five-arched bridge (a submerged stone bridge just upstream is sometimes visible). Continuing up the road towards Grassholme Farm, a finger sign shows the Pennine Way turning through the muddy farmyard, joining a faint path heading north-north-west over pasture. Crossing a broken wall to the left of a ruined barn, continue over cattle-churned pasture towards the B6276 (5 = NY 924 225). This road connects Middleton-in-Teesdale and Brough via the interestingly-named Grains o' th' Beck.

Harter Fell

The next part of the walk runs 2¾ miles (4¼ kilometres) around the flanks of Harter Fell. Crossing straight over the road, join a tarmac track leading to Wythes Hill Farm, then follow a faint path heading north-east over walled pasture. From a ruined barn, a quad track runs east then north-east over rough grazing, converging with a drystone wall that marks the crest of the ridge. Here the walk tops-out at a respectable 1,427 feet (435 metres). Passing through a gate, a good path heads north-east down gentle slopes, avoiding patches of limestone scree. Middleton-in-Teesdale can be seen down in the valley, while at the end of the ridge is Kirkcarrion – a Bronze Age tumulus, crowned with an enclosed stand of conifers. Eventually the path arrives at junction of Holwick road and the B6277 (this place will be remembered from the previous walk). Following the main road down towards the auction mart, cross over to join a tarmac track leading to Step Ends Farm (6 = NY 946 251).

Romaldkirk Moor

It is here that we leave the Pennine Way. The access road runs along the south bank of the River Tees, becoming a hardcore track as it passes the farm. Leaving the track at a marker post, head up a tree-covered bluff then diagonally across fields to emerge onto the B6277. Turning left, head along the road a short way. Passing Lonton Farm, a finger sign shows a path running over a field towards a ladder stile,

Tees Valley Railway

The railway line from Barnard Castle to Middleton-in-Teesdale was opened in 1868 by the Tees Valley Railway Company, then taken over in 1882 by the North Eastern Railway. It fell into disuse when Crossthwaite Quarry closed. The route is now open to the public as the Tees Valley Railway Walk, catering for walkers, cyclists and horse-riders, with lofty viaducts still spanning the wooded valleys of the Balder and the Lune.

where the Tees Valley Railway Walk is joined. Heading south-east along the pleasant, hawthorn-lined track, just after crossing the Lune Viaduct, turn off the railway walk onto Cote House Road (7 = NY 959 240).

A short way along the lane, a finger sign points up a hardcore track leading to Acres Farm. From the farmhouse, head south-west over fields, with the rolling terrain making for some tricky navigation. Converging with a drystone wall, follow this south for a way before crossing by a step stile. Continuing south-west over rough grazing, an unclassified road is soon met (8 = NY 954 228). Crossing straight over the lane, join a single track road heading steeply uphill beside an overgrown quarry. The next part of the walk follows the road for 2 miles (3¼ kilometres) as it runs over Romaldkirk Moor towards Baldersdale. The road is flanked by heather moorland then, as it tops-out, it passes an isolated farm (Botany). Passing another farm, the road heads down through pasture to arrive at a junction near the hamlet of Hury (9 = NY 958 199).

Turning left, head along the road, looking for a step stile on the right. This is difficult to spot, there being no waymarker, and should not be confused with a nearby gap stile (note that if daylight is failing, it is possible to follow quiet roads back to the start-

The view across Hury Reservoir.

ing point). Crossing the stile, head down the side of a field. Just before reaching a ruined farm, turn left over a gap stile. Hooking around a derelict barn, switch to a bridleway route following an overgrown farm track. Passing through a set of iron gates, Hury Reservoir north car park is reached. From here a track runs along the top of the dam, crossing an overflow channel by an iron bridge to arrive back at the starting point.

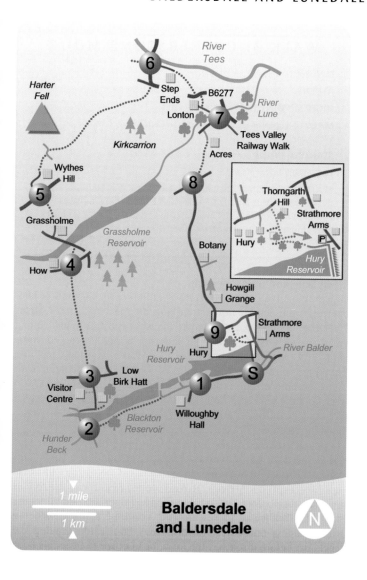

Baldersdale
and Lunedale

1 mile

1 km

WALK 3: COTHERSTONE MOOR

LENGTH 14 miles (22½ kilometres)

ASCENT 1,526 feet (465 metres)

HIGHEST POINT 1,385 feet (422 metres)

MAPS OS Explorer OL Map 31 ('North Pennines – Teesdale & Weardale') (East Sheet)

STARTING POINT Bowes village centre (NY 994 135)

FACILITIES Inn at Bowes.

FEATURES Combining the alternative Pennine Way routes of the 'Bowes Loop', this moorland walk can be hard-going in places. Points of interest include Bowes Castle and God's Bridge (a thick slab of limestone, spanning the River Greta).

Deep Dale and Goldsborough

Bowes is located on the A66 trans-Pennine route, 16 miles (26 kilometres) from Scotch Corner. Parking on the front street, cross over the A66 by a road bridge at the west end of the village and head up an unclassified road. Ignoring a right turn, continue along the road as it runs through an area of rough pasture. Flanking the road are the remains of Air Ministry buildings, with signs warning of poisonous gas buried here at the end of World War I. As the scattered farmsteads of Deep Dale come into view, a finger sign on the left shows the Pennine Way leaving the road, heading north-west over fields.

Cutting across pasture, drystone walls are crossed by stiles that can be hard to spot. A fenced enclosure surrounding a large cairn marks the location of Stonykeld Spring ('keld' being the Old Norse word for a spring). Arriving at West Stoney Keld Farm, the road is rejoined just before its end. Ignoring a finger sign marking the start of a bridleway to Pasture End, continue along a hardcore track heading north-west towards Levy Pool Farm. Leaving the track just before it reaches the farm, head down to Deepdale Beck (1 = NY 968 154).

Bowes

Bowes is located above the River Greta – a substantial tributary of the Tees. The ruined Norman keep dominating the village was built on the site of a Roman fort, Lavatris, which guarded the east end of the Stainmore Pass (its counterpart at Brough, Verteris, stood at the west end, a day's march away). The fort dates from the Flavian period (AD 69–96), and covered an area of 4 acres (1¾ hectares). Also of historical interest is the Ancient Unicorn, an old coaching inn where Charles Dickens stayed during 1838 while researching his novel *Nicholas Nickleby*. Dotheboys Hall, the school featured in the novel, was based upon Bowes Boys Academy, which stands at the top of the front street. The headmaster, William Shaw, was the model for the infamous Wackford Squeers. After serving as a transport café, the building was converted into private flats.

This tributary of the River Tees is prone to big spates, although it can now be crossed safely by means of a newly constructed footbridge. From here a marker post provides an indication of the route, although the best guide as the faint path heads generally north is a drystone wall off to the right. Progress over the rushy ground is made easier by following sheep tracks as the route rolls over a low ridge, dropping into the gully of Hazelgill Beck before climbing towards Ladyfold Rigg.

Heading north-west, MoD warning signs over a fence on the right mark the boundary of a firing range. Beside the path is a flat rock bearing cup and ring markings. Passing through a gate in a drystone wall, a narrow path runs across grassy moorland towards Goldsborough. It is possible to join a quad track running over the top of this distinctive hillock, although the literal route contours around its western flanks. From here the Pennine Way heads down to join an unclassified road running up Badersdale (2 = NY 947 179).

Levy Pool

Levy Pool supplied water to the Roman bath-house at Lavatris via an aqueduct – the River Greta being below the level of the fort. Its name is connected with that of the fort, and probably refers to a river bed. The farmhouse dates from 1736 and features the last surviving example of a heather-thatched roof in the Durham Dales.

Baldersdale

Heading along the road a short way, a finger sign shows the Pennine Way turning down a hardcore track leading to East Friar House Farm. Following a narrow passage down the side of a byre, a step stile marks the start of a steeplechase path running west over walled pasture. Crossing How Sike by a footbridge, the path continues over fields towards the bridge at Hunder Beck, where a finger sign marks the point at which the alternative Pennine Way routes meet (3 = NY 933 181). It is here that we begin our return journey. Heading south-east up a farm track, the road is re-joined at Clove Lodge Farm. Passing a small parking area, a finger sign shows the Pennine Way heading back onto Cotherstone Moor (4 = NY 935 176).

Race Yate and God's Bridge

The indistinct path runs south-east over tussocky grass, avoiding rushy areas as height is gained. Swinging around to head south, it

Goldsborough

Goldsborough is thought to be the site of an Iron Age hill-fort. At 1,276 feet (389 metres) it provides a grandstand view of Baldersdale with its chain of reservoirs and scattering of farmsteads. The Millstone Grit outcrops flanking the hillock are popular with rock climbers.

runs over the crest of Race Yate Rigg. Heading gently downhill beside a drystone wall, the path is easier to follow. Joining a quad track, continue down to the point where Deepdale Beck is crossed by a narrow footbridge (5 = NY 948 148).

From here a grouse shooters' track running to West Stoney Keld Farm offers a potential escape route. However, the Pennine Way turns off the track almost immediately, heading south-east over the moors. There is nothing to indicate the start of the route, although there are a few marker posts along the way. The narrow path runs through heather as it climbs towards an area known as Ravock Castle, where a cairn is all that remains of a shepherd's hut. From this point there are good views over Bowes Moor towards Tan Hill Inn. Continuing over ground that is mossy but firm, a few small cairns provide reassurance of the route. Arriving at Pasture End Farm, the Pennine Way passes under the A66.

Exiting from the underpass, the normally dry course of the River Greta can be seen down in the valley, as can the ponds of the nearby Otter Trust. Heading down a hardcore track leading to a bungalow, pass through a gap in an old railway embankment close to a lime kiln. Ahead is God's Bridge, where the River Greta is crossed with dry feet thanks to a quirk of geology (6 = NY 957 126). Ignoring a finger sign indicating a short-cut to Bowes, head south, following a drystone wall uphill. Passing through a gate in an inter-secting wall, the route runs onto heather moorland. Following the

The Stainmore Pass

The boundary between the North Pennines and Central Pennines is defined by the Stainmore Trough. This pass has long been used as a trans-Pennine route, with a Roman road linking Dere Street and Watling Street, guarded by a chain of forts, camps and signal stations. Close to the summit is the Rey Cross, which marks the location of the Battle of Stainmore, where Eric Bloodaxe was defeated in AD 95. England's highest railway once ran over the pass, reaching 1,370 feet (418 metres) at its summit. It was built by the South Durham & Lancashire Union Railway Company in 1861, and remained open until 1962. Today the busy A66 trunk road links the A1 at Scotch Corner and the M6 at Penrith. With an exposed summit at 1,467 feet (447 metres), it is frequently closed to high-sided vehicles.

boundary east for a way, the path turns south once more, with a couple of marker posts providing guidance. Close to Trough Heads Farm, a finger sign marks the point at which the alternative Pennine Way routes meet (7 = NY 962 114).

> ### God's Bridge
> God's Bridge is a thick slab of limestone, spanning the River Greta at the point where it re-emerges from a subterranean passage. The river is swallowed by fissures some way upstream, the dry bed recalling the origin of its name (which is connected with the Old Norse 'griota', 'stony').

River Greta

The final part of the walk follows the alternative Pennine Way route for 3½ miles (5½ kilometres) to Bowes. The path runs north-east then north beside a drystone wall, crossing rough pasture. Arriving at a hardcore track, turn right and head towards East Mellwaters Farm, before joining a made path that follows the south bank of the River Greta. Crossing a tributary (Sleightholme Beck) by a footbridge, head around West Charity Farm to join an access road running east (8 = NY 973 128).

Just past Lady Myres Farm, a marker post shows a path heading down to a newly constructed footbridge providing a safe crossing over the River Greta. This stands above a weir where the river was formerly crossed by means of limestone outcrops that served as stepping stones. On the north bank a rough track heads up to Swinholme Farm, then a walled lane continues towards the village. Half way up the lane, an acorn marker on the right shows the Pennine Way cutting across fields, passing the Norman keep before exiting onto the front street. If daylight is failing, from Lady Myers Farm simply stay on the access road as it continues towards Gilmonby, joining an unclassified road heading back into Bowes.

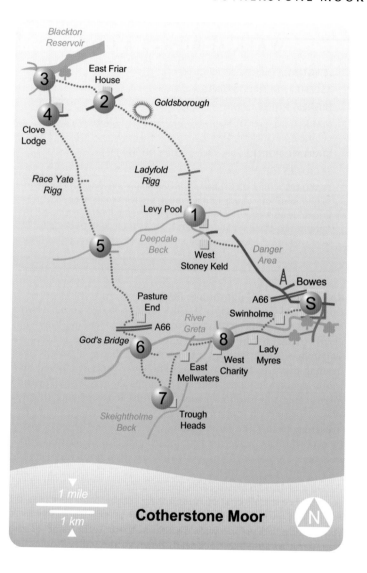

Blackton Reservoir

3

East Friar House

2

Goldsborough

4

Clove Lodge

Race Yate Rigg

Ladyfold Rigg

Levy Pool

1

Deepdale Beck

5

West Stoney Keld

Danger Area

Bowes

A66

S

Swinholme

Pasture End

A66

River Greta

God's Bridge

6

8

Lady Myres

East Mellwaters

West Charity

7

Skeightholme Beck

Trough Heads

1 mile

1 km

Cotherstone Moor

N

WALK 4: BOWES MOOR

LENGTH 17½ miles (28 kilometres)

ASCENT 1,263 feet (385 metres)

HIGHEST POINT 1,759 feet (536 metres)

MAPS OS Explorer OL Map 30 ('Yorkshire Dales – Northern & Central Areas') (North Sheet)

STARTING POINT Bowes village centre (NY 994 135)

FACILITIES Inn at Bowes.

FEATURES A long walk, once again combining alternative Pennine Way routes. An expanse of open moorland with some boggy ground leads to Tan Hill Inn – Britain's highest pub. Navigation is fairly straightforward and the return route is on good tracks and quiet roads.

River Greta and Sleightholme Beck

On the front street, next to St. Giles' Church, a sign points down a lane leading to Bowes Castle. From here, the Pennine Way runs across fields before turning onto a walled lane leading to Swinholme Farm. Passing the farmhouse, follow a rough track heading down to the point where the River Greta is crossed by a footbridge above a limestone weir. Joining an access road at Lady Myres Farm, this is followed west as it runs across pasture towards West Charity Farm (1 = NY 973 128).

Passing around the farm buildings, Sleightholme Beck is crossed by a footbridge. Leave the Pennine Way at East Mellwaters Farm. In a field used as a campsite a gate leads to a bridleway running south-west, parallel to the tree-lined gorge of Sleightholme Beck. Arriving at Trough Heads Farm, the Pennine Way is rejoined at the point where the alternative routes of the 'Bowes Loop' meet (2 = NY 962 114). Continuing south-west, the path is easy to follow as it runs beside a drystone wall. Switching to the other side of the boundary, a ramp-like track leads down to the valley floor, then contours around a bluff to arrive at a footbridge (Intake Bridge).

Bowes Castle

The Norman keep at Bowes was built by Alan, Earl of Richmond, in 1087 to guard the east end of the Stainmore Pass, just as Brough Castle covered the western approach. It was built using stones taken from Lavatris Fort, and at 53 feet (16 metres) high the ruins still dominate the village.

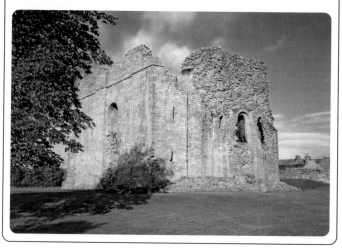

Cross the beck and continue over fields until a gate leads to an unclassified road (3 = NY 956 104).

Sleightholme Moor

The next part of the walk follows the Pennine Way for 4¾ miles (7½ kilometres) over Sleightholme Moor to Tan Hill Inn. Turning right, head along the road as it passes Sleightholme Farm. Climbing steeply, the road degenerates into a hardcore track as it continues parallel to the beck. There are fine views over the surrounding moorland. The heather is thick with grouse, which when startled call-out like mopeds being started on a cold morning! Arriving at a fork in the track, a finger sign shows the Pennine Way continuing south-west (4 = NY 941 093).

Passing an L-shaped bield, the track heads down to cross

Moorland Management

The Pennine moors are not the untamed wilderness that they might seem. They are in fact carefully managed for grouse shooting, with small areas of heather burnt-off every fifteen years or so to encourage the growth of young shoots that attract the birds. The North Pennines AONB includes nearly a quarter of the heather moorland in England and Wales, and 85 per cent of England's population of the rare black grouse. Other birds such as the lapwing, curlew and golden plover are more common, and add a lively dimension to the moors. Sheep numbers are maintained at a level that prevents over-grazing. An unfortunate side-effect of moorland management is the dearth of natural predators – in particular, stoats and weasels – which are culled to protect the grouse chicks. The result is a plague of rabbits, which compete with livestock for scarce pasture.

Frumming Beck by a flat bridge. From here a path follows the north bank, crossing moorland terrain that is an untidy mixture of heather, tussocky grass and cottongrass. Side streams have cut deep gullies that reveal a cross-section of the underlying peat. Passing a beehive cairn, the path becomes less well-defined as it runs over boggy ground. A few small cairns and some marker posts aid navigation, although it is sometimes necessary to stray in search of solid ground. Conditions improve as the path climbs towards Tan Hill Inn, its generator serving as an audible beacon. Joining an unclassified road, head past an ornamental windmill towards the inn (5 = NY 897 067), which stands on the watershed of streams destined for the Tees and Humber estuaries.

The Long Causeway

The return route can be tackled in failing daylight, so there should be time to visit the inn, where Millstone Grit outcrops provide a perch from which to look across the surrounding moors towards shapely fells (Mickle Fell and Little Fell are particularly prominent). The next part of the walk follows a quiet road and good tracks for 5 miles (8 kilometres) back to Sleightholme Farm (this is actually identified as an alternative 'foul weather' route for the Pennine Way). Heading north-east along the Long

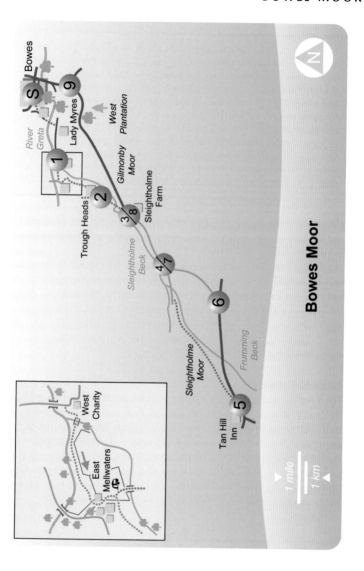

Bowes Moor

> **Tan Hill Inn**
>
> At 1,732 feet (528 metres), Tan Hill Inn claims to be the highest pub in Britain – although the owners of the Cat & Fiddle in the Peak District have issued a challenge. There has been an inn here since the sixteenth century serving the pack-horse routes, although the present building dates from 1737. It reached its heyday when coal was mined on the surrounding moors – at which point it was known as the King's Pit, after a nearby mine. Susan Peacock became landlady in 1903, and was known to keep a pistol behind the bar to control rowdy patrons. The annual Swaledale Sheep Fair has been held here on the last Thursday in May since 1951. Some of the inn's visitors will no doubt remember its appearance in a 1970s television commercial for double glazing.

Causeway, the upper reaches of Arkengarthdale can be seen in the distance. Eventually a road sign indicates a left turn onto a byroad to Bowes (6 = NY 929 075).

In places the former tarmac surface of Sleightholme Moor Road still shows-through, although the route is now classed as unsuitable for motors. Heading north-east then north, the track eventually arrives back at the fork passed earlier (7 = NY 941 093). Turning right, retrace your steps to Sleightholme Farm, then stay on the road, ignoring a finger sign showing the Pennine Way turning through a gate on the left (8 = NY 956 104).

Gilmonby Moor

The final part of the return route follows unclassified roads for 4 miles (6½ kilometres) back to the starting point. Heading north-east, the quiet road runs past isolated farmsteads and across open moorland. To the right is an area of heather-clad hillocks, while to the left is the broad valley of the River Greta. Passing through the charming West Plantation, turn left at a junction (9 = NY 995 127) and head north towards Gilmonby. Ignore a turning for Lady Myres Farm and continue along the road back to the starting point.

CENTRAL PENNINES

Walk 1: Stonesdale Moor
Walk 2: Upper Swaledale
Walk 3: Great Shunner Fell
Walk 4: Upper Wensleydale
Walk 5: Cam Fell
Walk 6: Upper Ribblesdale
Walk 7: Pen-y-ghent
Walk 8: Fountains Fell

The Yorkshire Dales

The Yorkshire Dales radiate outward from the Central Pennines — an area of shapely fells and moorland ridges. Most of the principal rivers rising in this area – the Swale, the Ure, the Nidd, the Wharfe and the Aire – flow south-east, joining the River Ouse before emptying into the Humber Estuary. The exceptions are the River Ribble, which flows south-west through Lancashire to enter the Irish Sea, and the River Lune, which runs down the western edge of the Central Pennines before turning towards Morecambe Bay.

In geological terms, the Central Pennines correspond to the area known as the Askrigg Block, which is bounded by the Stainmore Trough to the north, the Craven Fault System to the south and the Dent Fault to the west. The Millstone Grit of the Upper Carboniferous period caps much of the high ground. It rests upon the various strata of the Yoredale Series, recalling the old name for Wensleydale (where it is revealed in the characteristic profile of the valley sides). The Yoredale Series is of Lower Carboniferous age, and comprises a repeating sequence of limestone, shale and sandstone layers, with thin coal seams. Below this are thick layers of limestone known as the Malham and Kilnsey formations, also of Lower Carboniferous age.

The Malham Formation is also known as the Great Scar Limestone, and is spectacularly exposed by the vertical displacement of the Craven Fault System at locations such as Giggleswick Scar and Malham Cove. In addition to the usual eastward dip of the Pennines,

the Askrigg Block is tilted towards the north, so that the Malham Formation which outcrops so dramatically in the south of the area is seen only on the valley floor in Wensleydale. The Central Pennines exhibit some of the country's finest 'karst' scenery, with limestone scars, complex cave systems, disappearing and re-emerging streams, dry valleys and extensive areas of limestone pavement.

> **Limestone Pavement**
> The formation of limestone pavement began at the end of the last Ice Age, when limestone exposed by the passage of ice was dissolved by rainwater, creating a regular pattern of blocks ('clints') and crevices ('grikes'). The latter provide a sheltered habitat for plants such as dog's mercury and hart's tongue fern that are thought to be relics of the ancient woodland that covered much of the country.

People in the Central Pennines

The evidence of place names indicates that the upper dales were settled by the Vikings, who came from their settlements in Ireland and on the Isle of Man during the ninth and tenth centuries. They established a system of livestock rearing based upon seasonally alternating pastures, echoes of which are found in place names incorporating the element 'sett' (or 'seat'), which comes from the Old Norse 'saetr' ('spring shieling').

During the twelfth and thirteenth centuries, great monasteries were established in the lower dales. The Cistercians founded Fountains Abbey (1132) and Jervaulx Abbey (1145) in Wensleydale, and the Augustinians established Bolton Priory (1154) in Wharfedale. Coverham Abbey (1213) is Coverdale was built by the Premonstratensians. As well as being places of religious service, the monasteries were centres of economic activity, including sheep rearing and lead-mining. Fountains Abbey had grazing rights over a large area around Pen-y-ghent, Fountains Fell and Malham Moor, while Bolton Priory had extensive sheep-runs in Airedale.

The landscape of the dales is still strongly influenced by hill farming. A typical profile has rough grazing on the higher ground, walled pasture on the valley sides and hay meadows on the valley

The cliffs of High Clint in Upper Wensleydale.

The Fells of the Central Pennines

The Central Pennines rise to more than 2,000 feet (610 metres), with 24 hills in this class (this excludes 5 fells to the west of the Dent Fault, which are geologically distinct from the Pennine Chain). The highest peak, Whernside, stands at 2,415 feet (736 metres). Unlike the North Pennines, which takes the form of an interconnected system of ridges, the fells of the Central Pennines tend to stand in discrete groups of two or three. Many of the fells – as well as some of the valley sides – feature a distinctive stepped profile, owing to the differential weathering of the various strata of the Yoredale Series. The area to the west of the Dent Fault corresponds to the Howgill Fells, a compact group of steep-sided hills, fashioned by the elements from Pre-Carboniferous (Ordovician and Silurian) rocks, with highly compressed layers of mudstone, siltstone and sandstone.

floor. The field pattern often dates back to the earliest phase of enclosure, which established numerous smallholdings, each with a few fields enclosed by drystone walls, separated by walled lanes providing access to common land. The dales are separated by open moorland used only for sheep grazing and grouse-shooting – although here and there are traces of former lead- and coal-mining activity. With the exception of conifer plantations and shelter belts, tree cover is generally limited to scattered remnants of ancient woodland, surviving in sheltered gills and on the steep valley sides.

Looking at a map of the Central Pennines, it takes just a few moments to figure out what is missing. Due to the geology of the dales there are only two natural lakes of any size, namely Semer

Swaledale Sheep

The Swaledale is a hardy breed of black-faced sheep with a fleece of tight wool. It can be distinguished from similar breeds such as the Scottish Blackface by its white-tipped nose, although its trademark feature is its curling horns, which are most pronounced on the tups. The Swaledale is at home on damp ground, and has an agreeable tendency to stick to its heft, making it ideal for grazing on open moorland. Once it was seen only in Upper Swaledale, but thanks to the work of a breeder's association formed in 1920 it is now popular with hill farmers throughout Northern England.

Kisdon Hill in Upper Swaledale – arguably the finest of Yorkshire's dales.

Water in Raydale and Malham Tarn in Malhamdale. Only to the south-east, where Millstone Grit predominates, has the underlying geology permitted the creation of reservoirs.

The complex interaction of geology, landform and climate, combined with the influence of human activity, has fashioned a unique landscape. The Yorkshire Dales is not just a geographical area, but exhibits a distinct cultural identity associated with a particular way of life. Indeed, each of the dales has its own character. The main centres are Reeth (Swaledale), Hawes (Wensleydale), Grassington (Wharfedale), Skipton (Airedale) and Settle (Ribblesdale). Sedbergh stands among the Howgill Fells. However, most of the area is sparsely populated, with small villages and isolated farmsteads running up the dales. The Settle and Carlisle Railway is a solitary relic of the network of branch lines that once provided an alternative to the narrow, winding roads.

Walking in the Central Pennines

Whether an individual's tastes are for quaint villages sheltering in pastoral dales or for rugged fells offering unspoiled views, few would dispute that the Yorkshire Dales is one of the most beautiful areas in

Settle and Carlisle Railway

The Settle and Carlisle Railway was built entirely by hand by navvies working for the Midland Railway Company in 1870–6. A memorial stone at the parish church in Chapel le Dale remembers the 108 men who lost their lives during construction of Ribblehead Viaduct. This twenty-four arched viaduct is 440 yards (402 metres) long and 165 feet (50 metres) high. The nearby Blea Moor Tunnel is 1½ miles (2½ kilometres) long, and took four years to complete. Around 3,000 people lived in a shanty town on Batty Moss during construction of the line. The line was threatened with closure in 1983, but reprieved following a public outcry.

the country. Even the most tortuous car journey can be an enjoyable experience for those not in a hurry. It is a good place for walking, with terrain that is often more accommodating than that encountered elsewhere in the Pennines. Moreover, with one of the most extensive cave systems in Europe, it is also an important area for potholing. The Yorkshire Dales is heavily patronised by tourists, so a visit during the summer will not yield the wilderness experience that some crave. However, since the area is designated as a National Park, there is good provision for walkers in terms of accommodation and services. The Pennine Way itself follows old pack-horse routes and visits some of the principal fells.

The stone shelter on Great Shunner Fell – a welcome refuge for walkers.

Yorkshire Dales National Park

Yorkshire Dales National Park was established 1954, its symbol being the famous Swaledale tup. It covers an area of 680 square miles (1,761 square kilometres), encompassing Swaledale, Wensleydale, Wharfedale, Airedale and Ribblesdale, together with their various tributary valleys. Towards its western edge – which is marked by the Lune Valley – it includes the fells and dales around Ingleton and Sedbergh (the latter being perversely in Cumbria). Nidderdale lies to the east, and although outside the National Park boundary it has AONB status.

WALK 1: STONESDALE MOOR

LENGTH 11 miles (17½ kilometres)

ASCENT 1,608 feet (490 metres)

HIGHEST POINT 1,782 feet (543 metres)

MAPS OS Explorer OL Map 30 ('Yorkshire Dales – Northern & Central Areas') (North Sheet)

STARTING POINT Keld village centre, Upper Swaledale (NY 892 012)

FACILITIES Public toilets and refreshments.

FEATURES Starting at Keld – the uppermost village in Swaledale – the route crosses some difficult terrain as it navigates open moorland. The effort is rewarded by splendid views of Upper Swaledale and the surrounding fells. There are some fine cataracts along the way, most notably East Gill Force.

East Stonesdale

Keld is located just off the B6270 at the head of Swaledale. Park Lodge Farm in the village centre provides car parking for a modest charge. Following a link-path running south-east, the Pennine Way is joined as it heads down into the wooded gorge of the River Swale. Crossing a footbridge, the route climbs to the left of the charming East Gill Force before turning up a stony track leading to East Stonesdale Farm.

Keld

Keld is perhaps best known as the place where the Penine Way crosses Alfred Wainwright's Coast-to-Coast Walk. The name is Old Norse, recalling the Viking origins of the villages around Upper Swaledale, and was originally Appletre Kelde ('apple tree spring'). The grave of Susan Peacock, landlady of Tan Hill Inn, is in the churchyard at the URC chapel. Hers was the largest funeral ever held in Upper Swaledale, with a procession of more than forty cars making its way down Stonesdale Road.

From here the Pennine Way is followed for 4 miles (6¼ kilometres) to Tan Hill Inn. The path – an old pack-horse route – crosses rough pasture and open moorland as it heads north along the valley side, parallel to Stonesdale Beck. These routes were the vital arteries of the dales, with trains of ponies carrying wool, meat, limestone and coal to market, returning with commodities such as salt. After negotiating a rushy mire, a lively stream (Lad Gill) is crossed by a clapper bridge (1 = NY 887 045). Heading up beside a deep gully, the path continues over rough moorland. The general direction is north-east, with the remains

East Gill Force near Keld.

of a stony track showing through the peat in places. Arriving at the inn, we leave the Pennine Way (2 = NY 897 067).

Robert's Seat

Nearby is a junction, with a road signed for Keld heading down Stonesdale. Following this a short way, a finger sign on the right marks the start of a path running 3¼ miles (5¼ kilometres) over Robert's Seat to Ravenseat Farm (note that it is possible to follow the quiet road down the valley towards the turning for East Stonesdale Farm, cutting 1¾ miles/3 kilometres off the route). Heading south-west, the path runs down-

> **Coal Mining at Tan Hill**
> Stonesdale Moor was the scene of extensive coal mining, with poor quality 'crow' coal being dug here from the thirteenth century. Locally it was used for smelting lead and burning limestone. A row of miners' cottages near Tan Hill Inn was demolished after the last mine closed in 1929.

downhill on grassy moorland. Cross Tan Gill just before it enters Stonesdale Beck and follow the latter downstream until another finger sign marks the point at which it is forded (3 = NY 885 055).

From here the path heads west, climbing steeply beside the deep gully of Thomas Gill until a finger sign marks a turn onto a quad track heading south-south-west along Thomas Gill Rigg. The going is easy and the views are fine. As the track swings towards a fence between a pair of hillocks, look for a narrow path continuing south-south-west over tussocky grass (if this cannot be located, it is possible to follow the fence to the point where it is crossed). Running along a stony bluff marking the flank of Robert's Seat, the path eventually arrives at a fence stile (4 = NY 872 041).

Heading downhill, the direction is south-west. Ahead are fine views over Whitsun Dale, with a scattering of stone-built barns among walled pasture. Arriving at a fence stile, ignore a gate on the left (unless the stream below is in spate, in which case an emergency diversion might be in order). Cross Hoods Bottom Beck by a ford and follow a hardcore track above the gorge, which is home to a small waterfall (Jenny Whalley Force). Passing through a couple of gates, Ravenseat Farm is just ahead (5 = NY 863 034).

Wainwright's Coast-to-Coast Walk

The remainder of the return route follows Whitsundale Beck and the River Swale for a total of 3¼ miles (5¼ kilometres) back to the starting point. Crossing a narrow stone bridge and passing between a pair of barns, a finger sign marks the start of a path to Keld (at this

Hill Farming in Upper Swaledale

The hill farming methods encountered in Upper Swaledale can be traced back to the Vikings. They were a response to the harsh climate, which would normally have made cattle rearing impractical. Whilst the high ground is suitable only for grazing by hardy Swaledale sheep, the steep valley sides are used for pasture. Stone-built barns known as 'laithes', one in every second or third field, provide winter quarters for cattle. Hay from the riverside meadows is cut and dried, then stored in the barns as winter feed. Manure collected from the barns is used to fertilise the meadows.

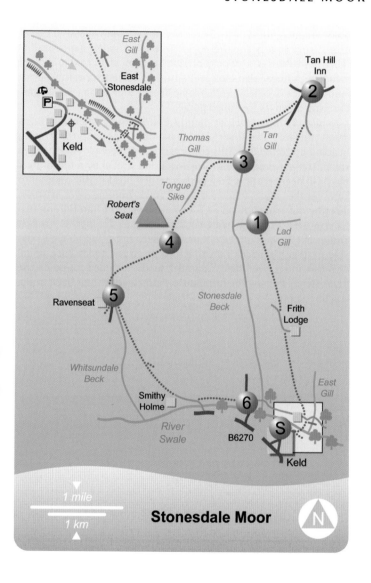

Stonesdale Moor

point Wainwright's Coast-to-Coast Walk joins our route as it comes down from Nine Standards Rigg). Through a gated gap stile, the faint path crosses a couple of side streams as it runs over wet meadow. A finger sign indicates a turn up towards a barn where a muddy track is joined. Whitsundale Beck is soon a long way below, hurrying down its tree-lined gorge.

Joining a stony track at Smithy Holme Farm, when this turns down towards the River Swale, a marker post shows a path heading up to the left. This continues along the valley side, above steep, tree-covered slopes. Crossing a side stream by a footbridge, the path degenerates into a muddy trench. Kisdon Hill comes into view as the route follows a quad track running over pasture, meeting Stonesdale Road as it comes down from Tan Hill Inn (6 = NY 886 016). Crossing straight over the road, the access for East Stonesdale Farm is joined. Stonesdale Beck is crossed above a sizeable cataract (Currack Force) before the track heads back uphill and continues over fields, parallel to the wooded gorge of the River Swale. Passing the farmhouse, retrace your steps back to the starting point.

WALK 2: UPPER SWALEDALE

LENGTH 7 miles (11½ kilometres)

ASCENT 1,247 feet (380 metres)

HIGHEST POINT 1,608 feet (490 metres)

MAPS OS Explorer OL Map 30 ('Yorkshire Dales – Northern & Central Areas') (North Sheet)

STARTING POINT Muker car park, Upper Swaledale (SD 911 978)

FACILITIES Public toilets, inn and refreshments.

FEATURES A short walk that visits the picturesque villages of Upper Swaledale as it criss-crosses the lovely Kisdon Hill. After a steeple-chase across meadows and an awkward path running around the steep hillside, the return route follows a good track over the top of the hill, offering exceptional views.

Usha Gap

Muker is located on the B6270 in Upper Swaledale. As well as a 'pay and display' car park, there is limited roadside parking to the west of the village. Opposite the public toilets, a ginnel runs up beside Swaledale Woollens to arrive at a back street. Turning left, just past a row of cottages a gate leads to a field. From here the route runs 1¼ miles (2 kilometres) over meadows towards Thwaite. Following the flagged path across fields, drystone walls are crossed by narrow gap stiles with spring-loaded gates that snap at you heals. Off to the left, beyond the tree-lined course of Straw Beck, pasture can be seen creeping up the steep valley side towards Muker Common. Pass through Usha Gap Farm and turn along the B6270.

A short way along the road, before it crosses Usha Gap Bridge, a finger sign marks the start of a path to Thwaite. This initially runs beside the beck, then continues over meadows, with signs requesting walkers to travel in single file so as to avoid trampling the grass. Just before reaching Thwaite, a finger sign shows the Pennine Way heading towards a gate in a drystone wall (1 = SD 894 982). Before continuing, however, a visit to Thwaite and the

Muker-in-Swaledale

Muker is another village with Viking origins, its name being derived from the Old Norse 'mjor-aker' ('cultivated enclosure'). The focal point of the village is the Church of St. Mary the Virgin. Before this was built in 1580 the dead of Upper Swaledale were carried along the old corpse way that ran from Keld to Grinton – a distance of 12 miles (19 kilometres). The literary institute in the village centre recalls the fact that Upper Swaledale – including the tributary valley of Arkengarthdale – was an important lead-mining area. At its height Muker had 1,450 parishioners, although this waned after lead-mining went into decline in the 1880s. More recently the village has found a new role serving the many visitors to Upper Swaledale.

famous Kearton Country Hotel for refreshments might be in order.

Kisdon Side

From here the Pennine Way is followed for 2¾ miles (4¼ kilometres) around the eastern flanks of Kisdon Hill. Heading over a couple of fields, cross a stream by a flat bridge and head up to a gated gap stile. At this point a finger sign marks the start of a stony path heading east up steep slopes clad in bracken and heather.

Upper Swaledale

The dramatic scenery of Upper Swaledale was fashioned during the last Ice Age. From its headwaters on Birkdale Common, the River Swale – the 'swirling river' – runs swiftly eastward through a deep, 'U'-shaped valley. The principal settlement in Upper Swaledale is Reeth. Downstream the River Swale flows through a beautiful wooded gorge en route to the Georgian market town of Richmond.

Pausing to look back, Great Shunner Fell and Lovely Seat dominate the view. Join a grassy track at Kisdon House Farm and head up beside a lime kiln. Arriving at a crossroads of tracks, a finger sign shows the Pennine Way turning north (2 = SD 904 986).

From here the route follows a path contouring around the side of the hill, picking its way awkwardly through belts of slippery scree. To the right are stunning views over the deep valley of the River Swale, with the gorge of Swinner Gill cutting down through the scarp of Ivelet Moor. The path runs above steep, wooded slopes, eventually passing through an overgrown quarry. A finger sign shows a muddy path heading down to Kisdon Force, offering an opportunity for a there-and-back detour. Continuing along our path, across the river are glimpses of towering limestone cliffs. When the Pennine Way turns down towards a footbridge, continue instead along the link path leading to the village centre at Keld (3 = NY 892 012). Heading up through the village, turn left along the B6270. Soon a finger sign beside an old barn marks the start of a bridleway to Muker (4 = NY 892 006).

Kisdon Hill

The final part of the walk runs 2½ miles (4¼ kilometres) over Kisdon Hill. Crossing a stream, a stony track heads steeply uphill towards an isolated farmhouse. The height gained affords good views over the valley, its steep slopes patterned with walled pasture. Ahead, the crumbling face of an abandoned quarry (Hooker Mill Scar) marks the hillside. Passing through a gate, a grassy track is followed over the broad crest of the hill. Turning sharply southward, the track heads downhill. Muker can be seen down in the valley, and beyond it the River Swale. On arrival back

Kisdon Hill

The lovely island-hill of Kisdon is almost entirely surrounded by streams. It is the jewel in the crown of Upper Swaledale, itself arguably the finest of Yorkshire's dales. Whilst it is a hill of relatively modest height (1,637 feet/499 metres), and the actual summit is seldom visited, its flanks provide a grandstand for views of the surrounding fells and dales.

at the crossroads of tracks passed earlier, follow the route signed for Muker (5 = SD 904 986).

Following a stony track heading south-east down a walled lane, this becomes tarmac as it zigzags steeply downhill. Approaching the village, it runs along a tree-shaded lane. Pass the tiny post office and continue down towards the village centre. Since this is a short walk, there should be plenty of time to sample the refreshments available locally, or else to go exploring (the remains of lead-mining operations in Swinner Gill are well worth a visit).

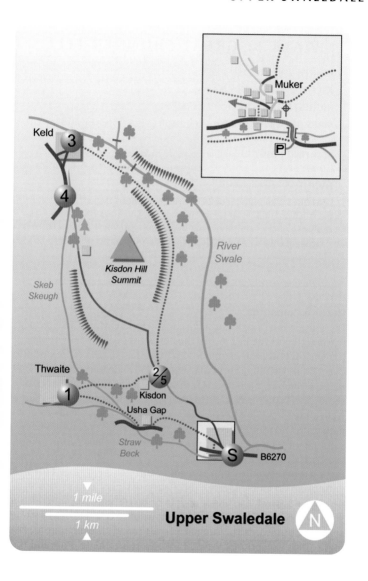

Muker

Keld

River Swale

Kisdon Hill Summit

Skeb Skeugh

Thwaite

Kisdon

Usha Gap

Straw Beck

B6270

1 mile

1 km

Upper Swaledale

WALK 3: GREAT SHUNNER FELL

LENGTH 16¼ miles (26¼ kilometres)

ASCENT 2,576 feet (785 metres)

HIGHEST POINT 2,349 feet (716 metres)

MAPS OS Explorer OL Map 19 ('Howgill Fells & Upper Eden Valley') (Howgill Fells [South] Sheet)

STARTING POINT Parking area beside Thwaite, Upper Swaledale (SD 893 980)

FACILITIES Refreshments.

FEATURES Although much of the route has been flagged, this is still a challenging hill-walk. Great Shunner Fell and Stags Fell offer extensive views, and there is an opportunity to visit Hardraw Force – England's highest waterfall. The return route passes the deep limestone fissures known as the Buttertubs.

Thwaite Common

There are a few rough parking spaces to the east of Thwaite, near the junction of the B6270 and the Buttertubs road. The first part of the walk follows the Pennine Way from the village centre up onto Great Shunner Fell, a total of 3½ miles (5¾ kilometres), with 1,500 feet (457 metres) of ascent. To the north of the village, a finger sign shows the Pennine Way turning onto a stony track heading up a walled lane. Arriving at the head of the lane, a gate leads to open moorland (1 = SD 876 984).

Joining a flagged path at some old mine workings, this follows the crest of a broad ridge as it swings around in a wide arc, crossing cottongrass mires and threading through peat hags crowned with heather and bilberry. The flagstones give out as the path heads south-west, passing a couple of cairns and dropping into a shallow dip. Heading steeply uphill towards a beehive cairn, stone steps climb towards the summit (2 = SD 848 972), which unsurprisingly offers exceptional views. To the west are the fells around the headwaters of the River Eden (the precipitous scarp of Wild Boar

Thwaite

Thwaite is a lovely little village of stone-built cottages. It is another place established by the Vikings – 'thwaite' being the Old Norse word for a woodland clearing. The village is famous for its association with the Kearton brothers, Richard and Cherry, who pioneered wildlife photography. They were born at the Corner House, the sons of a gamekeeper. The house can still be identified by the animals and birds carved into the lintel over the front door (the brothers' initials and years of their birth – 1862 and 1871 respectively – are below). At the centre of the village is the Kearton Country Hotel. Scenes from the television series *All Creatures Great and Small* were filmed around the village.

Fell being prominent), while to the south are early views of the three peaks.

The Long Ridge

From here the Pennine Way is followed down a long, broad ridge, 4¾ miles (7¾ kilometres) to Hardraw. The path initially continues south-west, with more flagstones and stone steps. As it levels-out, the route swings around to head south over grassy moorland terrain. Dunlin and golden plover are common in this area. Flagstones provide passage of cottongrass mires, although the going is generally easy. Looking to the left, the deep valleys of Hearne Beck and Fossdale Gill converge beneath the steep scarp of Stags Fell. To the right is the valley of Cotterdale Beck. Approaching a drystone wall, a finger sign points through a gate (3 = SD 847 932).

Join a stony track running south-east. Ahead are fine views over Upper Wensleydale. Passing

Great Shunner Fell

Great Shunner Fell reaches 2,349 feet (716 metres), its summit being marked by a cross-shaped stone shelter built around an OS pillar. The fell is capped in Millstone Grit, which resisted erosion as the surrounding valleys were formed by the passage of ice. Crow coal was mined on the flanks of Great Shunner Fell until the early twentieth century, with the pits being temporarily re-opened during the General Strike of 1926.

Hardraw Force

At the Green Dragon Inn, payment of a modest fee secures access to Hardraw Force, which is reached by following a path leading to the head of a wooded gorge. Hardraw Beck here drops nearly 100 feet (31 metres), creating the highest above-ground waterfall in England (there are bigger drops underground, notably at Gaping Gill). The original lip was washed away in the floods of 1890, but was subsequently restored by the landowner, Lord Wharncliffe. The surrounding cliffs offer an interesting cross-section of the different layers of rock, while the gorge has provided a venue for brass band concerts since the nineteenth century.

through another gate, the track enters a walled lane, heading down through pasture towards Hardraw. Arriving at an unclassified road, turn left and cross a stone bridge leading into the village centre. Beside Hardraw Beck is a pleasant public garden with tree-shaded benches offering an opportunity to stop for lunch (4 = SD 867 912).

Across the road is the Green Dragon Inn, which provides access to Hardraw Force (this involves a there-and-back detour of ¾ mile/ 1¼ kilometres). Just past the public garden, a sign shows the Pennine Way turning through a gate on the right, joining a flagged path running across meadows. The River Ure can be seen beyond a stand of mature broadleaf trees on the right. Passing through a gated gap stile, head down Burnt Acres Road. The Pennine Way continues down the road towards Hawes, although we cross over to join a path signed for Sedbusk (5 = SD 877 905).

Stags Fell

Heading north-west, the faint path crosses a tree-shaded stream before continuing over meadows towards a road. Straight over the road, a gated gap stile leads to pair of finger signs. Taking the route signed for Sedbusk Lane, head north over rolling pasture towards another road. Note the mosaic embedded in the drystone wall opposite. To the left the lane connects with the Buttertubs road, offering a shortcut if daylight is failing, although we turn right and head towards Sedbusk. Passing through the village, a finger sign marks the start of a track heading up a walled lane. Just before reaching a gate, turn over a ladder stile on the left (6 = SD 888 915).

Heading north-west up the steep scarp of Stags Fell, the rough track passes a walled enclosure of stunted sycamores. Pausing to look back, the height gained affords fine views over Upper Wensleydale, with Hawes sitting encamped beside the River Ure — a fair-sized town given the remoteness of the location. Ahead it is the crags of High Clint that dominate the view. Pass through a couple of gates and continue up a grassy track until a finger sign marks a sharp turn to the left (7 = SD 884 925).

Joining a quad track heading west over the springy turf of North Rakes Hill, the plateau reaches 1,750 feet (533 metres), with a short diversion to the cairned top being rewarded by wonderful views. The track swings around to head north-west, passing beehive cairns marking the steep scarp. High-quality sandstone mined here was used in the construction of Manchester Victoria Station. Arriving at a gully, ignore a hardcore track turning downhill, and instead continue around the edge of the plateau, with marker posts providing guidance. Crossing another gully (Shiveny Gill), a finger sign shows the path turning down towards the Buttertubs road (8 = SD 866 937).

Buttertubs Pass

The final part of the walk follows the unclassified road as it runs over the Buttertubs Pass, 3¾ miles (6 kilometres) back to the starting point. Turning right, head up the road, which runs above the deep valley of Fossdale Gill. The road is normally quiet, and the views towards Great Shunner Fell are splendid. The watershed between Wensleydale and Swaledale reaches 1,726 feet (526 metres), with the height of the snow poles beside the road hinting at the severity of winter conditions (9 = SD 869 957).

As the road starts downhill, fenced enclosures on either side mark the location of the famous Buttertubs. Continuing down the road, the deep gorge of Cliff Beck is to the right, with the flanks of Lovely Seat beyond. Ahead are early views of Kisdon

---

The Buttertubs

The Buttertubs are a group of large fissures, up to 90 feet (27 metres) deep, created by the erosion of limestone. The name probably refers to their shape, although there is a story that farmers returning from Hawes market used to lower unsold butter into the holes in order to keep it cool until the following week. Care is needed when approaching the unfenced holes.

Hill. For a way there is no verge, and beyond the crash barriers on the right are steep slopes, so stay alert for traffic. The road runs steeply downhill, passing through a belt of walled pasture before arriving back at the starting point.

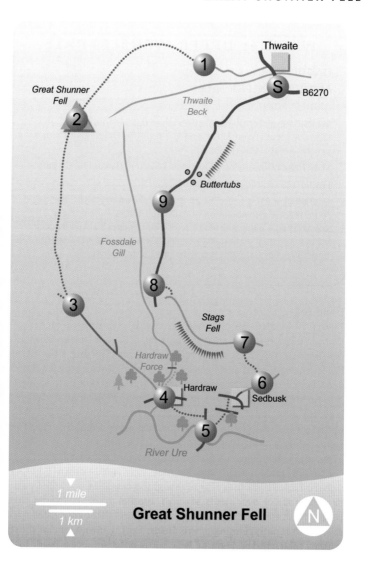

Thwaite

S B6270

Great Shunner Fell

Thwaite Beck

Buttertubs

Fossdale Gill

Stags Fell

Hardraw Force

Hardraw

Sedbusk

River Ure

1 mile

1 km

Great Shunner Fell

N

WALK 4: UPPER WENSLEYDALE

LENGTH 13½ miles (21½ kilometres)

ASCENT 1,411 feet (430 metres)

HIGHEST POINT 1,926 feet (587 metres)

MAPS OS Explorer OL Maps 2 ('Yorkshire Dales – Southern & Western Areas') (West Sheet) and 30 ('Yorkshire Dales – Northern & Central Areas') (Central Sheet)

STARTING POINT Dales Countryside Museum, Hawes (SD 875 898)

FACILITIES Full range of services.

FEATURES Starting at the bustling market town of Hawes, the route follows a combination of paths and tracks – including a Roman road – along a series of intersecting ridges flanked by deep valleys. The final section is a steeplechase across the meadows of Upper Wensleydale, so it is essential to finish before dark.

Dodd Fell

Hawes is located on the A684, towards the upper reaches of Wensleydale. As well as on-street parking, there is a 'pay and display' car park at the Dales Countryside Museum. Starting from here, follow the main road as it heads into the town centre, crossing Gayle Beck below sizeable cataracts. Passing the churchyard, look for a sign on the left showing the Pennine Way turning along a passageway. Heading up steps beside the churchyard, follow a flagged path across a field, parallel to the beck. Wensleydale Creamery is to the right, while a short way upstream is Gayle Mill (this was built in 1784, and is the oldest unaltered cotton mill in the country).

Crossing over a road, the Pennine Way heads down a ginnel between council houses. Through a gated gap stile, a flagged path runs diagonally over fields towards another road. Following this past some farm buildings, a finger sign points through a gated gap stile, with a path running across fields. Exiting into a lane, a short way to the right the Pennine Way turns onto an access road. Just before this reaches Gaudy House Farm, a finger sign points over a

Hawes

The bustling market town of Hawes is the capital of Upper Wensleydale. Whilst the area was settled by Vikings, the name is actually Anglo-Saxon and refers to a mountain pass. Hawes received its charter in 1700, and a market is still held every Tuesday. The town grew in importance after the arrival of the Wensleydale Railway in 1878, linking the East Coast Main Line at Northallerton to the Settle and Carlisle Railway at Garsdale. Following closure of the line, the railway station was reopened as the Dales Countryside Museum. Hawes is perhaps best known as the home of Wensleydale Cheese – of 'Wallace and Gromit' fame. The art of cheese-making was brought to the dales by French monks, who used ewes' milk. However, today it is produced at the creamery using cows' milk.

fence stile on the left (1 = SD 860 887).

From here the Pennine Way heads 4 miles (6½ kilometres) up a trailing ridge of Dodd Fell Hill. The summit reaches 2,192 feet (668 metres), although we avoid the peaty mires blanketing the Millstone Grit cap. Climbing steadily through a landscape characterised by the vague enclosure of rough grazing, there are good views over Upper Wensleydale towards Great Shunner Fell and its neighbours. Passing through a gate, a rough track continues to the right of a drystone wall, swinging around to head south-west. Turning across the foot of a steep slope, continue above the deep valley of Snaizeholme Beck, joining a stony track coming up from the right (2 = SD 843 868).

The track is an old pack-horse route known as West Cam Road, which is followed as it contours around the side of Dodd Fell Hill. Across the valley, the slopes of Great Knoutberry Hill are marked by angular conifer plantations. A small lake on the valley floor can

Upper Wensleydale

Wensleydale is broader than its northern neighbour, although the valley sides are equally steep. It was once known as Yoredale, after the River Ure – the current name being related to the village of Wensley, which in 1202 was the first place in the dale to be granted a market charter. Wensley failed to recover from an outbreak of the plague in 1563, and it remains a village of modest size. Upper Wensleydale is reckoned to start at Aysgarth, which is the location of an attractive series of cataracts. Associations with James Herriot have helped to establish Upper Wensleydale as a popular tourist destination, with the village of Askrigg being the location for scenes in the television series *All Creatures Great and Small*.

be seen among a scattering of farm buildings. Eventually the track runs onto the crest of the broad ridge, following this south-south-west until an access road is met (3 = SD 830 834).

Cam High Road

This is Cam High Road, which is followed east then north-east along a broad ridge for 3¾ miles (6 kilometres). Taking a moment to enjoy the distant views of the three peaks, turn through a gate and head along the road. In the deep valley on the right is the ill-defined watershed between Oughtershaw Beck, which feeds the River Wharfe, and Cam Beck, which joins the River Ribble – their waters being destined for the North Sea and the Irish Sea respectively. Passing an area of limestone pavement, the road runs between walls of white limestone towards a junction (4 = SD 861 847).

Turn left and head along the unclassified road. This leads down

Cam High Road

Cam High Road was once known as the Devil's Causeway. It was part of a Roman road originating at the regional headquarters at Lancaster, running north-east via Ingleton to the fort at Bainbridge (Virosidum) in Wensleydale, reaching 1,926 feet (587 metres) on Dodd Fell. Later it served as a droveway and pack-horse route. Cam High Road is one of the famous 'green lanes' of the Yorkshire Dales, although like many of these historic routes, recreational use by off-road vehicles has left the un-surfaced sections so badly eroded that the term is a misnomer.

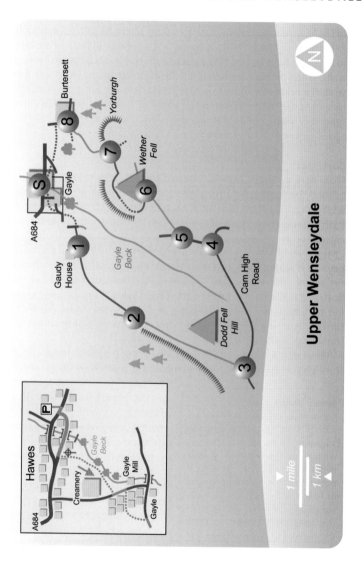

Upper Wensleydale

N

Burtersett

Yorburgh

S

Gayle

A684

Gaudy
House

Wether
Fell

Gayle Beck

Dodd Fell
Hill

Cam High
Road

Hawes

A684

Creamery

Gayle Beck

Gayle Mill

Gayle

P

1 mile

1 km

219

to Gayle, offering a potential escape route, although a finger sign soon indicates a right turn onto a byway – a continuation of the Roman road (5 = SD 863 853). The stony track heads north-east between broken walls. When the wall on the left fails, a finger sign on the left marks the start of a bridleway route (6 = SD 873 865). Before leaving the lane, try to spot Semer Water down in the valley of the River Bain. Also, the summit of Wether Fell (Drumaldrace) is just a short way to the north, and is well worth a visit if daylight and enthusiasm permit.

Burtersett

From here a rough track is followed for 1½ miles (2½ kilometres) around the northern flanks of Wether Fell. Initially the track heads west alongside a drystone wall, then as it crosses broken ground it swings around to run north-east. Passing some old workings, it zigzags downhill to join another track (7 = SD 883 875). Ahead is a distinctive hillock marked by a prominent scar (Yorburgh), and beyond it wonderful views over Upper Wensleydale. Passing an old tin shack, the stony track heads down towards the village of Burtersett. Whilst the track itself is hard going, it is usually possible to follow the verge. Arriving at a farm, the track becomes tarmac. Ignoring a finger sign on the left showing a path to Gayle, the village centre is reached (8 = SD 891 892).

Burtersett is a pleasant little place of stone-built cottages. Pass through the village and continue down the road (New Lane) until a finger sign on the left marks the start of a path to Hawes. This heads west over meadows, crossing drystone walls by gated gap stiles. Crossing straight over an unclassified road, continue across fields. Passing to the rear of some cottages, note the decorative use of limestone pavement on the garden walls. Upon reaching the main road, follow the pavement back to the town centre.

> **Semer Water**
> Semer Water is one of only two natural lakes of any size in the Yorkshire Dales. It was formed when a retreating glacier deposited a moraine, creating a natural dam. A local legend tells of how a village was lost beneath the lake, and when the water level was temporarily lowered in 1937, the remains of a Bronze Age settlement were indeed discovered.

WALK 5: CAM FELL

LENGTH 13 miles (21 kilometres)

ASCENT 1,444 feet (440 metres)

HIGHEST POINT 1,910 feet (582 metres)

MAPS OS Explorer OL Map 2 ('Yorkshire Dales – Southern & Western Areas') (West Sheet)

STARTING POINT Fleet Moss parking area, near Hawes (SD 860 838)

FACILITIES None.

FEATURES This walk can be hard-going at times, with a badly eroded track, boggy moorland and forest firebreaks to negotiate. However, much of the route is on quiet roads and there are fine views from the ridges. Unusually, the walk starts at its highest point.

Oughtershaw Side

Fleet Moss parking area is located on the crest of the broad ridge separating Wensleydale and Wharfedale, 4 miles (6½ kilometres) south of Hawes, and is reached by following a steep road connecting Gayle and Oughtershaw. Heading down the road, turn onto a stony track leading to some old workings. Join a quad track. This is not shown on all maps, but runs west over grassy moorland until it meets Cam High Road (1 = SD 850 838). Following the road for 1¼ miles (2¼ kilometres) along Oughtershaw Side, a finger sign shows the Pennine Way joining from the right (2 = SD 830 834).

Cam Fell

The route follows a broad ridge identified on the map as Cam Fell, although it is in fact a spur of Dodd Fell. Arriving at a fork, the Pennine Way continues straight ahead (to the left is the access for Camm Farm – marked on the map as Cam Houses). The stony track is badly rutted in places, although it is usually possible to follow the verge. Looking over the deep valley on the left, the view is already marred by the sprawling conifer plantation around

Langstrothdale. Passing a finger sign, the next part of the route is shared with the Dales Way (a 73-mile/118-kilometre trail connecting Ilkley and Bowness-on-Windermere) (3 = SD 813 817).

Arriving at Cam End, another finger sign shows the Dales Way continuing down the ridge, while the Pennine Way turns south (4 = SD 801 804). From here there are splendid views of the three peaks area, with Ribblehead Viaduct spanning the valley between the great ridge of Whernside and the ominous, sphinx-like form of Ingleborough (the top of which was the well-chosen site of a Brigantian settlement). Heading down the stony track as it weaves through a swarm of drumlins, the Pennine Way follows an old pack-horse route that connected Hawes and Settle. Rounding a bluff, the track heads down towards Cam Beck, which is crossed by a pack-horse bridge. Limestone outcrops beside the beck provide an opportunity to stop for lunch. Continuing along the track, to

Ling Gill

A close examination of the sixteenth-century pack-horse bridge at Ling Gill reveals the inscription: 'this bridge was repaired at the charge of the whole West Riding, anno 1765'. Ling Gill itself is a National Nature Reserve managed by English Nature. It is a fine example of a wooded gorge, its steep sides providing shelter and protection from overgrazing.

the right is the wooded gorge of Ling Gill. A dry gully on the left is home to a few sycamore trees, marking the point at which we leave the Pennine Way (5 = SD 803 787).

Langstrothdale Chase

The first part of the return route runs 1 mile (1½ kilometres) over Sike Moor, with some difficult terrain to negotiate. Following a faint path up the left-hand side of the gully, continue north-east along a quad track heading towards a ruin. Fording a small stream, the route turns east-south-east, keeping to the left of another gully. Ahead can be seen the distinctive cairned ridge of High Green Field Knott. Following a quad track over tussocky grass, this runs beside a drystone wall before veering to the left to avoid a cottongrass mire. Arriving at a broken wall marking the edge of the forest, pass between stone gate posts and cross a fence stile (6 = SD 815 789).

From here a path runs ¾ mile (1¼ kilometres) through the forest. Following a firebreak separating walls of densely-packed sitka spruce, the peaty ground is carpeted in heather and cottongrass. Crossing over a hardcore track, the path resumes a short way to the right, joining another firebreak. The ground here can be very slippery, so exercise caution. Eventually the way ahead opens out, with the faint path crossing rough grass to arrive at a forestry road close to a stone bridge (7 = SD 827 789).

Langstrothdale must once have been a beautiful place, with Green Field Beck flowing through meadows to its confluence with Oughtershaw Beck (where the River Wharfe is formed). However, the steep valley sides are now lost beneath a thick blanket of conifers. The track runs north-east towards the isolated High Green Field Farm, which stands at the end of an unclassified road. Following the road down the valley, off to the right is a tiny reservoir – a rare stopping place for wildfowl in the limestone dales. Passing Low Green Field Farm, a finger sign marks the start of a footpath to Oughtershaw, crossing a fence stile on the left (8 = SD 851 802). Note that it is also possible to reach the hamlet by continuing down the valley to Beckermonds, then turning onto Oughtershaw Road (this adds about 1 mile/1½ kilometres to the route, although there is some charming limestone scenery).

Following a hardcore track running east-north-east through the forest, a few rowan trees planted beside the route do little to improve what is otherwise just another coniferous tunnel. Leaving the track as it swings to the left, a finger sign marks the start of a path running down a

> **Langstrothdale Chase**
> Langstrothdale Chase – the hunting area of Langstroth – was part of Litton Forest. Among the isolated hunting lodges scattered throughout the area were Beckermonds and Oughtershaw, which subsequently evolved into small agricultural settlements.

firebreak. Emerging from the forest, there are fine views over Upper Wharfedale. A finger sign indicates the direction of the path, which heads north-east over rough grass. Heading downhill as though towards a chapel, a stony track is joined just before it crosses Oughtershaw Beck by a bridge (9 = SD 870 814).

Oughtershaw Road

The final part of the walk runs 2 miles (3 kilometres) up a steep road. This is normally quiet, although there are occasional spates of tourist traffic. Turning left, follow the road as it passes through the handful of stone-built cottages and farm buildings that together constitute the hamlet of Oughtershaw. Ignore a tarmac track turning along the valley of Oughtershaw Beck (the route of the Dales Way). A marker stone beside the road dates its construction to 1887. As height is gained there are good views over the valley, with Ingleborough once again visible in the distance. Eventually the road levels out, just before it arrives back at the starting point.

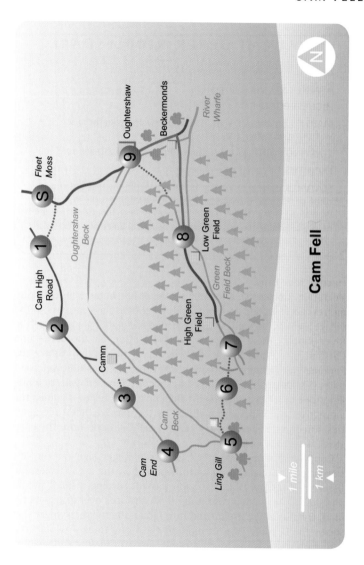

Cam Fell

WALK 6: UPPER RIBBLESDALE

LENGTH 13½ miles (22 kilometres)

ASCENT 1,575 feet (480 metres)

HIGHEST POINT 1,437 feet (438 metres)

MAPS OS Explorer OL Map 2 ('Yorkshire Dales – Southern & Western Areas') (West Sheet)

STARTING POINT Horton-in-Ribblesdale car park (SD 808 726)

FACILITIES Full range of services.

FEATURES Starting at Horton-in-Ribblesdale in the heart of the three peaks area, this highly enjoyable walk follows the Pennine Way along stony tracks, passing a series of deep limestone fissures, before returning through an area of beautiful limestone scenery.

Harber Scar Lane

Horton-in-Ribblesdale is located on the B6479, about 5 miles (8 kilometres) north of Settle. There is a 'pay and display' car park in the village centre, as well as limited roadside parking just over the River Ribble. There is also a railway station on the Settle and Carlisle line. Close to the Crown Inn, a finger sign shows the Pennine Way heading up Harber Scar Lane, which is followed for 3 miles (5 kilometres). The stony track climbs between walls of white limestone as it heads north-east then north. As height is gained the views over the valley are blighted by the massive limestone quarries. Cutting through the dry gully of Sell Gill Beck, note the limestone fissures (1 = SD 812 744).

Continuing along the track, ignore a finger sign on the left showing a footpath to Birkwith. Another of the area's limestone fissures – Jackdaw Hole – is soon passed. Fording a small stream and passing through a gate, the track continues over grassy moorland. Over another stream and through another gate, a finger sign shows the Pennine Way turning off the stony track – which continues on towards the forest around Langstrothdale – and heading up towards a small cairn (2 = SD 813 772).

Horton-in-Ribblesdale

Horton-in-Ribblesdale is the focal point of the three peaks area. The name of the village is Anglo-Saxon, and signifies a 'mucky farm'. The most prominent building is Saint Oswald's Church, which dates from the early twelfth century and today leans noticeably southward! Some of the cottages date from the seventeenth century. The opening of the Settle and Carlisle Railway triggered further development – this time on the west side of the river – and from the 1890s houses were built for the workers at the limestone quarries.

Ling Gill

From here a rough track heads west, down to a derelict structure then alongside a drystone wall. Meeting a hardcore track, turn left and head towards Old Ing Farm (3 = SD 804 774). From here the Pennine Way is followed north along another stony track – an old pack-horse route, 2¼ miles (3½ kilometres) to Cam End. Heading along the walled lane, a ladder stile on the right provides access to Calf Holes (note that the outcrops around the opening can be slippery). Further along the track a stile on the left provides the option of a 'there and back' detour to Browgill Cave. Passing the wooded gorge at Ling Gill, cross over the pack-horse bridge and continue up the track to Cam End, where we leave the Pennine Way (4 = SD 801 804).

Limestone Fissures

The Pennine Way heading north out of Horton-in-Ribblesdale passes a series of deep limestone fissures. At the head of Harber Scar Lane are Sell Gill Holes, which descend 210 feet (64 metres). Further along is Jackdaw Hole, which has an opening measuring 70 feet (21 metres) by 40 feet (12 metres). Nearby are Cowskull Pot (70 feet/21 metres deep) and Penyghent Long Churn (180 feet/55 metres deep). Calf Holes provide access to Dry Laithe Cave, where Brow Gill Beck drops 35 feet (11 metres) to a passage running under Cave Hill, re-emerging at Browgill Cave. Cavers are often encountered around the openings, or else their disembodied voices are heard echoing up from below.

The Dales Way

This fine vantage point will be remembered from the previous walk. The first part of the return route follows the Dales Way down the broad ridge, heading west along the course of Cam High Road for 1½ miles (2½ kilometres). As the track nears Gayle Beck, steep cobbles lead down to a slippery ford, with a footbridge providing an easier option. Arriving at the B6255, turn left and follow the verge. A marker stone identifies this as the Lancaster & Richmond Road – an old turnpike. Ignoring a farm access on the right (where the Dales Way leaves our route), Gearstones Lodge is soon reached (5 = SD 780 800).

> ### Gearstones
>
> During the Middle Ages, Upper Ribblesdale was grazed by sheep from Furness, Fountains and Sawley abbeys. Gearstones developed as a small farming community at the heart of the Furness Abbey sheep-runs. Gearstones Lodge itself was once an inn, located at the meeting place of a number of droveways, with the surrounding walled paddocks serving as holding pens for cattle. The building is now an outdoor activities centre.

The Ribble Way

A finger sign beside the building marks the start of a path to Nether Lodge. This is part of the Ribble Way – a 70-mile (113-kilometre) trail from the river's source to the Irish Sea. Here it is followed south-east for the next 4¼ miles (7 kilometres). Crossing a meadow and passing through a gate, ignore the rickety footbridge straight ahead and instead turn along a quad track leading down to a ford (Gayle Beck – the infant River Ribble – can be deep, so it may be necessary to backtrack a short way to the footbridge).

The quad track resumes on the far side of the beck, wrapping around a low hillock. Arriving at a ladder stile, a short section of lane runs between moss-covered walls under the shade of mature sycamore trees. Turning over a gated gap stile on the left, a finger sign confirms the route to Nether Lodge, crossing a ladder stile and heading uphill beside a drystone wall. Arriving at a ruined barn, a step stile leads to a quad track. Fording a small stream,

Upper Ribblesdale

The sizeable river flowing through Lancashire to the Irish Sea has humble beginnings high up on Gayle Moor. It runs as Jam Sike, Long Gill and Gayle Beck, eventually becoming the River Ribble at Ribblehead. The distinctive forms of Whernside, Ingleborough and Pen-y-ghent over-shadow the broad valley, which serves as an important tourist destination, despite the extensive quarrying of the Great Scar Limestone.

head up to a fence stile then follow a faint path over rough terrain. Navigation is straightforward, however, with Nether Lodge now visible ahead as a group of farm buildings. Crossing a rushy mire at the bottom of a broad trough, a quad track leads to the farm (6 = SD 793 778).

Taking the route signed for Birkwith, pass through the farmyard and cross a tree-lined stream (Cam Beck). Over a step stile beside a gate, a finger sign confirms the route to High Birkwith, following a stony track to God's Bridge. Here a thick slab of limestone spans Brow Gill Beck, recalling its namesake on the River Greta. Continuing beside a drystone wall, the route soon arrives at another stony track. A short way to the right is High Birkwith Farm, standing at the end of an unclassified road that offers a potential escape route, although the Ribble Way turns left, towards Old Ing Farm. Before reaching the farm, a finger sign marks the start of a path to Sell Gill (7 = SD 803 772).

This follows a terrace of lush grass beneath limestone outcrops, beside an extensive area of limestone pavement. When a deep gully cuts across the terrace, ignore a track veering off to the left and instead head down to a small footbridge. After a stiff ascent the terrace is regained, although the limestone pavement is now turf-covered. Crossing a succession of drystone walls by ladder stiles, when a farmhouse sheltering among mature broadleaf trees appears to the right, turn through a gate (8 = SD 808 750).

New Houses

Passing the buildings of Top Farm, a hardcore track zigzags down through pasture to arrive at an unclassified road (9 = SD 803 745). Nearby is a small fishing lake known appropriately as 'Tarn' (it is an indication of the geology of the area that this is sufficient for identification purposes). Heading along the quiet road, just past the hamlet of New Houses a redundant clapper bridge stands beside a dry ford. Following the road through meadows towards the village, the river can be seen a short way to the right.

Limestone outcrops in Upper Ribblesdale.

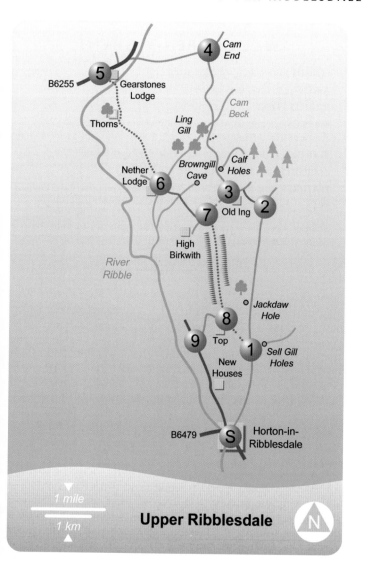

Upper Ribblesdale

WALK 7: PEN-Y-GHENT

LENGTH 15¼ miles (24½ kilometres)

ASCENT 2,051 feet (625 metres)

HIGHEST POINT 2,277 feet (694 metres)

MAPS OS Explorer OL Map 2 ('Yorkshire Dales – Southern & Western Areas') (West Sheet)

STARTING POINT Horton-in-Ribblesdale car park (SD 808 726)

FACILITIES Full range of services.

FEATURES A challenging hill-walk following pack-horse routes and difficult paths around Pen-y-Ghent, with an exhilarating clamber up onto the summit, where the views are spoiled only by nearby quarries. Deep limestone fissures passed along the way include the country's largest natural hole (Hull Pot).

Foxup Road

Starting at the car park, turn right and follow the pavement beside the B6479. Crossing over the road, a finger sign shows the Pennine Way passing between cottages and heading up a stony track lined with ash and hawthorn. Arriving at a fork in the lane, take the left-hand track (that on the right is part of the three peaks challenge route). The track climbs steadily as it heads north-east, with the distinctive stepped profile of Pen-y-ghent coming into view ahead. To the right of the lane is an incised valley flanked by limestone crags. Passing through a gate, a finger sign on the left marks the start of a bridleway route running over Foxup Moor (1 = SD 823 743).

This is Foxup Road – an old pack-horse route – which is followed for 3¾ miles (6 kilometres) around the northern flanks of Plover Hill. Leaving the Pennine Way for now, head north-east along a shallow trough leading to Hull Pot. Over a ladder stile, follow a quad track towards an elbow in a drystone wall, where it cuts across the three-peaks challenge route. Continuing straight ahead, the track crosses a cottongrass mire as it runs beside the

The Three Peaks Challenge

Pen-y-ghent Café is the traditional starting point for the three peaks challenge. Since it began in 1887 with a pair of schoolmasters from Giggleswick undertaking the circuit of Pen-y-ghent, Whernside and Ingleborough, the walk has grown in popularity to become a national phenomenon. Despite improvements to the paths it remains a significant undertaking, with a standard route of 23 miles (37 kilometres) and around 5,000 feet (1,524 metres) of ascent. Participants can clock out and back in again at the café, which doubles as a tourist information centre.

wall. A narrow causeway of compacted hardcore provides a safe crossing of the worst part of the bog. Ignoring a finger sign showing a path heading up onto Plover Hill, continue along the valley side (2 = SD 846 761).

Following a quad track beside a broken wall, eventually this turns steeply downhill (the ground is slippery, so take care). Passing through a gate, a finger sign confirms the route as the track continues along the valley side above Foxup Beck. Eventually the hamlets of Foxup and Halton Gill come into view ahead. These were originally lodges in the Forest of Litton, before developing into agricultural settlements around the sheep-runs maintained by Fountains Abbey. Arriving at a drystone wall, the track turns downhill again before continuing over pasture. Passing through a gate, finger signs show bridleway routes heading left and right (3 = SD 871 764).

Pen-y-ghent Gill

From here the route runs 3¾ miles (6 kilometres) around the

Hull Pot

At 300 feet (91 metres) long, 60 feet (18 metres) wide and 60 (18 metres) feet deep, Hull Pot is the largest natural hole in the country and the most dramatic of the limestone fissures that riddle the ground hereabouts. The spectacle is completed by an intermittent waterfall, which crashes into the chasm before disappearing underground. In times of severe spate, Hull Pot has been known to fill up and overflow!

eastern flanks of Plover Hill. Heading south-east, the track runs to the right of a drystone wall. Looking ahead, there are good views down the beautiful 'U'-shaped valley of Littondale. Continuing over grassy moorland, the track eventually converges with an unclassified road. Turning right, follow the quiet road as it heads up the valley of Pen-y-ghent Gill. The deep valley is flanked by the long ridge of Fountains Fell and the more shapely form of Pen-y-ghent. Ignoring a route signed for Nether Hesleden, stay on the road until a finger sign on the left marks the start of a path to Silverdale Road (4 = SD 872 745) (it is possible to stay on the road, although this misses the best what the valley has to offer).

Heading steeply downhill, the narrow path turns across the bracken-covered slope. Continuing along the valley side, still far below the stream hurries down its constricted gorge. Finger signs confirm the route as the path hooks around gullies. Passing a farm (Pen-y-ghent House), keep to the left of a drystone wall, following a narrow ledge. A side stream cutting across the route is usually dry, but can cause difficulties in times of flood. From here the path runs through an area littered with limestone outcrops. The location of the Giant's Grave – a communal burial mound of Neolithic age – is difficult to identify among the natural features, its stones having been plundered for building material. Crossing an area of limestone pavement, the road is rejoined, although a finger sign on the right soon indicates the continuation of the path (once again, it is possible to stay on the road) (5 = SD 856 732).

Following a drystone wall (on the far side of which the stream disappears underground), the faint path runs over springy turf and wet meadow. To the right are fine views of Pen-y-ghent. Approaching a barn (Blishmire House), the path veers somewhat to the left. Arriving at a hardcore track, this provides an easy route back to the road, avoiding a difficult section of path (the literal route turns along the foot of a bluff, following an overgrown path beside a drystone wall). Either way, the road is met at the point where the Pennine Way comes down from Fountains Fell (6 = SD 853 723).

Pen-y-ghent

At 2,277 feet (694 metres), Pen-y-ghent is the lowest of the three peaks. The addition of a secondary top, Plover Hill (2,231 feet/680 metres), creates a long ridge. The stepped profile of the fell reveals its geology, with rocks of the Yoredale series underlying a Millstone Grit cap. The meaning of the name is uncertain, and whilst many claim Welsh origins – 'pen' being the word for a hilltop – the modern spelling is in fact fanciful (older sources have 'Pennigent'). Pen-y-ghent is famed for the rare purple saxifrage that flourishes among its limestone cliffs, flowering during early spring.

Pen-y-ghent

Follow the road past Rainscar Farm. Eventually a finger sign indicates a right turn along a walled lane (7 = SD 843 714). Passing the buildings of Dale Head Farm, this place was originally a pack-horse inn. Continuing along the stony track as it crosses undulating terrain, Churn Milk Hole is reached. Here a finger sign shows the Pennine Way turning onto a gravel path heading towards the foot of Pen-y-ghent. Crossing a section of boardwalk, another finger sign indicates a path to Brackenbottom, offering a potential escape route for anyone unable to undertake the stiff climb ahead.

The path becomes very steep, heading up stone steps to the right of limestone cliffs. Care is required, and in winter conditions an ice axe and crampons might be in order! A broad shelf covered in boulders from the shattered cliffs above provides a welcome break. Continuing up the made path, this soon degenerates into a scramble up limestone blocks. Cresting the rise, the path continues towards an OS pillar marking the summit, from where the views are unsurprisingly exceptional (8 = SD 838 733).

Horton Moor

The final part of the walk follows the Pennine Way down paths and lanes, 3½ miles (5½ kilometres) back to the starting point. Crossing a ladder stile, a finger sign shows the route heading north-north-west down a stony path. Unfortunately, the view ahead is now blighted by the limestone quarries above Horton-in-Ribblesdale. A few cairns provide guidance as the stony path – an old miners' track – turns north and heads down through a breach in the limestone cliffs. Note the prominent needle sheering away from the rock face ahead.

Arriving at the bottom, a finger sign marks a turn onto an improved path, heading west over grassy moorland. Pausing to look back, the magnificent silhouette of Pen-y-ghent is now brought into sharp relief by the westering sun. Crossing a ladder stile, continue along the gravel path, with a short diversion to the left providing an opportunity to visit Hunt Pot (just follow the sound of the waterfall). Eventually a finger sign shows the Pennine Way turning down a walled lane – the same route that was followed earlier (9 = SD 823 743). From here simply retrace your steps back to the village.

Hunt Pot

Whilst Hunt Pot is smaller than Hull Pot, it is deeper, reaching down 200 feet (61 metres). The streams that empty into the two fissures percolate down towards their outflow near Horton-in-Ribblesdale, their courses apparently crossing underground.

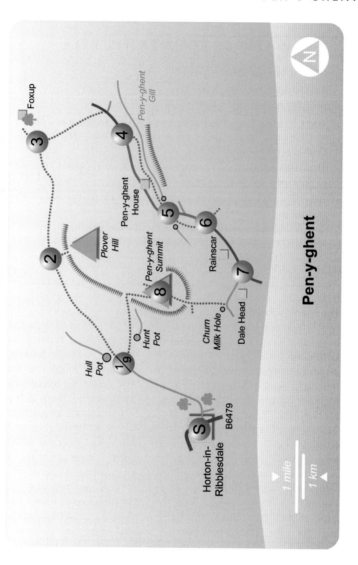

Pen-y-ghent

WALK 8: FOUNTAINS FELL

LENGTH 16 miles (25¾ kilometres)

ASCENT 1,903 feet (580 kilometres)

HIGHEST POINT 2,139 feet (652 metres)

MAPS OS Explorer OL Maps 2 ('Yorkshire Dales – Southern & Western Areas') (South Sheet) and 30 ('Yorkshire Dales – Northern & Central Areas') (Central Sheet)

STARTING POINT Arncliffe village centre, Littondale (SD 932 718)

FACILITIES Inn and refreshments.

FEATURES Starting at Arncliffe in Littondale – the original Emmerdale – this highly enjoyable walk follows a monastic way over limestone moors to Malham Tarn before crossing the rugged moorland terrain of Fountains Fell by miners' tracks. The return route follows a stony track and a riverside path.

The Monk's Road

Arncliffe is reached by turning off the B6160 a short way to the north of Kilnsey Crag, then following a narrow road running up Littondale for 3 miles (5 kilometres). There is roadside parking around the village green. The first part of the walk follows an old monastic way south-west over beautiful limestone moors to Malham Tarn, a total of 4¼ miles (6¾ kilometres). This was the Monk's Road, which was originally used to access the sheep runs held by Fountains Abbey. Beside the Falcon Inn, a finger sign points along a lane. Following this out of the village, just after the point where a small stream crosses the track, another finger sign marks a right turn through a gap stile, joining a path heading steeply uphill.

The steep slopes above Cowside Beck are carpeted in lush grass, dotted with brightly coloured flowers. The path becomes somewhat exposed as it runs above Yew Cogar Scar, but it soon veers away from the valley side to pass through an area of limestone outcrops. Crossing a ladder stile, a National Trust sign marks the boundary of its land holding. To the right are views towards Fountains Fell and

Littondale

Down the glacial U-shaped valley of Littondale runs the River Skirfare – a tributary of the Wharfe. The steep valley sides are embellished with limestone scars and hanging woods, while the valley floor is patterned with riverside meadows. The Normans established a hunting chase here (Litton Forest), before the grazing rights were awarded to Fountains Abbey during the thirteenth century. The old name for the valley was 'Amerdale', recalling the fact that it was the model for 'Emmerdale Farm'. Arncliffe ('eagle cliff') is an unspoilt place of stone-built cottages arranged around a village green, beside which is an inn (The Falcon, not The Woolpack!).

Darnbrook Fell, the latter being identified by the unsightly conifer blocks high up on its flanks. The path weaves through an area of low hillocks, with limestone features everywhere. Heading towards a clump of mature sycamore trees sheltering a ruin, ignore a finger sign indicating a turn for Darnbrook (1 = SD 907 684).

Passing to the right of the abandoned farm (Middle House), a stony track is joined. Over a ladder stile, instead of continuing down towards a working farm, follow a grassy track as it contours around a bluff. To the left is the dome of Great Close Hill. Crossing a fence stile, the track continues south-west over pasture studded with erratics until Malham Tarn suddenly comes into view. Zigzagging down towards the lake, mature beech trees in walled folds provide an opportunity to rest in the shade. Joining a lakeside track, a finger sign shows the Pennine Way heading into woodland (2 = SD 897 671).

Malham Tarn

Following the tree-shaded track around the north side of the lake, bird song completes a most idyllic scene. Passing to the right of Malham Tarn House, the track runs through a limestone cutting that was originally dug as part of a job-creation scheme. Occasionally the lake comes into view through the trees, and at one point a path leads down to a bird hide that is well worth a visit. Eventually a finger sign shows the Pennine Way turning through a gate on the right (3 = SD 888 673).

Passing a row of mature sycamore trees, the path runs along the

---

Malham Tarn House

Malham Tarn House was built around 1850 by Walter Morrison, a wealthy industrialist and Liberal MP. It had previously been the site of a hunting lodge owned by Lord Ribblesdale (who was responsible for planting the surrounding woodland), and before that a sheep-farm under Fountains Abbey. Notable guests entertained at the hall included Charles Darwin and Charles Kingsley – the latter drawing inspiration for his novel *The Water Babies* during his visit. Today it operates as a field studies centre.

---

bottom of a dry gully. Crossing a ladder stile, continue north over pasture, with views over the broad valley of Cowside Beck towards Fountains Fell. A finger sign marks a left turn onto a rough track heading down towards a step stile, from where it continues over a meadow. Arriving at an unclassified road, cross straight over to join a farm access (4 = SD 884 691).

Fountains Fell

The track passes close to the limestone outcrops of Great Hill Scar as it runs towards Tennant Gill Farm. Passing around the farm buildings, a quad track heads up the middle of a field towards a drystone wall. Over a step stile, a finger sign a short way to the left shows a path heading north-west, up beside an overgrown dyke. Turning north, the Pennine Way follows a track created in late eighteenth century to access the coal mines on the fell. Crossing a deep gully by stone steps, the route turns north-west as it starts to climb. Reaching the plateau, the track runs over heather moorland and cottongrass mires towards a tall cairn standing among stony heaps raised by the miners (5 = SD 868 720).

At 2,139 feet (652 metres), this is the highest point on the walk. The actual summit can be visited by a relatively short 'there and back' detour, following a quad track heading south-west across the plateau. However, in poor visibility do not be tempted to deviate from the Pennine Way – there are many deep mine shafts hereabouts. The quad track passes a fenced shaft and a coke oven before arriving at a size-able cairn marking the summit. Unlike the false top visited by the

Fountains Fell

Fountains Fell and its joined top, Darnbrook Fell, reach 2,192 feet (668 metres) and 2,047 feet (624 metres) respectively. It takes its name from Fountains Abbey, recalling the monastic sheep-runs that once covered the area. The stony heaps and mine shafts on the plateau are relics of the mining operations that took place here from the early eighteenth century, working a thin coal seam at the base of the Millstone Grit cap.

Pennine Way, this wonderfully remote place offers fine views of the surrounding fells, Pen-y-ghent being particularly prominent.

Retracing your steps to the Pennine Way, cross a drystone wall by a step stile. Here it is necessary to switch maps, from Sheet 2 to Sheet 30. Passing a cairn, turn onto a stony path – another old miners' track – heading steeply downhill. There is momentarily a sense of exposure as it hooks around bare rock and is over-washed by a stream, before continuing diagonally down the hillside. Eventually the path swings around from west to north-west, following a drystone wall over boggy ground. Arriving at an unclassified road, it is here that we leave the Pennine Way (6 = SD 853 723).

Darnbrook Fell

The first part of the return route follows a short section of quiet road, then a good track running around the northern flanks of Darnbrook Fell – a total of 3¾ miles (6 kilometres). Turning right, head along the unfenced road, looking out for a finger sign marking the start of a bridle road to Litton (7 = SD 855 729). The hardcore track heads northeast, with fine views across the deep valley of Pen-y-ghent Gill towards limestone terraces and the distinctive ridge of Pen-y-ghent itself. The map reveals a series of potholes along the valley side, below the track. Fording a stony stream and crossing a normally dry gully by a flat bridge, continue around the flanks of Darnbrook Fell.

Entering a walled lane, the stony track heads downhill, with splendid views across Littondale. Arriving at the valley floor, the lane continues between meadow and pasture, with a stone bridge off to the left providing an escape route onto a quiet road if daylight is failing. Passing a farm, ignore a finger sign showing a path to Litton and instead turn through a gate on the right. Following a tree-shaded

The distinctive ridge of Pen-y-ghent.

track running alongside a drystone wall, when this fords a side stream beware of slippery stones. Continuing past some old farm buildings, once again turn through a gate on the right, with a finger sign marking the start of a path to Arncliffe (8 = SD 905 739).

Littondale

The final part of the walk follows the River Skirfare for 2¼ miles (3¾ kilometres) back to the starting point. Crossing a couple of fields, a gate leads to a stony path running along the tree-lined riverbank. In times of drought the river runs underground, its stony bed becoming a place of stagnant rock pools. Through another gate, the path continues over meadows, with ruined barns dotted about the valley floor. The waymarking is good, and the path is easy-going as it cuts across a broad meander in the course of the river.

Crossing a wall by a gated gap stile, an English Nature sign provides information about Scoska Wood, which climbs the steep slopes off to the right (this is apparently the largest ash and rowan wood in the Yorkshire Dales). The path continues along the foot of a bluff, then across fields, with clumps of sycamore and ash trees providing shade for sheep. Eventually a few flagstones lead to a ladder stile, where a muddy lane is joined. This soon meets an unclassified road running back into the village centre.

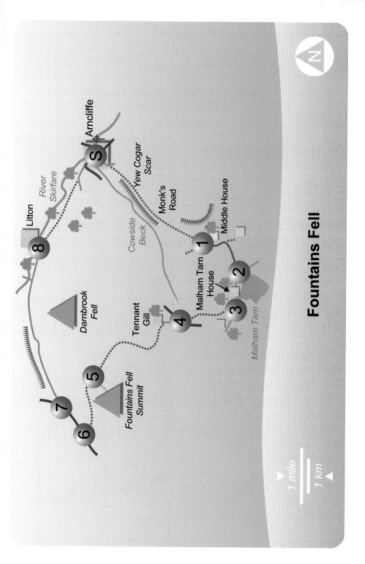

Fountains Fell

AIREDALE

Walk 1: Malhamdale
Walk 2: Upper Airedale
Walk 3: Leeds & Liverpool Canal
Walk 4: Elslack Moor

The Valley of the River Aire

Airedale separates the fells and dales of the Central Pennines from the moorland plateaus and industrialised valleys of the South Pennines. The River Aire rises amongst the karst scenery of Malhamdale. From its formation at the Aire Head Springs near the village of Malham, it flows south-east towards Skipton and the industrial areas of West Yorkshire. Unfortunately, by this point it is no longer recognisable as the sparkling stream that graces the landscape of Upper Airedale.

The geology of Malhamdale is dominated by the Great Scar Limestone, which was laid down during the Lower Carboniferous period and is exposed along the Middle Craven Fault at Malham Cove and Gordale Scar. The Craven Fault System marks the north-

The young River Aire, south of Airton.

ern boundary of the Craven Basin – a broad trough separating the Askrigg Block from the Millstone Grit plateaux of the South Pennines. To the east is high ground capped in Millstone Grit and flanked by steep scarps. To the west, the Bowland Shale that forms the valley floor is overlain by a thick layer of boulder clay marked by swarms of drumlins.

People in Airedale

Airedale possesses a character very different from that of any other part of the Pennines, with a landscape of gently undulating terrain clothed in lush pasture. Fields are bounded by hedges as much as by walls, and are home to breeds less hardy than those encountered on the neighbouring fells and moors. Dairy cattle are common, with Holstein Friesians being a particular speciality. Broadleaf species are common, with shelter belts along field edges and copses crowning

Leeds & Liverpool Canal

Construction of the Leeds & Liverpool Canal was authorised by an Act of Parliament in 1770, with the section from Leeds to Gargrave being completed in 1777. Work ceased due to a lack of funds, and did not recommence until 1790. It stopped again from 1804-05, and was not finally completed until 1816 – after forty-six years! The canal was built to carry vessels 62 feet (19 metres) long and 14 feet (4 metres) wide, transporting wool, cotton, limestone and coal. There are 91 locks on the 127 mile (205 kilometre) route, including the famous Bingley Five Rise. The canal reaches 488 feet (149 metres) above sea level, with a summit tunnel at Foulridge near Colne. Regular commercial traffic ceased in 1964 when the harsh winter made it unusable for several months. However, it never closed (unlike the two rival trans-Pennine canals), and it is still used extensively by pleasure craft.

hillocks. Attractive settlements of stone-built cottages are scattered throughout the area, sometimes clustering around pleasant village greens. Redundant mill buildings now serve for other uses.

The rivers Aire and Ribble come to within 3 miles (5 kilometres) of each other, forming an east-west corridor through the Pennines. This is the Aire Gap, which cuts the Pennine Chain in half, being approximately half way between Haltwhistle in Northumberland and Ashbourne in Derbyshire. The Aire Gap has long been used as a low-level route through the Pennines, with important road, rail and canal routes linking Yorkshire and Lancashire. The Leeds & Liverpool Canal was built as the longest in the country, connecting the Aire & Calder Navigation at Leeds to the west coast. At the Aire Gap, the Pennines can be traversed by road

> ### Skipton Castle
>
> Robert de'Romille built a timber fort at Skipton around 1090. Edward II put this under Robert Clifford in 1310, at which time he was appointed the first Lord Clifford of Skipton. However, he was killed at Bannockburn in 1314, prior to completing work on a new stone castle. During the English Civil War, Skipton Castle held out longer than any other Royalist stronghold in the North. It was besieged from 1642–5, when it was held by 300 men under the command of Sir John Mallory. In 1650 the castle was re-occupied by Lady Anne Clifford, who restored it to its present state – her legacy being seen in the family motto above the main gateway ('desormais', 'henceforth'). Today the castle is an important visitor attraction, enjoying an attractive setting beside the twelfth-century Holy Trinity Church.

at as little as 515 feet (157 metres) above sea level (on the A56, which tops-out near Thornton-in-Craven). By comparison, the M62 and A66 reach 1,221 feet (372 metres) and 1,467 feet (447 metres) respectively.

The focus of the Aire Gap has long been the bustling market town of Skipton, where several important trans-Pennine roads meet (A59, A65 and A629). Skipton, the 'Gateway to the Dales', has a population of around 16,000, although this swells significantly on market days when the cobbled streets are full of shoppers. The name means 'sheep-farmstead', and the town still hosts an auction mart. However, it was around the imposing Norman castle – built to control the passage of the Aire Gap – that the town developed.

Pendle Hill

Despite its relatively modest height (1,827 feet/557 metres), the isolated Millstone Grit dome of Pendle Hill is visible from almost every point in the Aire Gap. It casts an eerie shadow over the surrounding area, which is associated with the Pendle Witches – a group of local people hanged for witchcraft at Lancaster Castle in 1612. Pendle Hill is also famous as the place where George Fox received a vision in 1652, leading to the foundation of the Quaker movement: 'From the top of this hill the Lord le me see in what places he had a great people to be gathered.'

The Leeds & Liverpool Canal passes through the town centre, where there is a marina offering boat trips for tourists.

Walking in Airedale

Airedale is a popular tourist destination, with visitors drawn to natural features such as Malham Cove and Gordale Scar, as well as to man-made attractions including the Leeds & Liverpool Canal and the Worth Valley Railway. As far as hiking is concerned, the going is generally easier than in other parts of the Pennines, and the weather conditions are certainly more benign. However, paths often run across cattle-churned pasture, with endless gates and stiles to negotiate. To the south of the area are numerous low ridges, with paths that always seem to run against the grain of the terrain. One of the best walking routes in the area is the canal towpath. The section of the Pennine Way running through Airedale offers a pleasant interlude for long-distance walkers.

Worth Valley Railway

The railway line running up the Worth Valley from Keighley was opened in 1867 as a branch of the Lancaster to Leeds Railway, providing access to Haworth and Oxenhope. It closed in 1962, but was reopened in 1968 as a visitor attraction operating steam trains, and achieved fame when it was used as the backdrop for the film *The Railway Children*. To the north of Skipton is the terminus of the Embsay & Bolton Abbey Steam Railway, which links Airedale to Wharfedale and is another popular tourist route.

The double-arched bridge on the Leeds & Liverpool Canal at East Marton.

WALK 1: MALHAMDALE

LENGTH 11¼ miles (18 kilometres)

ASCENT 935 feet (285 metres)

HIGHEST POINT 1,329 feet (405 metres)

MAPS OS Explorer OL Map 2 ('Yorkshire Dales – Southern & Western Areas') (South Sheet)

STARTING POINT National Park Visitor Centre, Malham (SD 901 626)

FACILITIES Full range of services.

FEATURES A survey of the country's finest limestone scenery, including towering crags (Malham Cove and Gordale Scar), extensive areas of limestone pavement and a dry valley (Watlowes). The route also includes a circuit of Malham Tarn and a charming dene sheltering a lovely waterfall (Janet's Foss).

Malham Cove

Malham is a popular tourist village, serving as a base for visitors to Malham Cove and other nearby attractions. It is normally reached by following an unclassified road running 6 miles (10 kilometres) north from the A65 at Gargrave. The National Park visitor centre at the south end of the village provides tourist information, public toilets and a 'pay and display' car park. The first part of the walk follows the Pennine Way north for 1½ miles (2¼ kilometres) to Malham Cove. From the visitor centre, head through the village, ignoring a right turn leading towards a road bridge. It is possible to follow a tree-shaded path beside Malham Beck for a short way, before rejoining the road. Ignoring a clapper bridge (Moon Bridge) on the right, the village is soon left behind as the road heads up a walled lane.

Across the valley on the right, the remains of an old field system ('lynchets') can be seen. Soon Malham Cove comes into view – a spectacular amphitheatre of white limestone, the sheer scale of which is hard to comprehend. Passing through a gate, a finger sign marks the start of a path running down into the valley. Converging

Malham Cove

At Malham Cove the Great Scar Limestone is spectacularly exposed, with cliffs that tower more than 250 feet (76 metres) above the valley floor. Until the early nineteenth century, this place was the site of a tremendous waterfall. The stream concerned now flows underground from a point just south of Malham Tarn to emerge, not at the foot of the cliffs, but at Aire Head Springs, south of Malham village. This has left a dry valley (Watlowes) running from the Water Sinks to an expanse of limestone pavement at the head of the Cove. Malham Beck, on the other hand, drains into the ground on Malham Moor to re-appear beneath the cliffs of Malham Cove.

with the beck, as the Pennine Way turns uphill, instead continue a short way to the point where the crystal clear water emerges from the foot of the cliffs. Rejoining the Pennine Way, a seemingly endless series of stone steps heads up beside the Cove. As height is gained, the ash and hazel of the valley floor give way to rowan and hawthorn. At the top, continue across the expanse of limestone pavement that wraps around the head of the Cove (1 = SD 897 642). Hopping carefully from block to block, note the ferns sheltering in the deep crevices. The terraced outcrops provide a fine perch, with Pendle Hill visible in the distance.

Malham Tarn

From here the Pennine Way is followed for another 3 miles (5 kilometres), up a dry valley and around the side of Malham Tarn. Head north-west along a deep defile between craggy terraces. This was once the course of the infant River Aire, but is now dry. To the right are the remains of a waterfall (Comb Scar), now overgrown with vegetation. As the valley narrows, stone steps lead up to a fence stile, where a finger sign shows the path doubling back towards the head of the dry waterfall. Turning north along another defile, follow this as it swings to the right. Crossing a swathe of lush grass, the path runs past the Water Sinks, where the outflow from Malham Tarn soaks into the ground. Arriving at an unclassified road, turn right and head over a flat bridge towards a car park (2 = SD 893 658).

Heading through the car park, follow a path running across rough grazing. Ahead is Malham Tarn, with a couple of boathouses visible on the far shore. Passing the outflow from the lake (Tarn Foot), veer to the right of a copse and join a hardcore track running between the lakeside and Great Close Hill, the latter with its distinctive scar. The point at which the track enters the woodland around the north side of the lake will be remembered from the previous walk. Continuing along the tree-shaded track as it runs past Malham Tarn House, eventually a finger sign shows the Pennine Way turning through a gate on the right, although we continue straight ahead (3 = SD 888 673).

Malham Moor

The first part of the return route completes the circuit of Malham Tarn. Just past a barn, turn onto a gravel track running along a tree-lined lane (marked on the map as a permissive path). Passing the

---

Malham Tarn

Standing water is a rare sight among the limestone scenery of the Central Pennines. At end of last Ice Age, glacial meltwater pooling behind a moraine of boulder clay led to the formation of a lake, which rests upon a bed of Silurian slate. Although it extends to 153 acres (63 hectares), Malham Tarn is at most only 14 feet (4 metres) deep. Towards the end of the eighteenth century an embankment and sluice were added at the outflow, helping to maintain the water level. Today the surrounding area is managed by the National Trust as a 337 acre (138 hectare) National Nature Reserve. At 1,229 feet (375 metres) above sea level, Malham Tarn is the highest lime-rich lake in the country, creating a unique habitat.

access to Tarn Moss wetlands, an unclassified road is met. Turning left along the quiet road, then left again at a junction, head south past High Trenhouse. Arriving at a crossroads, take another left turn and follow a road running east across Malham Moor. Off to the left is Malham Tarn, while to the right is an old chimney – the remains of a smelt mill that operated in 1815–60. The road follows the route of the historic Mastiles Lane, passing Low Trenhouse Farm as it heads towards the car park passed earlier (4 = SD 893 658).

From here an old monastic way (Trougate) is followed south-south-east over limestone moors for 1½ miles (2½ kilometres). Across the road from the car park, a finger sign marks the start of a path to Malham Rakes. Passing to the left of some small ponds, the path runs along a shallow trough between slopes flanked by limestone outcrops. Over a ladder stile, the path becomes stony as it runs down a miniature dry valley. Looking to the right, the area of limestone pavement around the head of Malham Cove comes back into view. Eventually the path converges with a snaking road (5 = SD 903 638).

Gordale Scar

Crossing straight over the road, a finger sign shows a path to Gordale Scar, wrapping around the hillside. Passing the mouth of another dry valley, ahead are views of a terraced field system, beneath the limestone crags of Cross Field Knotts. Another finger sign shows the route turning through a gate and heading down a few steps to join a path running gently downhill on grassy slopes towards Gordale Bridge (6 = SD 913 635).

At this point a 'there-and-back' detour of less than 1 mile (1½ kilometres) provides an opportunity to visit the dramatic limestone ravine of Gordale Scar. Turning left, head along the quiet road a short

> **Mastiles Lane**
> Mastiles Lane is a green lane running from Kilnsey in Wharfedale up onto Malham Moor. During the Middle Ages it was used by the monks of Fountains Abbey to access their sheep runs, although it was originally a Roman road. The remains of a marching camp extending to 20 acres (8 hectares) can still be seen close to Gordale Beck.

Gordale Scar

Opinion differs as to whether Gordale Scar is a collapsed cavern or the product of scouring by glacial meltwater. However, few would argue that it is one of the most stunning geological features in the country. The boulder-strewn floor of the narrow ravine is shaded by overhanging limestone cliffs, up to 300 feet (91 metres) high. These are home to stunted yew trees, as well as buzzards and kestrels. Through the defile runs Gordale Beck, which at one point cascades down slabs of tufa – a substance formed from deposits of calcium carbonate. A route running up the side of the falls connects to Mastiles Lane, although this involves scrambling up a near-vertical buttress. Whilst the handholds are good, the ascent is dangerous or even impossible in times of flood.

---

way. Passing through a gate on the left, a sign warns of a difficult ascent ahead (although we only go as far as the foot of the waterfalls). Crossing a field used as a campsite, to the left is Gordale Beck, running swiftly down its stony channel. As the valley narrows, scree fields intrude upon the path. Continuing into the ravine, the route picks its way through rocks as it runs between overhanging cliffs. Soon the lowest of the waterfalls is reached (7 = SD 915 641). Having taken time to enjoy the spectacle, retrace your steps to Gordale Bridge (8 = SD 913 635).

A short way along the road (Gordale Lane), a finger sign on the left marks the start of a riverside path to Malham – now just 1½ miles (2¼ kilometres) away. At the head of the dene is a charming waterfall known as Janet's Foss. Here the beck falls over a slab of tufa, behind which is a cave that was once thought to be the home of a fairy queen called Janet! At the foot of the waterfall is a lovely pool of clear water. Continuing along the tree-shaded path, garlic, ferns and mosses carpet the ground. As the path emerges from the dene it continues south then south-west over meadows. Arriving at a crossroads of tracks, ignore a lane on the right and continue straight ahead through a waymarked kissing gate. Joining the Pennine Way, follow a hardcore path running beside Malham Beck. A ford leads back to the starting point, although a clapper bridge a little further along might be preferred.

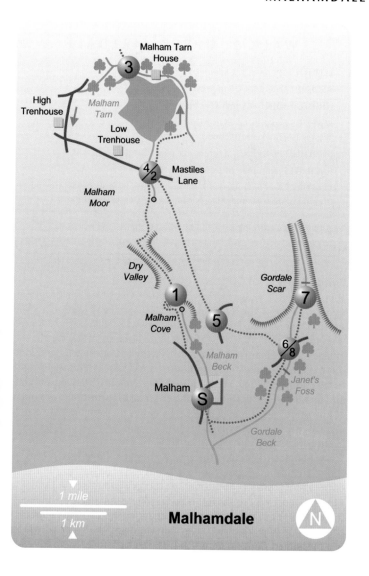

Malham Tarn House

3

High Trenhouse

Malham Tarn

Low Trenhouse

4/2 Mastiles Lane

Malham Moor

Dry Valley

1

Malham Cove

5

Malham Beck

Malham

S

Gordale Scar

7

6/8

Janet's Foss

Gordale Beck

1 mile

1 km

Malhamdale

N

WALK 2: UPPER AIREDALE

LENGTH 14¼ miles (23 kilometres)

ASCENT 1,066 feet (325 metres)

HIGHEST POINT 804 feet (245 metres)

MAPS OS Explorer OL Map 2 ('Yorkshire Dales – Southern & Western Areas') (South Sheet)

STARTING POINT North Street car park, Gargrave (SD 932 543)

FACILITIES Full range of services.

FEATURES An enjoyable walk through pleasant countryside, linking a string of picturesque villages running up the valley. The route follows the Pennine Way over pasture and beside the infant River Aire before returning by a combination of paths and tracks.

Eshton Moor

There are two free car parks close to the village hall at Gargrave, signposted from the A65. There is also a railway station to the south of the village. The first part of the walk follows the Pennine Way to Airton, a total of 3¾ miles (6¼ kilometres). Starting at the village hall, a quiet road heads north-west out of the village, crossing the Leeds & Liverpool Canal just above a lock. Ignoring a right turn, continue along Mark House Lane, which is flanked by lime and maple trees. Continuing along the lane as it runs out into open countryside, eventually a finger sign shows the Pennine Way crossing a step stile on the right (1 = SD 925 550).

From here the route runs north-west over pasture, crossing a series of fence stiles along the way. A couple of finger signs confirm the route, although navigation is still fiddly. Looking to the right, Barden Moor with its Millstone Grit scenery can be seen in the distance. A short way to the left is an OS pillar standing atop a hillock (Haw Crag). Arriving at a finger sign marking a crossroads of paths, the Pennine Way here runs over Eshton Moor, the name of which is a misnomer. Continuing north-west over pasture, the path converges with a road, with Newfield Hall not far ahead. Turning

Gargrave

Gargrave ('Gara's grove') sits uncomfortably on the busy A65 trans-Pennine route, with the Leeds & Liverpool Canal to the north and the Lancaster to Leeds railway to the south. Although blighted by traffic, it is an attractive village of stone-built cottages, standing on either side of the River Aire. At the south end of the village stands St Andrew's Church, which alone among the seven churches in the area was not torched by raiding Scots – it being dedicated to their patron saint. There are pleasant riverside walks, with stepping stones crossing the river, and a canal towpath that is always popular with visitors.

through a gate, the River Aire is crossed by a footbridge then followed upstream. Heading along the tree-shaded riverside, cross an area of rough grazing and climb a few steps to arrive at Newfield Bridge (2 = SD 907 581).

Over the bridge, a finger sign shows the Pennine Way heading through a gate. Following the river upstream, the clear water runs swiftly down a stony bed between banks lined with sycamore, ash and hawthorn. Crossing drystone walls by step stiles, the path runs beneath the wooded river terrace. Eventually another stone bridge is encountered, this time opposite the village of Airton (3 = SD 904 592).

Hanlith

Instead of crossing the bridge, a finger sign shows the Pennine Way continuing along the east side of the river, 2½ miles (4 kilometres) to Malham. Crossing a side stream by a footbridge, continue north over rough grazing and along the tree-lined riverbank. Approaching Hanlith Hall, the flood plain takes on the character of parkland, with sycamore, beech and horse chestnut dotted about. Eventually the path arrives at Hanlith Bridge (4 = SD 900 612).

Here a finger sign shows the Pennine Way turning right, following a steep road up through the hamlet of Hanlith. At a sharp bend another finger sign marks the start of a path heading north over fields, with the view ahead now dominated by the limestone scenery of Malhamdale. The path runs above the wooded valley side before hooking around a dry gully and heading down to a concrete bridge near the confluence of Malham Beck and Gordale Beck. Continuing upstream beside Malham Beck, once again use either the ford or the clapper bridge to reach the National Park visitor centre (5 = SD 901 626).

Kirkby Malham

The first part of the return route runs 3½ miles (5¾ kilometres) back to Airton, this time on the west side of the valley. A finger sign opposite the visitor centre marks the start of a path to Hanlith Bridge, crossing a step stile and heading over meadows towards Aire Head Springs (the official birth-place of the River Aire and the point at which the outflow from Malham Tarn re-emerges from its underground passage). Passing a reed-choked mill pond, the path follows a race towards an old mill (Scalegill). Joining an access road, continue along the tree-lined riverbank to arrive back at Hanlith Bridge (6 = SD 900 612). This time follow the road towards Kirkby Malham, crossing over a busy road to reach the parish church.

Beside the church's parking area, a finger sign shows a path heading down into a dene, where Kirkby Beck is crossed by a footbridge. Climbing slippery steps towards a gate, the path heads south-west over fields. Over a small footbridge at the head of another dene, cross a step stile and continue beside a drystone

The Cathedral of the Dales

The parish of the Church of St Michael the Archangel covers seven districts, earning it the title 'Cathedral of the Dales'. It was built during the fifteenth century on the site of an earlier (eight century) structure. One of the church bells – cast in 1601 – weighs over a ton and is the second largest in country. In the churchyard is a preaching cross and a set of stocks. The church is usually open and welcomes visitors who remove their boots. One visitor was Oliver Cromwell, who witnessed three marriages here in 1655.

wall. Eventually a finger sign marks a left turn through a gate. There is some fiddly navigation ahead, so follow the map carefully. Arriving at a barn, turn right and follow a field boundary until a step stile is met. From here the faint path runs down through fields, crossing intersecting walls by step stiles. Passing some farm buildings to arrive at an unclassified road, head towards some stone-built cottages marking the outskirts of Airton. Before reaching the village centre, turn onto a ginnel signed as a bridleway to Town End. Arriving at another road, turn right, then left, following the Bell Busk road a short way before turning onto a hard-core track (7 = SD 902 588).

Bell Busk

The remainder of the return route follows lanes for 4¼ miles (6¾ kilometres) back to the starting point. The track is flanked by sycamore and ash trees as it runs towards Kirk Syke Farm, where it fords a shallow stream and continues south. Eventually the route

Airton

Airton is an attractive little village with long-standing Quaker associations. A meeting house in the centre of the village is still in use. On the village green is a 'squatters house' dating back to the seventeenth century (at that time there was a law that anyone who could build a house and have smoke rising within twenty-four hours was entitled to the freehold!). Beside the river is a converted linen mill that was once owned by the canons of Bolton Priory.

259

narrows to a path running along the side of a field. A finger sign marks a left turn through a gate, joining a quad track running over rushy grazing. Crossing Otterburn Beck by a bridge, the track continues towards Raven Flatt Farm, passing the derelict farm buildings to arrive at an unclassified road. Turning left, follow the road as it runs parallel to the beck. At a junction, cross over the beck by a stone bridge (Red Bridge). Here a finger sign marks the start of a bridleway (Mark House Lane) (8 = SD 904 565).

Crossing the River Aire, the track heads uphill. Just before reaching a barn, turn left onto a stony track following a walled lane (ignore a waymarked gate on the right). As the lane veers to the right (south-east), a gate on the left offers a 'there and back' detour to Haw Crag, which provides a good viewing point. Continuing down the lane as it runs through pasture, the stony track becomes uncomfortable for a way. Passing the point where the lane was left earlier in the day (9 = SD 925 550), retrace your steps along a quiet road leading back to Gargrave.

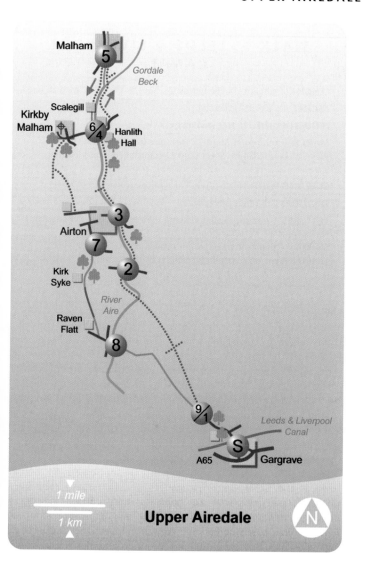

Upper Aairedale

Malham
Gordale
Beck
Scalegill
Kirkby
Malham
Hanlith
Hall
Airton
Kirk
Syke
River
Aire
Raven
Flatt
Leeds & Liverpool
Canal
A65
Gargrave
1 mile
1 km
Upper Airedale
N

WALK 3: LEEDS & LIVERPOOL CANAL

LENGTH 11¼ miles (18 kilometres)

ASCENT 574 feet (175 metres)

HIGHEST POINT 525 feet (160 metres)

MAPS OS Explorer OL Maps 2 ('Yorkshire Dales – Southern & Western Areas') (South Sheet) and 21 ('South Pennines') (North Sheet)

STARTING POINT North Street car park, Gargrave (SD 932 543)

FACILITIES Full range of services.

FEATURES A pleasant walk following the Pennine Way over gently rolling pasture, returning on the towpath beside the Leeds & Liverpool Canal as it winds lazily through an area of drumlins. Entertainment is provided by canal boats negotiating the locks.

The 'Bers'

The first part of the walk follows the Pennine Way south-west from Gargrave to East Marton, a total of 2¾ miles (4¼ kilometres). Over the busy A65, join an unclassified road heading south, crossing the River Aire by a stone bridge and heading towards St Andrew's Church. Passing the Masons Arms Inn, ignore a turning on the right. A finger sign shows the Pennine Way joining a path running across fields. Meeting the tree-shaded Mosber Lane, turn left and cross over the railway by a bridge. As the lane opens-out, stay on the hardcore track as it heads towards a tall marker post (1 = SD 923 531).

Leaving the track at this point, continue south-west, as though towards the Green Bank transmitter. The faint path runs over fields of lush grass that are home to dairy cattle. Crossing a drainage channel by a footbridge, head diagonally over another field to join a lane. The Pennine Way soon leaves the track, crossing fields used for show-jumping practice and skirting a wood. Rejoining the lane – now a tree-shaded road – Williamson Bridge (canal bridge 162) is soon reached. Over the bridge is the hamlet of East Marton, although the Pennine Way turns down onto the canal towpath (2 = SD 910 511).

Thornton-in-Craven

The next part of the walk follows the Pennine Way south for 1¾ miles (3 kilometres) to Thornton-in-Craven, initially on the canal towpath. Passing the East Marton visitor moorings, the canal soon runs under a curious double-arched bridge (161). The top deck was added when the road (now A59) was upgraded to make it suitable for motorised traffic. A marker stone gives the distances to Leeds (38¼ miles) and Liverpool (89 miles). Further along the way an arched bridge (160) is passed. Turning off the towpath just before meeting a gate, head down to a fence stile (3 = SD 907 503).

Over a boggy field, a steep climb leads to the crest of a hillock (Langber Hill). Heading downhill, an old marker stone is passed. Crossing a stream by a slab bridge, head up to a gate and continue over fields towards some farm buildings. Turning left onto an access road, this eventually becomes a lane (Cam Lane) flanked by attractive cottages. Arriving at the busy A56, turn right and follow the pavement through Thornton-in-Craven, looking for a driveway leading to the start of a farm track (4 = SD 907 485).

East Marton

The first part of the return route runs 2½ miles (4¼ kilometres) back to East Marton, rejoining the canal towpath along the way. Passing between cottages, follow the track north-west down the side of a field before turning onto a beaten path running across a meadow towards a drumlin (Castleber Hill). Crossing a small stream by a slab bridge, head up onto the domed hillock. Cresting the rise, aim towards a gate at the corner of the field, where the towpath is rejoined (5 = SD 899 492).

The canal runs along an embankment lined with ash and hawthorn as it heads north-east. Anglers are a common sight, while ducks and swans shelter among the reeds. Eventually the point at which the Pennine Way earlier left the towpath is met (6 = SD 907 503). Arriving back at bridge 160, this time leave the towpath and cross over the canal. Passing through the churchyard at St Peter's Church, exit onto an access road leading up to the A59. Crossing the busy main road, head down the pavement towards the Cross Keys Inn, turning onto an unclassified road signed for Bank Newton. The tree-lined lane runs past the Abbot's Harbour café, stables and cottages before crossing the canal by Williamson Bridge (162) (7 = SD 910 511).

> **Canal Boats**
> The brightly painted boats that frequent the Leeds & Liverpool Canal feature a wonderful assortment of names, including Pineberry, Loch Maree, Rubyann, Jester, Pearl Barley, Green Frog and Saffron. A dredger operating in the area is appropriately named *The Pennine Way*.

Bank Newton

From here the return route follows the canal towpath, 4 miles (6½ kilometres) back to Gargrave. Heading back down to the canal side, this time pass under the bridge and follow the towpath north through a wooded cutting. Emerging from the cutting, the Green Bank transmitter is just ahead. Passing under another bridge (163), the canal runs along an embankment, snaking about as it seeks a level course through an area of drumlins. Passing bridge 164, then some moorings, a leafy lane is joined before the canal is crossed by bridge 165 (8 = SD 912 528). Here there is the option of following a quiet road back to Gargrave – but only if failing daylight means there is a real danger of falling into the canal!

Beside the bridge, a gate leads back down to the towpath, which now follows the left-hand side of the canal, passing the Bank Newton long-term moorings. Ahead is a procession of seven locks. These are always busy during summer, and you may be called upon to lend a hand! The towpath runs gently downhill as the canal swings around to head north-east. Passing an old lock-keeper's cottage and some moorings, a gate leads to the road, which runs beside the canal for a way. Crossing Priest Holme Bridge (168), turn onto a path spiralling back down to the towpath, which returns to the right-hand side of the canal (9 = SD 918 537).

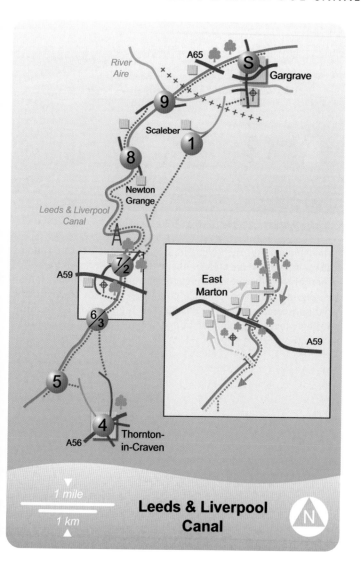

Bank Newton Locks, on the Leeds & Liverpool Canal.

The canal crosses the River Aire by an aqueduct, before running under a railway bridge (168A). Ahead is another series of locks, the second of these beside moorings for patrons of the Anchor Inn on the edge of Gargrave. Down a cobbled section of towpath, the canal runs under the A65. Passing the Higherlands Lock visitor moorings, leave the canal at bridge 170 and head down the road back to the starting point.

WALK 4: ELSLACK MOOR

LENGTH 13¼ miles (21½ kilometres)

ASCENT 2,838 feet (865 metres)

HIGHEST POINT 1,273 feet (388 metres)

MAPS OS Explorer OL Map 21 ('South Pennines') (North Sheet)

STARTING POINT Gill Lane, Ickornshaw (SD 968 430)

FACILITIES Public toilets and inn.

FEATURES This arduous walk is a prelude to the Millstone Grit landscapes of the South Pennines. It runs over pasture and moorland, crossing and re-crossing ridges that add greatly to the ascent but provide compensation in the form of extensive views. There is some fiddly route-finding along the way.

Lothersdale

The starting point is reached by turning off the A6068 at the west end of Cowling and heading down a steep bank leading to the Holy Trinity Church. There is roadside parking along Gill Lane. The first part of the walk follows the Pennine Way for 2¼ miles (3½ kilometres) to Lothersdale. Heading along the quiet road as it runs past the Millstone Grit cottages of Middleton, the Pennine Way joins from the left. Arriving at a junction, turn right and follow the road down to Gill Beck. Just over the bridge, a finger sign shows the Pennine Way turning onto a driveway. Instead of re-crossing the tree-lined beck, join a faint path heading north-north-west, up through walled pasture. Pausing to looking back, there are good views towards Earl Crag with its distinctive monuments. Crossing a step stile, cut across the top corner of a field to arrive at another stile lost among holly bushes (1 = SD 963 440).

Continuing gently uphill, aim to the left of a ruined farm building (High Stubbing), where a finger sign shows the route continuing over fields. Exit onto an unclassified road. A short way to the right is a junction, where we turn down a lane. Another finger sign marks the point at which the Pennine Way leaves the road, crossing a step

Cowling

Cowling is located on the A6068, midway between Keighley and Colne. It grew up during the industrial revolution, and on either side of the busy main road there are long terraces of houses that were built to provide accommodation for the mill workers. Close by is Ickornshaw, an older and smaller settlement of stone-built cottages, located off the main road, beside a tree-lined stream (Ickornshaw Brook). At the boundary between the two villages is the Holy Trinity Church, established in 1845 under the Diocese of Bradford. Lord Philip Snowden, the first Labour Chancellor of the Exchequer, was born at the adjacent hamlet of Middleton in 1864.

stile. Over a field, the path heads steeply downhill before veering towards a wooded clough at the foot of bracken-clad slopes. Fording Surgill Beck, follow a row of oak trees towards Woodhead Farm cottages, where an access road is joined. As the track swings to the left, turn onto a faint path heading steeply downhill, following a line of telephone poles. Passing under mature broadleaf trees, the path meets an unclassified road at the west end of Lothersdale (2 = SD 959 460).

Elslack Moor

From here the Pennine Way is followed for 4½ miles (7 kilometres) over pasture and moorland to Thornton-in-Craven. Across the road from the old mill, a sign shows the Pennine Way heading north over fields, gaining height at a steady rate, with the dene of Stansfield Beck off to the right. Crossing straight over an unclassified road, a finger sign shows the route continuing along a farm access. As this swings towards Hewitts Farm,

Lothersdale

Lothersdale is a quiet little village, hidden away in an isolated valley. Beside a tree-shaded beck, buildings of Millstone Grit cluster around an old woollen mill with a prominent chimney. The mill retains its waterwheel, although this is no longer operational. Quakers settled here during the reign of King Charles II, and their meeting house is still in use. A Georgian house to the east of the village – Stonne Gappe – was the basis of Gateshead Hall in Charlotte Brontë's *Jane Eyre*.

cross a step stile and continue straight ahead. The path soon runs onto Elslack Moor, with walled pasture on the left and heather moorland to the right. Continuing over open moorland, a few small cairns confirm the route. When the path divides, take the left-hand branch (a sign here is a source of confusion), which soon arrives at an OS pillar marking the 'summit' (3 = SD 944 472).

This place is known as Pinshaw, and although it stands at just 1,273 feet (388 metres), the views are splendid. Looking to the north, the fells of the Central Pennines mark the horizon. Airedale appears as a patchwork of fields, spread over gently undulating terrain. To the east is Ilkley Moor, forming the watershed between Airedale and Wharfedale. To the south is Earl Crag, although it is principally west-wards – towards the enigmatic Pendle Hill – that the eye is drawn. From this apparently remote spot it is in fact just a short way down to a road, following a track that initially runs south-west, turning alongside a drystone wall to arrive at a junction. Crossing straight over, join a quiet moorland road (Clogger Lane) heading north-west, looking out for a ladder stile on the left (4 = SD 934 475).

Here a sign indicates a link to Earby Youth Hostel, although the Pennine Way continues north-west, weaving through clumps of rushes. There are short sections of flagstones and boardwalk as the path heads gently downhill beside a drystone wall. Eventually a finger sign shows the route turning over a footbridge, before continuing down beside a deep gully lined with oak, hawthorn and holly. Crossing cattle-churned pasture leading to Brown House Farm, an access road is joined. Cutting through an old railway embankment, turn left and head up a tree-shaded road (Old Road) towards Thornton-in-Craven. Passing a row of stone-built cottages, a finger sign marks the point at which we leave the Pennine Way (5 = SD 907 485).

Thornton Moor

The first part of the return route follows lanes and crosses pasture, heading south-east for 3¼ miles (5¼ kilometres). Following the pavement beside the busy main road, turn down Booth Bridge Lane, which runs through fields towards Booth Bridge Farm. Passing the farm buildings, ignore a lane on the right and instead cross Earby

Beck by a bridge. Ignore a kissing gate on the left and head up a farm track. Turning off the track as it swings towards Booth House Farm, continue south-east, heading steeply uphill beside an over-grown dyke. Passing a large cairn, the transmitter on Proctor Height Hill comes into view ahead. A short section of walled lane leads to a crossroads of routes, where we ignore tracks to left and right (the latter being signed for the youth hostel) and join a hard-core track leading to Oak Slack Farm. Approaching the farm build-ings, turn through a gap stile on the right (6 = SD 924 474).

Over a paddock, head down to Wentcliff Brook, which is crossed by a flat bridge. Passing through a gate into a field, head uphill beside a tree-lined gully. Crossing over the gully, pass an old farm building and continue south-east over grazing land. Joining a farm track (Dodgson Lane), this becomes an access road as it passes Dodgson's Farm, heading up to a road. Turn left and follow the grass verge towards the Proctor Height Hill transmitter. Before reaching the mast, turn through a gate leading to the access for Proctor Height Farm. Leaving the track as it swings towards the farm build-ings, look for a step stile straight ahead. Heading down through a field, a gate leads to a hardcore track at Bent Laithe Farm. Cross straight over the track and head diagonally across a field then down to the left of a drystone wall. Eventually a step stile leads to an unclassified road (Winter Gap Lane) (7 = SD 941 458).

Hawshaw Moor

From here the return route continues south-east over pasture, a distance of 3½ miles (5½ kilometres) back to the starting point (note that it is also possible to follow quiet roads south to Stone Head, then east to the junction at Gill). Crossing straight over the road, a finger sign points through a gate to a path running down the side of a field. Passing Raygill Farm, turn left onto an access road. A fishing lake to the right of the leafy lane occupies part of Raygill Delf — a former limestone quarry where hippopotamus bones were discovered in 1880. Continuing towards The Fold, a finger sign marks a right turn over a step stile. Crossing Lothersdale Beck by a flat bridge, a faint path heads south, running uphill through fields. Eventually a step stile leads to an unclassified road,

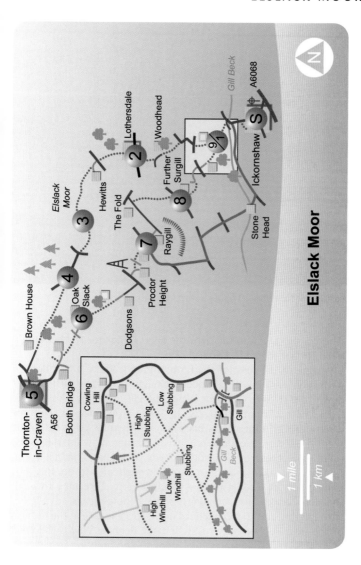

Elslack Moor

Pasture meets moorland above Lothersdale.

where a short way to the right the access track for Further Surgill Head Farm is joined (8 = SD 949 449).

Passing to the right of the farm, a gate leads to a corridorised path. Converging with a wooded clough, a narrow path zigzags down to a stream. Climbing out of the gill, head towards a byre, from where a farm track zigzags up Sweet Brow ridge. As the track levels-out, Earl Crag comes back into view, while Keighley can be seen to the east. Crossing an unclassified road (Cowling Hill Lane), follow an access track leading down to Higher Windhill Farm. Approaching the farmhouse, turn through a gate on the left, joining a track leading to Low Windhill Farm. Threading through the abandoned farm buildings, some cobbles leads to a gate. Through this, turn right and head down to a gap stile at the bottom of the field. A short way to the left the Pennine Way is re-joined (9 = SD 963 440). Retrace your steps to the junction at Gill and follow the quiet road back to the starting point.

SOUTH PENNINES

Walk 1: Ickornshaw Moor
Walk 2: Withins Height
Walk 3: Upper Calderdale
Walk 4: Stoodley Pike
Walk 5: Cragg Vale
Walk 6: Millstone Edge and Blackstone Edge

The Moors of the South Pennines

The South Pennines is an area of sprawling moorland plateaux, cut by deep valleys occupied by linear settlements that sprang up during the industrial revolution. The landscape of the area is dominated by Millstone Grit. Outcrops of this hard, coarse-grained sandstone appear on the steep scarps flanking the moorland plateaux. Soot-blackened gritstone is also seen in the drystone walls marking the valley sides, and in the terraced streets and dark, satanic mills crowding the valley floors. It is an essential part of the rugged charm of the area, although it contributes to its grim appearance when seemingly endless drizzle smudges-out the views. Millstone Grit is less permeable than limestone, so the high ground is overlain with blanket bog and wet heath. It weathers to produce acid soils, encouraging the spread of heather, bilberry and bracken on drier ground.

People in the South Pennines

The industrial revolution brought about a wholesale transformation of the South Pennines. The area had long been associated with the manufacture of cloth, although this took the form of a cottage

Tamed Rock.
Millstone-grit – a soul-grinding sandstone.
Roof-of-the-world-ridge wind
And rain, and rain.
Ted Hughes, 'Wild Rock'.

industry using locally produced wool and domestic spinning and weaving. During the eighteenth century the process was mechanised and production was concentrated in mills. Initially these used water-power for spinning wool, and so were located beside fast-flowing streams. However, since waterwheels could not deliver a constant speed, pedal-driven looms were needed for weaving until the advent of steam power. Whilst

> This whole country, however mountainous, and that no sooner we were down one hill but we mounted another, is yet infinitely full of people; these people all full of business. . . . This business is the clothing trade, for the convenience of which the houses are thus scattered and spread upon the sides of the hills.
>
> Daniel Defoe, *A Tour Through the Whole Island of Great Britain*.

Yorkshire was the focus of woollen manufacture, Lancashire became the main centre for the production of cotton cloth (the raw material being imported through the west coast ports). During the first half of the nineteenth century, cotton cloth production spilled over into Yorkshire, with new centres of production established away from the guild restrictions of the old towns.

The large-scale mechanisation of cloth production necessitated the creation of an effective transportation system. The earliest communications had been based upon a network of pack-horse routes, with flagged 'causeys' (that is, 'causeways') criss-crossing the moors. The pack-horses ran in trains of up to forty animals, carrying goods as diverse as wool, salt and lime. Turnpike roads were eventually built to facilitate travel by stagecoach, but the tolls were too high to permit the transportation of goods. Consequently, during the industrial revolution canals and railways were built along the valley floors. The three trans-Pennine canals were tremendous feats of engineering, being constructed entirely by hand by armies of navvies (a term derived from 'navigators', because they built navigations).

All three were completed during the early nineteenth century,

Gibson Mill in Hebden Dale, built around 1800 as a water-powered spinning mill.

Rochdale Canal

The Rochdale Canal connects the Calder & Hebble Navigation at Sowerby Bridge with the Bridgewater Canal at Manchester, traversing the Pennines by the valleys of the River Calder and the River Roch. Following an Act of Parliament in 1794, construction began in 1799 and continued until 1804. The canal was built 14 feet (4 metres) wide, with 92 locks and more than 100 bridges along the 32 mile (52 kilometre) route. It reaches 600 feet (183 metres) above sea-level near the village of Summit. The canal has a summit level just ¾ mile (1¼ kilometres) long, so a number of supply reservoirs were created on the moors above the village. One of the canal's main roles was to deliver cotton and coal to the mills of Calderdale, returning with cloth for export. Despite the arrival of the railways during the mid-nineteenth century, traffic did not peak until the 1880s. The canal closed in 1952, but it has recently been re-opened for use by pleasure craft.

and played a key role in facilitating the industrial revolution (a single canal barge could carry as much as several hundred pack-horses). Crossing the Pennines became a pre-occupation with the foremost engineers of the day, despite the tremendous difficulties involved. The most northerly of the three is the Leeds & Liverpool Canal, running through the Aire Gap. However, the first to open

Huddersfield Narrow Canal

Work on the Huddersfield Narrow Canal was again authorised by an Act of Parliament in 1794. Thomas Telford was called in to complete the project when it ran into difficulties, and it finally opened in 1811. The canal covers 19¾ miles (31¾ kilometres) between Huddersfield and Ashton under Lyne, with a total of 74 locks maintained by ten reservoirs. It runs under the Pennine ridge between Marsden and Diggle by the country's longest (3¼ miles/5¼ kilometres), highest (645 feet/197 metres above sea level) and deepest (638 feet/195 metres underground) canal tunnel. This has no towpath, so while the horses were led around by an above ground route, 'leggers' walked the boats through. The canal had fallen into disuse by 1944, but following restoration work it re-opened in 2001. A visitor centre has been created at Marsden ('The Standedge Experience'), based around a converted transhipment warehouse.

was the Rochdale Canal, which cuts through the heart of the South Pennines. The Huddersfield Narrow Canal employs a tunnel, taking it deep beneath the Pennine ridge, and although built to 'narrow' dimensions, it was arguably the most technically challenging of the three routes.

The railways followed the canals during the mid-nineteenth century, and for a time there was plenty of trade for both. The Lancashire & Yorkshire Railway was opened in 1841 as the first trans-Pennine railway, connecting Leeds to Manchester via Calderdale. An extension to the Leeds & Bradford Railway was driven through the Aire Gap in 1848, and a route from Huddersfield to Manchester followed in 1849, using a tunnel running under the Pennine ridge at Standedge. The area is criss-crossed with busy A-roads. Some of these follow the same valley floor routes as the canals and railways, while others run over the moors. The M62 crosses the Pennine ridge between Huddersfield and Rochdale, and is still the country's highest motorway. There is a long-standing proposal to build a motorway through the Aire Gap, as an extension of the M65, although it now seems unlikely that this will come to fruition.

The industrial revolution substantially determined the modern settlement pattern, with linear settlements strung along the

SOUTH PENNINES

narrow valley floors and creeping up the steep valley sides. Significant towns include Keighley and Haworth in the Worth Valley, Hebden Bridge and Todmorden in Calderdale and Bacup and Rawtenstall in the valley of the River Irwell. The area is flanked by major centres whose fortunes were built upon the textiles industry, with Bradford, Halifax and Huddersfield to the east and Burnley, Rochdale and Oldham to the west.

The moors of the South Pennines have long been grazed by sheep, with the wool being hand-woven into cloth and the meat going to feed the people of the

The Brontë Sisters
The novels of Anne, Charlotte and Emily Brontë were inspired by the bleak, wind-swept moors of the South Pennines. The three sisters were the children of Reverend Patrick Brontë, who was minister at the Church of Saint Michael & All Angels at Haworth during the first half of the nineteenth century. Today the former mill town is the centre of an area branded as 'Brontë Country', with the former parsonage attracting hordes of visitors.

Walshaw Dean (Middle) Reservoir, with Withins Height in the distance.

nearby towns. Today the area mostly supports part-time farming. In some cases farms have been abandoned altogether, with smallholdings rendered uneconomic by reservoir construction. A distinctive feature of the South Pennines is the numerous small reservoirs scattered throughout the area, taking advantage of the high rainfall and favourable geological conditions. Some were built to serve the canals, while others were intended to slate the thirst of the nearby towns, which were experiencing rapid growth as a result of the industrial revolution.

Walking in the South Pennines

Today the traditional industries of the South Pennines are idle, leaving the towns and villages of the area searching for new roles – including tourism and recreation. The ruins left in the wake of industrial decline add to the unique character of the area, with seemingly every dene concealing the remains of an abandoned cotton mill with overgrown walls, toppling chimney and reed-choked millpond. Weather permitting, the South Pennines can be good walking country, although the terrain is not always as accommodating as the relatively modest altitude of the plateaux and the degree of urbanisation would suggest. The Pennine Way itself crosses bleak, featureless moorland as it passes through the area, periodically dropping into deep valleys which are negotiated by steep, overgrown causeys.

The South Pennines Heritage Area

The South Pennines is perhaps the least appreciated of the areas through which the Pennine Way passes. Whilst there are National Parks to north and south, the South Pennines itself carries no special landscape designation. This makes the area vulnerable to intrusive developments, with electricity pylons marching across the moors and sizeable wind farms already established at Ovenden Moor, Coal Clough and Royd Moor. This is despite a unique combination of attractive countryside and industrial heritage – the latter reflecting its role as the hub of the industrial revolution. A Heritage Area has been defined, although this does not deliver unified management of the area, which includes parts of North Yorkshire, West Yorkshire, Lancashire and Greater Manchester.

WALK 1: ICKORNSHAW MOOR

LENGTH 15½ miles (25¼ kilometres)

ASCENT 2,362 feet (720 metres)

HIGHEST POINT 437 metres (1,434 feet)

MAPS OS Explorer OL Map 21 ('South Pennines') (North Sheet)

STARTING POINT Gill Lane, Ickornshaw (SD 968 430)

FACILITIES Public toilets and inn.

FEATURES The route crosses windswept moorland by rough paths that can be boggy in places. Passing small reservoirs and a ruined cotton mill, points of interest include Ponden Hall (the inspiration for Thrushcross Grange in 'Wuthering Heights') and the Earl Crag monuments.

Ickornshaw Moor

Starting at the Holy Trinity Church, head west through the centre of Ickornshaw. A finger sign on the left shows the Pennine Way leaving the road, climbing a steep bank leading to the busy A6068. Over the main road, another finger sign points through a narrow gate and up the middle of a field towards Lower Summer House Farm. Following an overgrown lane, then a hardcore track running around the head of a deep gully, Lumb Farm is passed. Crossing a couple of side streams, head steeply uphill beside some ruined farm buildings, where a finger sign shows the Pennine Way turning over a ladder stile (1 = SD 972 418).

From here the route runs south over Ickornshaw Moor then south-east across Oakworth Moor, a total of 3¼ miles (5¼ kilometres). Whilst there is a real sense of isolation on these windswept moors, navigation is fairly straightforward. Initially the path follows a boundary as it runs past some grouse-shooters' huts. Crossing a small stream beside a stone-built hut, it heads onto open moorland. Flagstones provide passage of boggy ground as the cairned route climbs gently towards an old fence line marking the highest point on the walk (2 = SD 974 397).

This is not the highest place on Ickornshaw Moor, however, which is at the Wolf Stones, a short way to the south-west (a 'there and back' detour is rewarded with fine views, but crosses some very difficult terrain). The Pennine Way continues along a rough but well-defined path, which soon swings around to head south-east. Passing a pond and a few old boundary stones, a shallow

> **The Wolf Stones**
>
> The Wolf Stones is a small group of Millstone Grit outcrops surmounted by an OS pillar, standing 1,454 feet (443 metres) above sea level and marking the point at which three counties meet – North Yorkshire, West Yorkshire and Lancashire. The name recalls the fact that the surrounding area was inhabited by wolves until the sixteenth century.

drainage ditch is followed for a way as the surrounding heather is replaced by grassy moorland. Meeting a drystone wall, the route soon enters a walled lane. Crossing a stile, a track leads down through an overgrown quarry, with views over the valley of the River Worth. Arriving at the bottom, turn left along an unclassified road (3 = SD 984 379).

Ponden

Following the road past a row of cottages and around a wooded clough (Deep Clough), a finger sign marks the start of a path running along the valley side. When this meets a hardcore track, turn right and head down to Far Dean Field Farm, where a short alleyway leads to a ruined byre. Continuing down through fields, an unclassified road is met. A short way to the left a finger sign shows the Pennine Way crossing a bridge at the head of Ponden Reservoir. This was completed in 1877, and despite its relatively small size is home to a boat club. Joining a track running beside the reservoir then up a walled lane, the Brontë Way joins from the right (this 40-mile/64-kilometre route links various locations of significance in the lives of the family).

Turning left, follow the track as it heads towards Ponden Hall, where an access road is joined. This passes the outflow from a deep, incised valley (Ponden Clough), then continues towards the south end of the dam. Here a finger sign shows the Pennine Way turning

Ponden Hall

Ponden Hall is an imposing collection of Millstone Grit Farm buildings dating back to 1680. It is one of many locations in the area with links to the Brontë family – being the inspiration for Thrushcross Grange in Emily Brontë's *Wuthering Heights*. The present form of the structure owes to a restoration of 1801.

right, up a muddy track. Arriving at Buckley Farm, join a hardcore track heading east. Just past a cottage, the Pennine Way switches-back onto another track, then turns onto a stony path climbing a heather-clad slope. A stile in a short section of fence marks the point at which we leave the Pennine Way (4 = SD 998 364).

Stanbury

The first part of the return route heads north-east to Stanbury before re-crossing the Worth Valley. Turning left, follow a track (Back Lane) down to an unclassified road, then continue towards the village. Joining a back lane opposite the village school, turn through a gate on the left. Heading down through a couple of muddy fields, a sunken lane runs around a reed-choked millpond. The lane itself is very boggy, but a broken wall to the right offers firm footing. Passing a ruined cotton mill, follow the tree-lined river for a short way before crossing by a flat bridge.

On the north side of the river is an overgrown stone enclosure, the purpose of which is unclear. Heading uphill beside a stream, then a high wall, just past the entrance to Oldfield House an unclassified road is met. Turning right, follow the road as it runs through Oldfield. Passing through a gate on the left (opposite a telephone box), head up through a couple of fields. Crossing another road, a finger sign points to a hardcore track leading to Hare Hill Quarry. Zigzagging up through the overgrown quarry, there are good views down the valley towards Haworth. Continuing along a rough track, a marker post indicates a left turn onto a moorland path (5 = SE 006 386).

Keighley Moor

Following the remains of a drystone wall, the path runs between a stand of conifers (Pine Wood) and a line of grouse butts. Turning through a gap in the wall, the path continues alongside the boundary before heading north-west across open moorland, with a couple of marker posts confirming the route. Eventually the south end of the dam at Keighley Moor Reservoir is reached (6 = SD 989 393). The reservoir is located high up on the moors, with heather

A ruined cotton mill near Stanbury.

growing right up the face of the dam. Joining the access road at the far end of the dam, this runs north-east above the valley of Morkin Beck, across which can be seen the imposing remains of Clough Hey Farm. Passing a farmhouse, the track continues down towards an unclassified road. Turning left, the road runs through a wooded clough, then past a couple of farms (Slippery Ford). As it heads uphill, at a sharp bend, there is a choice of ways (7 = SE 001 409).

Sutton Moor

The first follows quiet roads for 3¾ miles (6¼ kilometres) back to the starting point, visiting the Earl Crag monuments along the way. Continuing along the road (Long Gate), this eventually joins Cowling Road as it heads north-west. Arriving at a crossroads, continue straight ahead before turning onto a track running through an overgrown quarry. Steps lead up the side of the quarry to the head of Earl Crag, where Lund's Tower stands sentinel. A spiral staircase provides access to a viewing platform, with wonderful views over Airedale. Following a path along the edge of the plateau, this is marked by great blocks of Millstone Grit that provide sport for rock climbers. Crossing a couple of difficult step stiles, Wainman's Pinnacle marks a left turn, heading towards a parking area (8 = SD 985 426). Turning right, follow the quiet road as it heads west (Buck Stone Lane) then north (Old Lane). Passing a scattering of farmsteads, cross straight over the A6068 and head down the steep bank leading back to the starting point.

Earl Crag Monuments

The steep scarp of Sutton Moor is marked by a line of Millstone Grit outcrops known as Earl Crag, and surmounted by a pair of monuments looking like over-sized chess pieces. Lund's Tower (or Sutton Pinnacle) was built as a folly during the late nineteenth century by James Lund of Malsis Hall, probably to commemorate Queen Victoria's Golden Jubilee. Wainman's Pinnacle (or Cowling Pinnacle) takes the form of an obelisk, and was supposedly built by Richard Wainman of Carr Head Hall after the Battle of Waterloo.

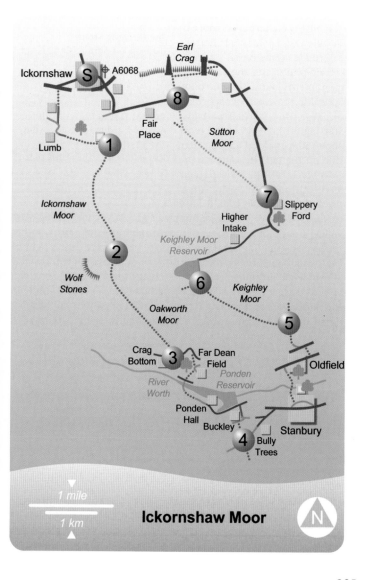

Ickornshaw Moor

285

Whilst the alternative route is ¾ mile (1¼ kilometres) shorter, it crosses some very difficult terrain and misses the Earl Crag monuments, so it will only appeal to those with a particular dislike for road-walking. Starting at the bend in the road above Slippery Ford, cross a step stile on the left. Heading north-west across a field, a sheep track leads through a rushy area towards a gap stile (this is hard to spot, and may be blocked-up). Ahead is a shallow, trough-like valley. Continuing north-west across rough grazing, join another sheep track running along the heather-clad terrace to the right of the trough. Eventually the Earl Crag monuments come into view ahead, while off to the left is the Hitching Stone. Heading across an area of tussocky grass, there is no path and it is easy to founder in the mires. Passing through a gate, follow a drystone wall heading north to arrive at an unclassified road opposite the parking area for Wainman's Pinnacle.

The Hitching Stone

High up on Sutton Moor is the Hitching Stone, which is said to be the largest boulder in Yorkshire. A great block of Millstone Grit, it stands more than 20 feet (6 metres) high and weighs around 1,000 tons/tonnes. It was deposited here by ice, and seems to have originated at Earl Crag.

WALK 2: WITHINS HEIGHT

LENGTH 13¼ miles (22 kilometres)

ASCENT 1,985 feet (605 metres)

HIGHEST POINT 448 metres (1,470 feet)

MAPS OS Explorer OL Map 21 ('South Pennines') (North Sheet)

STARTING POINT Gorple & Walshaw Dean reservoirs parking area, above Hebden Dale (SD 947 323)

FACILITIES Inn nearby.

FEATURES An enjoyable walk following the Pennine Way beside reservoirs and over moorland, returning by an old pack-horse route. Among the many features associated with the Brontë sisters is the isolated ruin of Top Withins (the inspiration for the Earnshaw residence in *Wuthering Heights*).

Walshaw Dean Reservoirs

The starting point is located 5 miles (8 kilometres) north-west of Hebden Bridge, close to the Pack Horse Inn on the Colne road. The first part of the walk follows the Pennine Way for 2 miles (3¼ kilometres) around the Walshaw Dean reservoirs. A finger sign points up a stony path, joining an access road heading north-east towards the reservoirs. The Pennine Way actually follows a corridorised path beside the tarmac track, although the latter is preferred by many walkers. Ignoring another track leading off to the right, continue towards the lower reservoir, where a finger sign marks a right turn over the dam. Following a gravel path above the eastern shore, ignore a hardcore track starting at the middle dam and instead continue along a narrow strip of land between the reservoir and a drain. A short way along a track, a finger sign shows the Pennine Way turning onto a moorland path (1 = SD 969 339).

Withins Height

From here the Pennine Way runs north-east for 2¾ miles (4¼ kilometres) over the heather-clad slopes of Withins Height. The path is

Hebden Water Reservoirs

The six reservoirs in this area were built to supply Halifax. The oldest and largest is Widdop, built 1871-78. A horse-drawn tramway 5½ miles (9 kilometres) long carried materials to site, running up Hebden Dale and Walshaw Dean. The engineer, Edward La Trobe Bateman, had attended the Suez Canal opening in 1869, and the design of the valve house shows Egyptian influence. When the three reservoirs in Walshaw Dean were constructed in 1900–13, a stone circle was submerged. The two Gorple reservoirs were built in 1927–34, with fourteen narrow gauge locomotives used on the site.

easy-going as it climbs gently, with flagged sections along the way. Arriving at the watershed (2 = SD 980 348), there are fine views towards the Worth Valley. Whilst this is the highest point on the walk, the actual summit of Withins Height (Round Hill) is a short way to the north-west (in fact, it is only marginally higher).

Ignoring a path heading east along the watershed, the Pennine Way turns north, with flagstones providing easy passage of the rough grass. The ruin of Top Withins – the highest of a chain of abandoned farmsteads – is now just a short way ahead. To the right is the valley of South Dean Beck, separating Stanbury Moor and Haworth Moor. Arriving at the ruin, it is not hard to see how its remote location might have inspired Emily Brontë. Continuing past another ruined farm building, a hardcore track is eventually joined. A white-washed farm (Upper Heights) dates from 1761 and is famed for the bearded head sculpture adorning the wall. Just past Lower Heights Farm, a crossroads of routes marks the point at which we leave the Pennine Way (3 = SD 998 364).

Haworth Moor

The first part of the return route follows the Brontë Way to Penistone Hill Country Park, before joining the Haworth to Hebden Bridge Walk. Turning onto a path heading south through heather, cross straight over a hardcore track. A finger sign shows the path heading steeply down into the valley of South Dean Beck, which is crossed by a slab bridge (the 'Brontë Bridge'). This sheltered clough

– a favourite haunt of the Brontë sisters – might make a good place to stop for lunch. Following a narrow path up the steep, bracken-covered valley side, the route broadens into a hardcore track. Ruined farm buildings punctuate the slopes of the broadening valley, and Lower Laithe Reservoir can be seen downstream. Ahead are the heather-clad mounds of Penistone Hill – a former quarry and now a country park. Eventually the track arrives at an unclassified road (Moor Side Lane) (4 = SE 016 365).

Crossing straight over the road, a gravel path runs towards the overgrown spoil heaps. Joining a hardcore track (part of the Haworth to Hebden Bridge Walk), head through a car park and back to the road. Here a

The remote ruin of Top Withins – thought by many to be the inspiration for the Earnshaw residence in Emily Brontë's *Wuthering Heights*.

finger sign points along the access road leading to Drop Farm, which is home to some popular tea rooms. Passing the farmhouse,

Brontë Bridge

The current Brontë Bridge was built after the original was washed away during a flash flood in 1989. A small waterfall on a side stream is identified as Emily Brontë's falls, while a nearby rock is named the Brontë Chair (it was here that Charlotte often sat while she wrote). It seems that every feature hereabouts, no matter how insignificant, is branded for the benefit of visitors. Indeed, many of the signs hereabouts are written in English and Japanese – the Brontë sisters' novels being particularly popular in Japan.

climb over a fence stile and turn left, heading south-east down the edge of a field. Joining a track at Westfield Farm, this leads to an unclassified road (Lee Lane) (5 = SE 018 353).

Stairs Lane

From here the walk follows an old pack-horse route running south-west for 3¼ miles (5½ kilometres) over a moorland ridge. The road becomes a stony track as it hooks around Lee Shaw Reservoir and heads up a walled lane. The track deteriorates as it passes Bodkin Farm and climbs Stairs Lane towards the watershed (which is appropriately named 'Top of Stairs') (6 = SE 004 337). Looking across the valley on the left, the curious apparatus on Oxenhope Moor is a Bradford University field station. The wind turbines beyond are located on Ovenden Moor. The track improves as it heads steeply downhill, eventually becoming an unclassified road (Old Road) leading to Grainwater Bridge (7 = SD 996 324).

Here a finger sign shows the old pack-horse route turning off the road, following a stony track as it crosses a stream and continues along the steep valley side. The deepening valley is home to Crimsworth Dean Beck, with the charming Lumb Falls (although these unfortunately cannot be seen from the track). Arriving at the ruin of Nook Farm, a marker post shows our route turning right, leaving the Haworth to Hebden Bridge Walk (8 = SD 990 313).

Walshaw

From here it is just 3 miles (4¾ kilometres) back to the starting point. A stony track heads west around a spur of Shackleton Moor, which forms the ridge between Crimsworth Dean and Hebden Dale. Heather climbs the steep slopes on the right, while to the left is walled pasture. Ahead are distant views of Heptonstall, with its prominent church tower. A finger sign shows the route turning through a gate in the drystone wall on the left, before continuing along the top of a field. Crossing cattle-churned pasture, a rough track leads towards Walshaw Farm (9 = SD 974 313).

Here a hardcore track threads between the farm buildings and continues west-north-west through pasture, parallel to the beautiful wooded valley of Hebden Dale. Passing a byre, the track follows

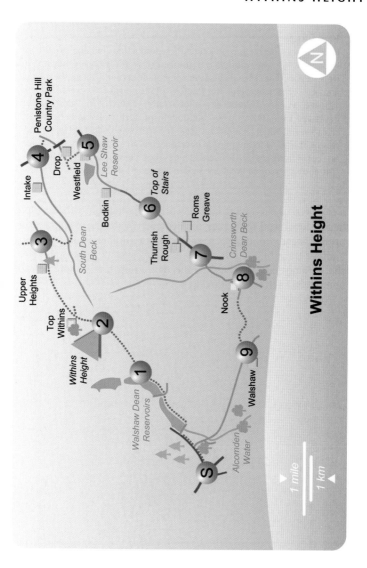

Withins Height

Heptonstall

Prior to the mechanisation of textiles production and the growth of Hebden Bridge, Heptonstall was the centre of the woollen industry in Upper Calderdale. The village developed on dry ground above the valley, and was centred around the Church of St Thomas à Beckett, built in 1256–60 as an offshoot of Halifax Parish Church. The church was destroyed in a storm in 1847, although the shell still stands beside its replacement, which was built in 1854. The Wesleyan Chapel at Heptonstall was built in 1764 to an unusual octagonal design – apparently to provide no corner in which the Devil could hide! The collection of lovely Millstone Grit cottages around Weaver's Square is a delight to see.

a causeway over grazing land, eventually swinging north-west as it heads down into the valley of Alcomden Water. Crossing a stone bridge, head up beside a ruined barn (Holme Ends). Ignoring another track on the left, continue past a sycamore copse towards the turning passed earlier in the day. From here simply retrace your steps back to the starting point.

WALK 3: UPPER CALDERDALE

LENGTH 13½ miles (21¾ kilometres)

ASCENT 1,952 feet (595 metres)

HIGHEST POINT 373 metres (1,224 feet)

MAPS OS Explorer OL Map 21 ('South Pennines') (North & South Sheets)

STARTING POINT Pennine Way car park, near Charlestown (SD 972 265)

FACILITIES Full range of services at Hebden Bridge.

FEATURES This walk offers an unequalled combination of beautiful countryside and industrial heritage. The varied route includes narrow lanes and open moorland, as well as a beautiful wooded valley (Hebden Dale), a visit to the centre of Hebden Bridge and the towpath beside the Rochdale Canal.

Colden Clough

The starting point is on the north side of the A646, 1½ miles (2½ kilometres) west of Hebden Bridge, opposite the Rochdale Canal workshop (a street sign marks the access for Underbank Avenue). The first part of the walk follows the Pennine Way up and down steep causeys, heading north for 2 miles (3¼ kilometres). Passing through a tunnel under a railway embankment, climb a steep alley-way on slippery cobbles to arrive at an access road. Turning left, the height already gained affords good views across the deep valley, with Stoodley Pike visible beyond steep, wooded slopes.

Arriving at a retaining wall, a finger sign shows the Pennine Way turning hard right. Ignoring an alternative route heading up beside an overgrown graveyard, follow a narrow path running along the steep, bracken-covered valley side. Climbing steps beside a tree-shaded gully, a stone privy stands perched above a small waterfall. Turning left onto another access road, then left again along a lane, a finger sign marks a right turn over a stile, joining a path running across meadows towards an unclassified road (1 = SD 967 275).

Upper Calderdale

The River Calder rises on the moors above Todmorden, from where it flows eastward down a deep, incised valley, passing Hebden Bridge and continuing on towards Halifax (confusingly, a nearby tributary of the River Ribble has the same name). John Wesley visited Upper Calderdale in 1747, and compared it to the Garden of Eden. Today it is a place of stark contrasts, where beautiful countryside is juxtaposed with the remains of the industrial revolution. Until the eighteenth century, wool from the sheep that grazed the surrounding moors was turned into rough cloth on domestic hand looms, then transported to market by pack-horse. During the first half of the nineteenth century the cotton industry spilled over from Lancashire, bringing industry to the valley floor. Water-powered, then steam-powered mills were built, eventually transforming Upper Calderdale into the world centre for fustian production. To serve the rapidly growing textiles industry, the Rochdale Canal and the Lancashire & Yorkshire Railway were driven up the valley during the first half of the nineteenth century.

This is Badger Lane, part of a medieval route running over the Pennines known as the Long Causeway. Crossing straight over the road, a path heads north along the edge of a field. Following an overgrown causey towards Colden Clough, at the bottom of the wooded valley a narrow pack-horse bridge leads to a muddy path. Here a marker post indicates a left turn onto another path, climbing out of the clough and heading over fields towards a tidy farmhouse. Arriving at an unclassified road, cross straight over and join a gravel path leading to another road. Here a finger sign shows the route heading up a steep path to arrive at a waymarked gate (2 = SD 966 289).

Heptonstall Moor

For the next 3 miles (5 kilometres) the Pennine Way runs north-west across Heptonstall Moor. Following a track beside a drystone wall, a cairn soon marks a turn onto a path running through the heather. Crossing a gully at the head of a clough, continue north-west, with a few slabs providing passage of boggy ground. Contouring around the side of Standing Stone Hill (named for the guide stones that mark a pack-horse route running over its summit), Gorple Lower Reservoir comes into view ahead. Arriving at a broken wall, turn left along a corridorised path. A finger sign shows the Pennine Way turning north, along a stony track, passing through a set of iron gates to arrive at a crossroads of routes beside Gorple Cottages (3 = SD 947 312).

Continuing straight ahead (we will return to this place later), join a path signed for Clough Foot. Stone slabs embedded in the grass recall the origins of this path as a pack-horse route. Care is needed as the stepped path drops into a rugged clough, where Reaps Water and Graining Water are crossed by footbridges. Heading up the far side of the clough, ignore a fence stile on the right (this provides access to the Pack Horse Inn). Arriving at an unclassified road, turn left and head towards the parking area for the Gorple & Walshaw Dean reservoirs, where we leave the Pennine Way (4 = SD 947 323).

Hebden Dale

The first part of the return route connects with Hebden Dale. Opposite the parking area, a finger sign marks the start of a concrete track following Graining Water south before swinging towards the dam at the foot of Gorple Lower Reservoir. Crossing over the dam, the track turns towards Gorple Cottages and the crossroads of routes passed earlier (5 = SD 947 312). During the 1960s, a reservoir keeper who lived at the cottages perished in a blizzard on the surrounding moors.

Continuing straight ahead (east), follow an access road signed as a permissive route to Blake Dean. To the right of the tarmac track is a drain, while off to the left Millstone Grit outcrops mark the edge of the deep clough of Graining Water. A marker post shows a path turning off the access road, heading steeply downhill to arrive at an unclassified road. A short way to the left the stream is crossed by a stone bridge (6 = SD 958 313).

Ignoring a track turning off the road, instead pass through a narrow gate and head down a few steps to join a tree-shaded path running beside the stream. Arriving at a confluence, Alcomden Water is crossed by a footbridge. This lovely place is Black Dean, at

Black Dean

Black Dean marks the point at which Hebden Water is formed through the confluence of two streams. It is a beautiful place, with a scattering of rowan and birch beneath steep slopes covered in bracken and heather. Not surprisingly, it is a favourite spot for picnickers. A short way downstream are the remains of a pitch pine trestle bridge, built in 1900 to carry a narrow gauge railway from Dawson City (a shanty town near Heptonstall) to the reservoir construction sites in Walshaw Dean. This was 105 feet (32 metres) high and 700 feet (213 metres) long.

the head of Hebden Dale. Heading up the steep valley side, cross an old track-bed before continuing over rough pasture. Passing through a gate, the path runs under tree cover, above an overgrown quarry. Emerging into the open, follow the narrow path as it runs down heather-clad slopes towards a ruined cottage (Over Wood) (7 = SD 973 310).

Here the route enters Hebden Dale proper, with the tree-shaded track covered in oak leaves and pine needles. At a fork, take the left-hand track, heading uphill (south). Soon another track joins from the left – part of the Haworth to Hebden Bridge Walk. Some rock outcrops among the trees off to the right gave the valley its

Hebden Dale

Hebden Dale, or Hardcastle Crags as it is popularly known, is a beautiful wooded valley owned by the National Trust. It was formed by glacial meltwater at the end of the last Ice Age, and together with the tributary Crimsworth Dean, it reaches up into the moorland plateau to the north of Hebden Bridge. Much of the woodland was planted during the nineteenth century to provide fuel for charcoal burners. Today the valley is home to every kind of broadleaf tree, as well as a scattering of scots pine. On three occasions it has been threatened with being flooded to create a reservoir, but its future now seems secure. The National Trust maintains visitor facilities and a network of paths. Swiss residents of Britain visit Hebden Dale for their open air forum, giving it the title 'Little Switzerland'.

popular name – Hardcastle Crags. When an abandoned mill comes into view ahead, it is possible to turn off the track and walk along the top of the millpond dam. Otherwise, continue along the track until it arrives at Gibson Mill (8 = SD 973 298).

A quaint hump-back bridge behind the mill is worth investigating, before rejoining the track as it runs down the wooded valley towards New Bridge (note that there is also a riverside path, if there is plenty of time). Passing the National Trust car park at the head of an unclassified road (and close to some public toilets), an access road turns down a lane on the right (9 = SD 988 291).

Gibson Mill

Gibson Mill was built as a water-powered cotton mill by the second Abraham Gibson, around 1800. It was powered by a water-wheel fed from a millpond. During summer the flow became inadequate, and in winter the pond often froze, so a steam engine was installed in the 1860s. The mill closed at the end of the 1890s due to competition from larger mills downstream. Afterwards it was used as a dining saloon, a roller-skating rink and a dance hall (complete with boating on the pond). The last Abraham Gibson died in 1956, leaving the mill to the National Trust.

Hebden Bridge

From here a it is also possible to reach the centre of Hebden Bridge by following Midgehole Road then the pavement beside the A6033. However, the next part of the return route proper follows a riverside path for 2 miles (3¼ kilometres). Heading down the access road, cross the river by a stone bridge and turn through the Blue Pig WMC car park. Ignoring an alleyway heading steeply uphill on the right (part of the Calderdale Way), a finger sign marks the start of the riverside path. Crossing back over the river by a footbridge, head over a meadow then up a farm access to rejoin the road.

Turning onto a tree-shaded alleyway running parallel to the road, a marker post eventually points down a stepped path. Passing some houses at the bottom of the slope, cross another footbridge. Turning left, follow the riverside path as it runs beside sports fields before crossing a charming little pack-horse bridge. From here the route weaves through a maze of back streets. Heading along Windsor Road, then Victoria Road, re-cross the river by a road bridge and turn right, off Valley Road, to join Hangingroyd Lane. This is followed towards the Old Bridge and the town centre. Once over the A646 by a signal controlled crossing, head along Holme Street to arrive at the Rochdale Canal (10 = SD 941 271).

Hebden Bridge

Hebden (formerly Hepton) Bridge is a product of the industrial revolution, and is in many respects the archetypal South Pennines mill town. As early as the fifteenth century, settlement began spilling into valley, focussed around river-crossings on the pack-horse routes. Indeed, the town is named after the Old Bridge, which has provided a crossing on Hebden Water since around 1510. However, it was not until the first half of the eighteenth century that Hebden Bridge achieved dominance over its forerunner, Heptonstall. Industrialisation brought about the rapid growth of the town, and due to a shortage of flat land, homes for the mill workers were built on the steep valley sides in the form of four-storey terraced housing.

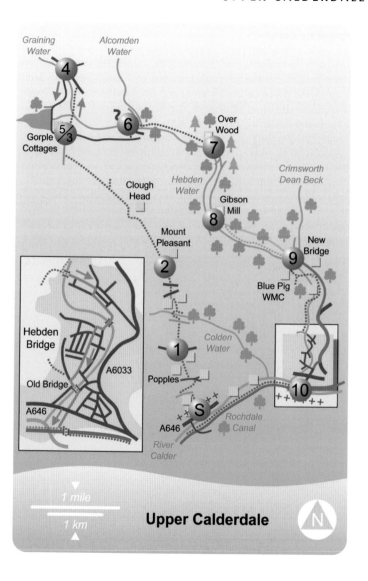

Graining Water

Alcomden Water

Gorple Cottages

Over Wood

Clough Head

Hebden Water

Gibson Mill

Crimsworth Dean Beck

Mount Pleasant

New Bridge

Blue Pig WMC

Colden Water

Hebden Bridge

Old Bridge

A6033

A646

Popples

Rochdale Canal

A646

River Calder

1 mile

1 km

Upper Calderdale

Rochdale Canal

Ahead is a pleasant 1½ mile (2½ kilometre) stroll along the canal towpath. Ignoring a bridge leading to Calder Holmes Park, turn right and follow the towpath past Blackpit Lock. Here the canal crosses the River Calder by an aqueduct. Passing Stubbing Lower and Upper locks, a sign gives the distances to Manchester (26 miles) and Sowerby Bridge (6 miles). Stubbing Wharf Inn is a favourite stopping place for boat crews. To the right of the towpath is the river, lined with old mills and terraced housing. To the left is the canal, with wooded slopes above its reedy banks. Passing another lock (Cawden Mill), moored barges mark the location of Rochdale Canal Workshop. Just before reaching the bridge that carries the Pennine Way over the canal, turn off the towpath and follow an access road leading to the A646, where the car park is on the far side.

WALK 4: STOODLEY PIKE

LENGTH 6¾ miles (10¾ kilometres)

ASCENT 968 feet (295 metres)

HIGHEST POINT 400 metres (1,312 feet)

MAPS OS Explorer OL Map 21 ('South Pennines') (South Sheet)

STARTING POINT Pennine Way car park, near Charlestown
(SD 972 265)

FACILITIES Full range of services at Hebden Bridge.

FEATURES A short but varied walk encompassing a wooded valley side, a moorland ridge, an attractive dene and a canal towpath. The imposing monument on Stoodley Pike is the principal landmark in the area, offering spectacular views over Upper Calderdale.

Callis Wood

The first part of the walk follows the Pennine Way for 1¼ miles (2¼ kilometres) as it heads up through Callis Wood. Starting at the car park beside the A646, this time cross over the busy main road and join an access road crossing the River Calder and the Rochdale Canal before heading up the wooded valley side. As the track turns towards Oaks Farm, the Pennine Way cuts the corner, following a path threading through birch trees. Rejoining the track, a finger sign marks a choice of ways, with one route heading steeply uphill and another taking a more circuitous course through a materials store. Continuing south, the track eventually emerges into the open before entering a walled lane running through pasture. Ahead are views of Stoodley Pike, while the group of farm buildings off to the north-east is Erringden Grange, a seventeenth-century model farm. At Lower Rough Head Farm, as the lane turns left, the Pennine Way crosses a stile on the right (1 = SD 980 253).

Stoodley Pike

From here the Pennine Way is followed over Stoodley Pike for 2 miles (3¼ kilometres). Heading south-west along the edge of a

Stoodley Pike

Stoodley Pike is a promontory above a steep, boulder-strewn scarp, reaching 1,312 feet (400 metres) above sea level. The name is popularly applied to an imposing monument, taking the form of a stone obelisk some 120 feet (37 metres) high. This was built in 1814 to commemorate Napoleon's abdication and the Peace of Ghent, but collapsed in 1854, being rebuilt two years later to mark the end of the Crimean War. Stoodley Pike is thought to have been a prehistoric burial site, and human remains were discovered here when the monument was erected. Up close the soot-blackened monument is

not particularly appealing, although it does offer tremendous views. A viewing platform is gained by means of a winding staircase, although this is pitch-dark and few brave the ascent.

field, then diagonally over rushy ground, the path swings around to head south-east beside a drystone wall. Crossing straight over a stony track (London Road), a finger sign shows the path heading uphill, passing an overgrown quarry set among grassy moorland. Climbing over a tall ladder stile, turn right (west) and head towards a narrow gap in an intersecting wall. From here a cairned path runs towards the monument on Stoodley Pike (2 = SD 973 242).

The moorland ridge is cut off sharply, with a steep scarp running away from Stoodley Pike. This is a rugged place, but it is by no means remote. Below the escarpment is modern housing estate, hopelessly out of character, occupying the site of the former Stansfield View Hospital (which was built as a workhouse for Todmorden's poor). A ribbon of development running up the valley floor leads towards Todmorden. Wind farms can be seen on the moorland plateaux to the north-east (Ovenden) and north-west

(Cliviger), while to the south is the Windy Hill transmitter.

After taking time to enjoy the views and perhaps have lunch, a cairned path runs south-south-west along the edge of the scarp. Looking ahead, Gaddings Dam can be seen on the moors above Langfield Edge. Many of the reservoirs in this area were built to supply the Rochdale Canal, although this example was created for the benefit of the cotton mills. Continuing through an overgrown quarry, the path heads down towards a

> **The Long Causeway**
>
> The Long Causeway (or Long Stoop) originated as a corpse road and pack-horse route crossing the ridge between Cragg Vale and Mankinholes. Most of the flagged causeys in this area were created during the early eighteenth century. This is a particularly fine example, with scuffed stones recalling centuries of use. Today it is part of the Calderdale Way – a 50-mile (81-kilometre) circular walk created in 1978, starting at Halifax.

saddle, passing a tall standing stone. Ahead is Withens Gate, where we leave the Pennine Way and turn onto the Long Causeway (3 = SD 968 231).

Mankinholes

The causey zigzags steeply downhill, then continues in a westerly direction between a drystone wall and a rushy gully. Looking ahead, the tower at Lumbutts Mill can be seen. At a gate, turn right, leaving the flagged path and joining a walled lane heading north through pasture towards Mankinholes, where it meets an unclassified road (4 = SD 960 235).

Ignoring a turning on the right signed as the Pennine Bridleway, follow the quiet road through the cluster of attractive Millstone Grit cottages. This place was the location of a Quaker meeting place from 1667. Beside the road is a row of stone water troughs once used by pack-horses. Passing the

> **Lumbutts Mill**
>
> The tower at Lumbutts once contained three waterwheels, stacked vertically, providing 54 horsepower for the adjacent cotton mill. It was fed by water siphoned from the nearby Lee and Heeley Dams. The buildings now serve as an activity centre.

youth hostel, continue along the road as it leaves the village. The stone cross in a field on the left was placed here to commemorate a visit by John Wesley. The road (New Road) was built during the cotton famine to provide a route for a local mill-owner (Honest John Fielden) to travel to his lodge in Cragg Vale. Continuing along an avenue of sycamore trees, another road is met at the head of Shaw Wood. Ignoring a gap in the low wall opposite (which marks the start of an overgrown path with very slippery steps), follow the road down through the dene. Arriving at the bottom, cross over the canal next to Shawplains Lock (5 = SD 959 247).

Rochdale Canal

The final part of the return route follows the towpath for 1½ miles (2¼ kilometres). At Holmcoat Lock, cross straight over an access road and continue along the towpath. Passing another lock (Callis), head under a stone bridge and turn off the towpath, rejoining the access road before it crosses the river to reach the A646. Arriving back at the starting point, there should be plenty of time to visit Hebden Bridge, with its range of specialist shops.

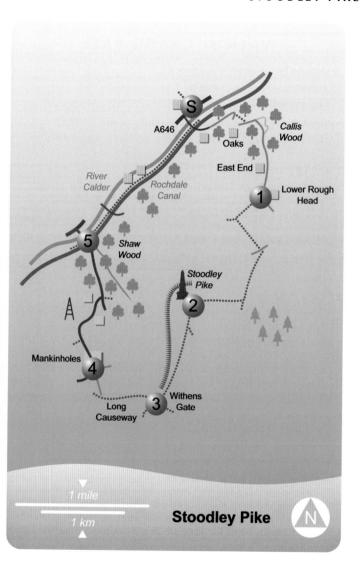

Stoodley Pike

1 mile

1 km

WALK 5: CRAGG VALE

LENGTH 15½ miles (25¼ kilometres)

ASCENT 1,312 feet (400 metres)

HIGHEST POINT 452 metres (1,483 feet)

MAPS OS Explorer OL Map 21 ('South Pennines') (South Sheet)

STARTING POINT Baitings Reservoir car park, near Ripponden (SE 011 191)

FACILITIES None.

FEATURES Although this walk crosses bleak moorland, navigation is fairly straightforward and the Pennine Way itself follows good tracks beside a chain of moorland reservoirs. Sections of the route use permissive paths created by Yorkshire Water, including a path above the village of Cragg Vale.

Rishworth Moor

The starting point is located on the A58, 2 miles (3 kilometres) west of Ripponden. Crossing the towering concrete dam, the views towards the surrounding moors are marred by electricity pylons. Arriving at Upper Schole Carr Farm, a sign shows routes heading right and left. Taking the latter, pass through the farmyard and head east across fields towards Higher Wormald Farm. Following the farm access up to an unclassified road, the Heights picnic place is a short way to the left (1 = SE 010 184).

From here the route runs 3 miles (5 kilometres) over Rishworth Moor to join the Pennine Way at Blackstone Edge, following a

The Ryburn and Baitings Reservoirs

The twin reservoirs on the River Ryburn were built to supply Wakefield. Ryburn Reservoir was built in 1925–33, and has a dam 128 feet (39 metres) high. The present Baitings Reservoir was built 1948–56, replacing an earlier construction. The concrete dam is 174 feet (53 metres) high and 1,550 feet (472 metres) long, and is used for abseiling events.

permissive path created by Yorkshire Water in 1993 (unfortunately, this is not shown on the Landranger map). Crossing over the road, a finger sign points along a short section of lane. As this gives out, the path continues south-west across open moorland, with marker posts confirming the route. To the left is an old drainage channel, snaking about as it seeks a level course. Hooking around a pronounced bluff, Blackstone Edge comes into view, its humpback strewn with boulders. Eventually a finger sign marks a right turn, joining a path running beside a concrete drain (2 = SD 981 177).

Another finger sign shows a link to the Pennine Way, crossing the drain and following the course of a Roman road that once ran over Blackstone Edge. Heading uphill on a rough track, bits of blockwork show through the peat here and there. Passing a fallen marker stone, the stony track runs over the watershed to arrive at the Aiggin Stone, where the Pennine Way is finally joined (3 = SD 973 171).

The Aiggin Stone

The Aiggin Stone stands near the summit of a Roman road that ran over Blackstone Edge. It was placed here around 600 years ago as a guide for travellers, at the crossroads of old trans-Pennine routes linking Rochdale and Halifax, and Oldham and Burnley. The stone was recently re-erected, although only the top three of its seven feet are above ground. The name evidently comes from 'agin', meaning 'edge' – a reference to its location.

Summit Reservoirs

From here the Pennine Way is followed for 5½ miles (8¾ kilometres) beside a chain of moorland reservoirs built to supply the Rochdale Canal. Following the course of the Roman road downhill, the blockwork is now distinct. Looking to the left, great towers of Millstone Grit buttress the flanks of Blackstone Edge. Crossing a drain, the Pennine Way turns right, joining a path following the watercourse through boulder-strewn moorland as it swings around from north-west to north-east. Turning down a stony path leading to the A58, head up the road towards the White House Inn. Just past the former coaching inn, a finger sign shows the Pennine Way joining a hardcore track running beside Blackstone Edge Reservoir (4 = SD 970 179).

The track runs north-west in the lee of the low dam, with Chelburn Moor on the left falling away towards the valley of the River Roch and the village of Summit. Continuing north alongside Head Drain, to the right are the massive outcrops of Light Hazzles Edge, with one large boulder surmounting a Millstone Grit block resembling a wolf's head. Passing under some pylons, the track divides. Ignoring a route signed for White Holme Reservoir, continue along a causeway running beside Light Hazzles and Warland reservoirs. Looking to the north-east, an OS pillar marks the location of Little Holder Stones, close to the highest point on the plateau. Arriving at the head of Warland Reservoir, ignore a path on the left (5 = SD 955 215).

Continuing north beside Warland Drain, ignore a flagged path

The Roman Road

The Roman road over Blackstone Edge reaches 1,483 feet (452 metres). Daniel Defoe records (in *A Tour through the Whole Island of Great Britain*) how he crossed the ridge in a blizzard one day in August. This is a testimony to the impact of climate change since the early eighteenth century, although conditions can still be difficult, and the ridge is often shrouded in hill fog. It is not surprising that it became known as the Devil's Pavement. Whilst the route itself is Roman, the visible remains are medieval. On the western side of the ridge it is remarkably well preserved, with regular blockwork on either side of a drainage channel.

Summit Reservoirs

During 1801–4, a number of reservoirs were built on the moors above Summit to supply the Rochdale Canal. Blackstone Edge, White Holme, Little Hazzles and Warland reservoirs are located at around 1,250 feet (381 metres), and now supply drinking water for Oldham and Rochdale.

taking off through the heather on the left. Staying on the Pennine Way as it turns east then north-east with the stone channel, eventually a finger sign marks the point at which we leave the drain, joining a flagged path heading north over rushy ground (6 = SD 964 220). Passing a couple of boundary stones, the path runs across boulder-strewn moorland. Nearing the edge of the plateau, Mankinholes and Lumbutts come into view down in the valley – although it is the monument on Stoodley Pike that dominates the view. Heading down towards Withens Gate, the Pennine Way continues towards Stoodley Pike, although we turn right, joining the Calderdale Way (7 = SD 968 231).

Turley Holes Edge

The first part of the return route runs past Withens Clough Reservoir and around Turley Holes Edge, a total of 3¼ miles (5¼ kilometres). Heading east along old causey slabs, through a gate in a high wall, a stone bearing a cross and the inscription 'te Deum laudamus' ('we praise thee O God') marks the spot where coffins were rested at the summit of the corpse road. From here the path heads gently downhill, turning left as it passes the entrance to a walled lane. A dirt path follows broken walls, then causey slabs, along the top of some fields, before turning down towards the reservoir. Joining a walled lane, continue past Pastures Farm to arrive at the north end of the dam, where a finger sign marks the start of a permissive path (8 = SD 984 232).

At this point we leave the Calderdale Way, which continues along an access road heading down towards Cragg Vale. Crossing over the dam, turn left and join a narrow path running beside a drain, heading east along the steep, bracken-covered slopes beneath Turley Holes Edge. Below is an old mill chimney, while ahead the terraced streets of Cragg Vale can be seen creeping up

Withens Clough Reservoir

Withens Clough Reservoir was built in 1891–4 to supply Morley, and continued in this role until 1989. Since then its water has been transferred through the Manshead Tunnel to Baitings Reservoir. At one time the surrounding valley was home to seventeen farmsteads, although these were cleared to avoid contamination of the drinking water.

the valley side. The path turns hard right as it meets a drystone wall, continuing above the wooded valley. After swinging around to head south-west, the path eventually drops into Turvin Clough. Although it is quite wide, the stream is usually easy to ford thanks to boulders that form a natural bridge. Heading up out of the clough, cross over a track and climb a bracken-covered slope. Turning left at an elbow in a drystone wall, head through a gate and up the side of a field to arrive at the B6138 (9 = SD 997 215).

Coal Gate Road

The final part of the return route follows a combination of lanes and roads, 3¼ miles (5 kilometres) back to the starting point. A short way to the right, opposite Sykes Gate Farm, is a junction. Joining an unclassified road heading east then north-east, ignore the access for Sykes Farm and continue straight ahead until a finger sign on the right points along a walled lane. This heads

The Cragg Vale Coiners

Cragg Vale is best known for its associations with counterfeiting. When the growth of trade during the early eighteenth century led to a shortage of currency, foreign coins became legal tender. The Cragg Vale Coiners used metal clipped from the edge of gold guineas to forge Portuguese moidores. The ringleader, 'King' David Hartley, lived at Bell House above the village. His brothers, Isaac and William, were known as the dukes of York and Edinburgh respectively. When an exciseman named William Deighton began investigating their activities in 1770, they had him murdered. David Hartley was later hanged for the crime, his body being buried at Heptonstall. At the Hinchcliffe Arms in Cragg Vale there is a display of coiners' equipment found in the wall of a local cottage.

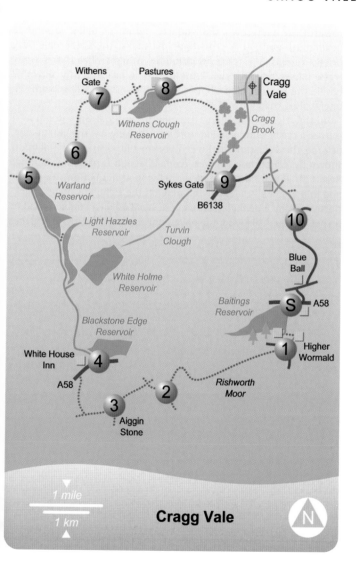

Cragg Vale

towards an overgrown slate quarry before swinging around to head south-east. At a crossroads of tracks, the Calderdale Way briefly rejoins our route. Continuing straight ahead, the stony track passes an old brick structure as it heads gently downhill beside the heather-clad slopes of Great Manshead Hill towards an unclassified road (10 = SE 012 207).

Turning right, head along the quiet road (Coal Gate Road) as it passes a farm with a wind turbine. Looking to the north-east, beyond the valley of the River Ryburn, the location of Halifax is shown by Wainhouse's Tower. A small lagoon is passed as Baitings Reservoir comes back into view. Arriving at a junction, turn right and join Blue Ball Lane. The building on the right was once a pack-horse inn (the Blue Ball). Turning left, head down a cobbled road to arrive at the A58, where a pavement leads back to the starting point.

WALK 6: MILLSTONE EDGE AND BLACKSTONE EDGE

LENGTH 17½ miles (28 kilometres)

ASCENT 2,704 feet (825 metres)

HIGHEST POINT 472 metres (1,549 feet)

MAPS OS Explorer OL Maps 1 ('The Peak District – Dark Peak') (West Sheet) and 21 ('South Pennines') (South Sheet)

STARTING POINT Standedge parking area, Saddleworth (SE 019 095)

FACILITIES Inn nearby.

FEATURES A long walk following the Pennine Way through a landscape of rugged charm, with moorland paths running along Millstone Grit scarps. The return route follows tracks and lanes through the Saddleworth area, with its scatter of reservoirs, functional villages and untidy farmsteads.

Millstone Edge

The starting point is located at the west end of the Standedge Cutting on the A62. The first part of the walk follows the Pennine Way north-west along Millstone Edge for 3¼ miles (5¼ kilometres). Crossing straight over the busy main road, a finger sign points along a hardcore track. Soon another sign marks a right turn over a fence stile, joining a path running along the edge of the moorland plateau towards an OS pillar (1 = SE 012 104).

This stands at 1,470 feet (448 metres) – not quite the highest point on Millstone Edge, but offering fine views over the Saddleworth area. Fixed to a nearby boulder is a memorial plaque celebrating the life of Ammon Wrigley (1861–1946), a poet and artist from Delph, whose ashes were scattered on the moors hereabouts. Continuing along the edge of the scarp, this is marked by blocks of soot-blackened Millstone Grit. Whilst the path itself is easy-going, to the right is an expanse of grassy moorland with areas of exposed peat. Dropping into a gully, a marker stone shows the Pennine Way turning right, joining a gravel path heading north-east.

> ### Standedge
>
> Standedge has long been an important transportation route. Since 1811, the Huddersfield Narrow Canal has run through a tunnel beneath the Pennine ridge, connecting Marsden in the Colne Valley and Diggle in Saddleworth. This was joined in 1849 by a railway tunnel, which at around 3 miles (5 kilometres) was then the world's longest. Another railway tunnel was added in 1871. The three tunnels are inter-connected – the canal being used to deliver materials and remove spoil during construction of the railway. A twin track railway tunnel opened in 1894 and is still in use today. The A62 Huddersfield to Oldham road running over Standedge was built as a turnpike by 'Blind' Jack Metcalf, replacing earlier toll roads. It was completed in 1839, with a cutting providing passage of the Pennine ridge at 1,273 feet (388 metres) above sea level.

Arriving at the head of the gully, the path turns north before dropping into Haigh Gutter. Ignoring a flagged path off to the right (part of the Station to Station Walk, which follows an old packhorse route from Marsden and Rochdale known as Rapes Highway) head up to a parking area beside the A640. Crossing straight over the road, a sign marks the edge of the National Trust's Marsden Moor Estate. The path runs alongside a broken wall before heading gently uphill towards the OS pillar marking the top of White Hill (2 = SD 991 132). This stands at 1,529 feet (466 metres) and offers wide views of a moorland landscape that is by no means pretty ('bleak' would be a more appropriate term), but it is nonetheless inspiring.

Blackstone Edge

From here the Pennine Way is followed north-west along Blackstone Edge for 3¾ miles (6 kilometres). A cairned path leads off in a westerly direction, crossing a mossy area (Green Hole Hill) as it swings around to head north-north-west, following the broad ridge down towards the A672. Passing through a parking area near the Windy Hill transmitter, a finger sign points along a gravel path. Crossing over the M62 by an elegant footbridge, turn left and join a stony path that soon swings around to head north-west (the Pennine Way used to head north, across the aptly-named Slippery Moss).

M62 Footbridge

The M62 is a brutal intrusion upon the moorland landscape of the South Pennines. Crossing the Pennine ridge between Huddersfield and Rochdale, the summit reaches 1,221 feet (372 metres), making it the country's highest section of motorway. Since the Pennine Way was already established when the road was built during 1966-71, a 220 feet (67 metres) long footbridge had to be provided. The combination of a high, narrow bridge, strong crosswinds and the roar of traffic below creates a sense of vertigo.

Stepping stones provide passage of a small stream at the head of Longden End Brook. Crossing another stream, the view ahead is now dominated by the boulder-strewn humpback of Blackstone Edge. Green Withens Reservoir can be seen off to the right. Following a chain of cairns, the path heads up onto the broad ridge, the flanks of which are once again marked by massive blocks of Millstone Grit. In hill fog the summit could be missed, so keep a

The summit of Blackstone Edge.

look out to the left for an OS pillar atop one of these blocks (3 = SD 972 164).

At 1,549 feet (472 metres), the top forms a fine vantage point and a good place to stop for lunch (the boulders serve as ready-made picnic tables). To the west, close to Littleborough, is Hollingworth Lake. To the north, beyond rough moorland strewn with boulders are the Summit

> ### Hollingworth Lake
> Hollingworth Lake was created around 1800 to supply the Rochdale Canal. Workers from the local cotton mills took their holidays beside the lake, which thus became known as the 'weavers' seaport'. It is now a country park and nature reserve, as well as a location for sailing and water-skiing.

reservoirs, among a forest of electricity pylons. Heading north-north-east from the summit, cairns and marker posts provide guidance in poor visibility, with the path weaving through the jumble of boulders as it heads gently downhill. In places the path is made of stone blocks – a discrete form of improvement that helps to reduce erosion. Arriving at the Aiggin Stone, turn left and head down the Roman road. When the Pennine Way turns along the line of Broad Head Drain, instead continue downhill (4 = SD 969 170).

Clegg Moor
The first part of the return route follows good tracks along the fringe of Clegg Moor for 3½ miles (5½ kilometres). Looking to the right, the A58 can be seen snaking down the steep slope. Crossing over a farm access, follow a path running through bracken then alongside a drystone wall towards the hamlet of Lydgate. Passing a row of cottages and a whitewashed farm, a finger sign marks a left turn onto an access road heading south (5 = SD 955 165).

Veering onto a hardcore track, follow a line of electricity pylons running along the edge of Clegg Moor. Ignoring a path on the right, stay on the track as it passes under the pylons and turns through a gate to arrive at a farmhouse perched above the M62. The roar of the traffic is deafening as the motorway is re-crossed. Following a hardcore track heading down into the valley of Longden End Brook, turn left and continue past a derelict mill and a farmhouse to arrive at a crossroads of routes. Switching-back onto a stony track heading steeply uphill, follow this south-west until it meets Tunshill Lane (6 = SD 952 133).

Station to Station Walk

The next part of the return route follows the Station to Station Walk for 2½ miles (4 kilometres). The stony track heads east, following a sunken lane bounded by broken walls. Ignoring a left turn through a gate, stay in the lane as it swings around to head south-east. The valley on the right is occupied by a group of reservoirs, built in 1858–1901 to provide water for Oldham. Veering right at another fork, follow the track as it heads down towards Piethorne Reservoir. Crossing over the dam, to the left is Norman Hill Reservoir. From here the track climbs steeply, passing a right turn leading to a supply reservoir. As the track levels-out, continue along a walled lane until arriving at the A672 beside the Ram's Head Inn (7 = SD 978 119).

Denshaw and Castleshaw

It is here that we leave the Station to Station Walk, following the road for ¾ mile (1¼ kilometres) down to Denshaw. There is no way to avoid this section of busy main road, although there is a grass verge, then a pavement on the right hand side. Several main roads meet at a staggered crossroads in the centre of the village, which is the location of the Junction Inn – a former coaching inn built to serve the turnpikes. Following the pavement beside the A6052 (Delph Road), as this leaves the village, cross over to join a hedge-lined lane (Wham Lane) heading east. As the narrow road turns right, join a stony

Castleshaw (Rigodunum) Fort

The Roman fort at Castleshaw was apparently named after a nearby Brigantian settlement, Rigodunum ('King's Fort'). It was built by Agricola around AD 80 on the trans-Pennine route between Chester and York, before being demolished and replaced by a fortlet during the Trajanic period. This in turn was abandoned around AD 125. Today little can be discerned without the benefit of an aerial view – just a trace of the grassy ramparts on the high ground above the Castleshaw Reservoirs.

track running along Ox Hey Lane (8 = SD 975 102). In the valley on the left is another group of reservoirs, this time capturing the waters of the River Tame. Eventually the track arrives at a cross-roads of routes (9 = SD 989 102).

Ignoring routes signed for the Pennine Way and Delph, turn right (south-east), heading down Low Gate Lane. The sunken lane runs steeply downhill between retaining walls, with views across Castleshaw Upper and Lower reservoirs and the site of a Roman fort. Turning left, follow an access road over the upper reservoir dam. Joining an unclassified road as it snakes uphill towards Bleak Hey Nook, another junction is soon met (10 = SE 005 094). Turning left again, follow the quiet road as it heads north-east through an area of untidy farmsteads. As the road turns down towards Globe Farm, instead continue up a hardcore track to rejoin the Pennine Way, which is followed back to the starting point.

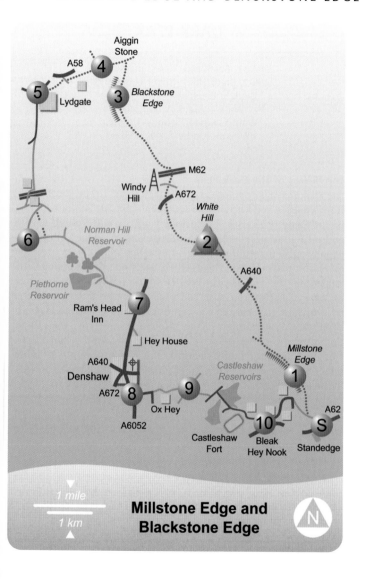

Millstone Edge and
Blackstone Edge

DARK PEAK

Walk 1: Black Hill – Wessenden Moor
Walk 2: Black Hill – Upper Longdendale
Walk 3: Bleaklow – Old Glossop
Walk 4: Black Ashop Moor
Walk 5: Kinder Scout – Hayfield
Walk 6: Kinder Scout – Edale

The Moors of the Dark Peak

The Peak District comprises two distinct areas. To the south of the Hope Valley – and forming the southern tip of the Pennine Chain – is the White Peak. This is limestone country, with rolling pasture and pleasant dales. Between Standedge and the Hope Valley is the equally aptly-named Dark Peak, a horseshoe-shaped area of rugged moorland plateaux and ridges where Millstone Grit dominates the landscape. The whole of the Peak District is underlain by limestone of Lower Carboniferous age, laid down when the area was covered by a shallow tropical sea. On top of this were deposited layers of shale and sandstone – the Millstone Grit of the Upper Carboniferous period – formed from mud and sand washed down from the mountains of Caledonia. The whole system was subsequently uplifted to create a great, dome-shaped plateau.

The Millstone Grit was then eroded away in the southern part of the area, exposing the underlying limestone to form the landscape of the White Peak. In the Dark Peak the Millstone Grit survived, although the great dome has been dissected by the passage of ice and water to form a tangle of smaller plateaux and ridges, with the underlying shale exposed around the valley floors. The differential

This, perhaps, is the most desolate, wild, and abandoned country in all England. The mountains of the Peak, of which I have been speaking, seem to be but the beginning of the wonders to this part of the country . . .

Daniel Defoe, *A Tour Through the Whole Island of Great Britain*.

Laddow Rocks in Upper Longdendale.

erosion of the hard sandstone and softer shale layers – the latter being susceptible to landslips – has contributed to the formation of the characteristic steep scarps. These are known as the 'edges', and are marked by gritstone outcrops that provide popular rock climbing routes.

During the period following the last Ice Age, the whole area was covered in woodland. When this was cleared by human settlers, a deterioration in the climate triggered the formation of blanket bog. Millstone Grit weathers to produce sandy soils that are wet and acidic. This limited the decomposition of vegetation, resulting in the accumulation of a thick layer of peat. As a result of the pollution generated by the industrial revolution, the sphagnum moss

The South Pennine Fells

The Peak District is part of the broader South Pennines area. Despite the forbidding appearance of the Dark Peak, there are only two hills of over 2,000 feet (610 metres) in this section of the Pennine Chain, namely Kinder Scout and Bleaklow Head. This recalls the fact that the plateaux of the South Pennines were formed through sedimentary in-filling, and subsequent uplifting, of a depression known as the Craven Basin.

that once provided the bulk of the vegetation on the high ground is now comparatively rare, so little new peat formation is taking place. Instead, the boggy ground is home to cottongrass, with white tufts that provide a pleasing embellishment to an otherwise bleak landscape. Nevertheless, the names of the different areas of moorland often retain the element 'moss'.

Intermittent streams running across the moorland plateaux have cut innumerable channels into the peat, reaching down to the bedrock. These are known locally as 'groughs', and can be up to 15 feet (4½ metres) deep. In places the sandstone itself has been exposed by erosion, then weathered to create strange rock formations. Vegetation on the drier ground includes heather, bilberry, crowberry and cloudberry. As well as grouse, the area is home to the usual range of moorland birds, most commonly lapwing, curlew and golden plover. Mountain hares were re-introduced to the area during the nineteenth century. Cutting down through the edges of the plateaux are fast-flowing streams, with steep-sided cloughs sheltering fragments of woodland.

Strange rock formations on Kinder Scout.

People in the Dark Peak

The moorland plateaux – which are known locally as 'gaits' – are exclusively used for grouse-shooting and sheep-grazing. The Derbyshire Gritstone is a big sheep which is identified by its lack of horns, black-and-white speckled face and legs clear of wool. Tucked in beneath the escarpments are farmsteads with in-bye pasture where landform permits. The sheltered valleys offer limited scope for cattle rearing. Conifer plantations are restricted to the valleys, in particular where there are reservoirs. A combination of high rainfall, valley floors of impermeable shale and proximity to a number of major conurbations has made the Dark Peak an important location for water collection, with around 50 reservoirs in the area. The largest of these are located in the Upper Derwent Valley and in Upper Longdendale.

During the Middle Ages, the area was criss-crossed with packhorse routes carrying salt from Cheshire to Sheffield (where it was used to preserve meat) and wool from Yorkshire to Cheshire. A number of trans-Pennine turnpikes were built during the eighteenth century, facilitating travel by stagecoach and providing the basis of the modern highway system. Later came the railways, with routes connecting Sheffield and Manchester being pushed through Upper Longdendale (1845) and the Vale of Edale (1894). Both involved the construction of long tunnels – with the 3-mile (5-kilometre) Woodhead Tunnel on the former and the 2-mile (3-kilometre) Cowburn Tunnel on the latter.

The high ground of the Dark Peak is devoid of habitation. Even the valleys are sparsely

Derwent Valley Reservoirs

Howden, Derwent and Ladybower reservoirs together cover 840 acres (340 hectares), and were built to supply Sheffield, Nottingham, Derby and Leicester. Construction of the first two dams was undertaken in 1901–12 and 1902–16 respectively, with the navvies being housed at a nearby shanty town appropriately known as 'Tin Town'. Ladybower was added in 1935–45, with World War II failing to prevent its completion. During 1943 the reservoirs were used by Lancaster bombers of the RAF to practice for the famous 'Dambusters' raid on Germany's Ruhr Valley.

populated, although there are a few sizeable villages, most notably Castleton in the Hope Valley. There are sizeable towns on the fringes of the area, including Chapel-en-le-Frith, Glossop and Holmfirth. Indeed, the major conurbations of Greater Manchester and Sheffield are nearby, accounting for the area's extraordinary popularity as a destination for day-visitors.

Walking in the Dark Peak

As well as being home to some very difficult terrain, the plateaux and ridges of the Dark Peak are prone to hill fog, making luck a significant factor in navigating around the grough mazes. The blanket bog that overlies much of the high ground is typically 80 per cent water, so 'bog-trotting' can be expected to result in peat-stained feet! Dry conditions and good visibility are therefore definitely advisable for any but the most experienced hill-walkers. The starting point for the Pennine Way is the village of Edale, and the most heavily used parts of Britain's first National Trail fall within the Dark Peak. The resultant erosion has led to the creation of alternative routes on a number of sections. These avoid open moorland, and instead follow valley floors and the escarpment edges – which in any case tend to offer better views. However, the original routes are still available for more adventurous walkers.

Peak District National Park

Established in 1951, the Peak District was Britain's first National Park. It extends to 555 square miles (1,438 square kilometres), encompassing both the Dark Peak and the White Peak. The National Park is surrounded by conurbations, and is visited by 30 million people each year – only Mount Fuji National Park in Japan receives more visitors. Whilst it can no longer offer a wilderness experience, it is nevertheless an enjoyable place to visit. Within the National Park are 98 square miles (254 square kilometres) of 'access land' that is open to the public when grouse-shooting is not taking place. The symbol of the National Park is the millstone, recalling the geology of the Dark Peak.

WALK 1: BLACK HILL – WESSENDEN MOOR

LENGTH 12½ miles (20¼ kilometres)

ASCENT 1,657 feet (505 metres)

HIGHEST POINT 1,910 feet (582 metres)

MAPS OS Explorer OL Map 1 ('The Peak District – Dark Peak') (West Sheet)

STARTING POINT Standedge parking area, Saddleworth (SE 019 095)

FACILITIES Inn nearby.

FEATURES A challenging walk across open moorland, combining old and new Pennine Way routes. After following an easy path beside reservoirs and up onto Black Hill, the return route crosses dreadful terrain – including the infamous Saddleworth Moor – with difficult navigation making fair weather essential.

Wessenden Moor

The first part of the walk follows the Pennine Way over Wessenden Moor, a total of 5½ miles (8¾ kilometres). At the parking area, a finger sign points to a path climbing above Standedge Cutting. Joining a track heading east-south-east, this follows the course of an old turnpike, constructed in 1815 and subsequently replaced by the alignment now used by the A62. Off to the left, beneath the shapely form of Pule Hill, is Redbrook Reservoir, built to supply the Huddersfield Narrow Canal. Looking ahead, the Holme Moss transmitter identifies the location of Black Hill. Arriving at an old marker stone, the Pennine Way turns onto a flagged path heading towards a pair of small reservoirs (Black Moss and Swellands) (1 = SE 031 089).

Crossing a low dam above the neck of land separating the two reservoirs, follow a flagged path over cottongrass mires. The path swings around to head north-east, following Blakely Clough gently downhill towards the deep valley of Wessenden Brook. Switching to the right-hand side of the clough, the path follows a narrow

Holme Moss Transmitter

The BBC transmitter at Holme Moss is 750 feet (229 metres) high, with a base at 1,723 feet (585 metres) above sea level. When it was activated on 12th October 1951, it was the most powerful television transmitter in the world. The event was celebrated with a special programme appropriately entitled *Hello Up There*, hosted by Gracie Fields.

ledge around a bracken-covered bluff to enter the gully of Short Grain. Hooking around the head of the clough, the stream is crossed beneath a small waterfall. Joining a track heading down towards Wessenden Reservoir, cross over the dam (2 = SE 058 088).

Joining a track running south-east up the valley, this is home to a chain of reservoirs built to supply Huddersfield and the Colne Valley. Crossing a couple of side streams by footbridges, continue past Wessenden Head Reservoir to arrive at an unclassified road, which is followed towards its junction with the A635. Until the 1950s this was the location of the Isle of Skye Inn. Turning right, follow the grass verge beside the busy main road

Wessenden Reservoir, built to supply the Colne Valley and Huddersfield.

before crossing over to a finger sign pointing to a fence stile (3 = SE 075 072).

Black Hill

From here the Pennine Way runs over Wessenden Head Moor then up onto Black Hill, a total of 1¾ miles (2¾ kilometres). Joining a flagged path, this follows a dyke (Black Dike) running south-east across rough moorland. Stone steps lead in and out of Dean Clough, where the stream is usually easy to ford. The view ahead is dominated by Issue Edge, marking the steep scarp of Black Hill, with the Holme Moss transmitter beyond. Eventually the path turns south as it starts uphill. There is a stiff climb ahead, although the height gained affords good views back towards Holmfirth. As the path levels out, a few cairns confirm the route across the plateau. Despite being flanked by peat hags, the path itself is easy going. As ground conditions start to deteriorate, flagstones lead to the OS pillar marking the summit (4 = SE 078 047).

> ### Black Hill
>
> When surveyors from the Corps of Royal Engineers set up a triangulation point on Black Hill in 1784, the theodolite soon sank into the sea of peat covering the plateau. The summit still bears the name Soldier's Lump, although this may relate to another survey, undertaken in 1936. The hill seems higher than its 1,910 feet (582 metres), and although the official route of the Pennine Way has been improved with flagstones, the other approaches demand a significant degree of caution.

Wessenden Head Moor

The first part of the return route heads north-west off the hill, following the original line of the Pennine Way across 2 miles (3½ kilometres) of very difficult terrain. Even in good visibility, careful compass work is required in order to maintain a steady course while keeping to firm ground. The initial bearing is 310 degrees, with a few cairns providing guidance. Passing a ruined shelter that now serves as a cairn, the route heads downhill before continuing across rough moorland.

A number of gullies are crossed as the route runs against the grain of the terrain, and whilst there are one or two marker posts along the way, there is little trace of a path on what is a very remote expanse of open moorland. Here there is a taste of what the Pennine Way must have been like before it was tamed. However, as a fence line converges from the left, traffic can be seen moving on the A635 away to the right. Continuing north-west towards a fence stile, a hardcore track is joined. Upon reaching the road, turn left and head towards a parking area at the summit, which reaches 1,614 feet (492 metres) above sea level (5 = SE 051 063).

Saddleworth Moor

The Pennine ridge south of Standedge is covered by an expanse of open moorland and treacherous peat bog. To the east of the ill-defined watershed is Wessenden Moor, while to the west is Saddleworth Moor. The latter gained infamy during the mid-1960s through its association with the Moors Murders – a reputation which its bleak appearance has helped to reinforce. Beneath the scarp is the Saddleworth area of Oldham, with Uppermill at the centre of a cluster of villages, including the lyrically named Diggle, Dobcross, Delph and Denshaw.

Saddleworth Moor

The final part of the return route continues north-west across the infamous Saddleworth Moor, with another 3¼ miles (5¼ kilometres) of very difficult terrain. Crossing a fence stile, a long section of flagstones provides passage of a cottongrass mire (Featherbed Moss). The flagstones give out at the edge of a grough, with the route continuing straight ahead (north-west). Boot prints in the peat are now the only guide. At one point the route drops into a grough, following the sandy floor of the channel. Continuing over boggy ground, a couple of cairns are passed. Heading in and out of another couple of groughs, Pule Hill is now visible ahead. Arriving at Black Moss Reservoir, cross over the dam (6 = SE 031 089) and retrace your steps back to the starting point.

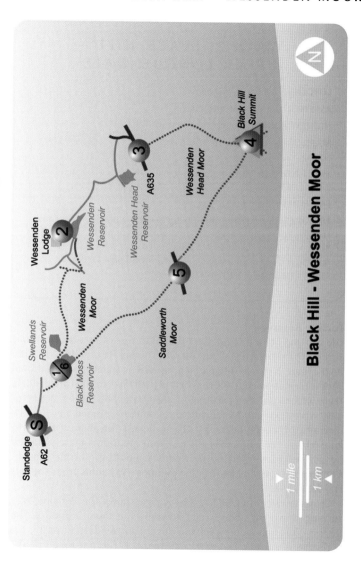

Black Hill - Wessenden Moor

WALK 2: BLACK HILL – UPPER LONGDENDALE

LENGTH 12½ miles (20 kilometres)

ASCENT 1,788 feet (545 metres)

HIGHEST POINT 1,910 feet (582 metres)

MAPS OS Explorer OL Map 1 ('The Peak District – Dark Peak') (West Sheet)

STARTING POINT Torside Reservoir car park, Upper Longdendale (SK 068 983)

FACILITIES Public toilets.

FEATURES An enjoyable hill-walk following a cliff-edge path above Laddow Rocks and a flagged route leading up onto the summit of Black Hill. The descent is via a broad ridge with some difficult terrain. A circuit of Torside Reservoir – including a section of railway trail – adds variety.

Torside Reservoir

The starting point is located on the south side of Torside Reservoir, 1 mile (1½ kilometres) along the B6105 from its junction with the A628. There is ample free parking, as well as toilets and a National Park information centre. From here a path links to the Longdendale Trail, which runs along a former railway track-bed. There are actually two tracks – an all-weather path on the right and a grassy bridleway to the left. Following the trail west for about 1 mile (1½ kilometres), the views over the reservoir are unfortunately marred by pylons. To the left is the dramatic gorge of Torside Clough. Converging with the B6105, the Pennine Way joins from the left (1 = SK 057 981).

Crossing over the road, a finger sign shows the Pennine Way turning down an access road towards the dam. Torside is the largest of a chain of reservoirs in Upper Longdendale, covering 160 acres (66 hectares). Climbing some steps at the north end of the dam, signs confirm the route as it runs through a pleasant stand of

Trans-Pennine Communications

Upper Longdendale has long been an important trans-Pennine route. From the Middle Ages, pack-horses carried salt from Cheshire to Sheffield and Wakefield. The construction of a turnpike was authorised in 1731. The railway followed in 1845, creating the first rail link between Manchester and Sheffield. This passed through the first Woodhead Tunnel, which despite being 3 miles (5 kilometres) long was built entirely by hand. Until its closure in 1981, the railway carried coal from Yorkshire and Nottinghamshire to supply the industries of Lancashire. In 1992 the track-bed was established as a recreational route – the Longdendale Trail – forming part of the Trans-Pennine Trail. The A628 remains one of the principal trans-Pennine routes, with lorries running bumper-to-bumper like modern-day pack-horses, straining to reach the summit.

fir trees. Turning up a stepped path leading to the A628, cross over the busy main road to where a finger sign points along a tree-shaded farm track heading towards Crowden. Passing a stand of conifers, another finger sign shows the Pennine Way leaving the track and turning over a fence stile on the left (2 = SK 068 991).

Laddow Rocks

From here the Pennine Way starts its long climb towards the summit of Black Hill, 4½ miles (7¼ kilometres) away. Heading north-north-west, the stony path runs along the bracken-covered

Upper Longdendale Reservoirs

Upper Longdendale is home to a chain of five reservoirs (Woodhead, Torside, Rhodeswood, Valehouse and Bottoms), with the impermeable shale of the valley floor permitting capture of the waters of the River Etherow. The chain was conceived as the world's largest, with the aim of helping to eradicate disease in Manchester. The engineer, John Frederic La Trobe Bateman, began work in 1848, with the first reservoir – Torside – being completed in 1864. Work did not finish until 1884. Some of the cotton mills built beside the River Etherow during the eighteenth and nineteenth centuries were submerged beneath the reservoirs.

slopes, with fine views up the valley towards the confluence of Crowden Great Brook and Crowden Little Brook. Gaining height, the path skirts a rushy mire before crossing a side stream (Oakenclough Brook) and zigzagging steeply uphill. Continuing above the terraced outcrops of Laddow Rocks, a small cairn marks a division in the path (3 = SE 056 013). At this point there is the option of a 'there-and-back' detour of 2¼ miles (3½ kilometres) to Chew Reservoir, following a cairned path running north-west over Laddow Moss. This was constructed in 1912, and at 1,607 feet (490 metres) is England's highest reservoir.

The Pennine Way continues north-north-east along the exposed cliff-edge path, with rough moorland to the left offering a poor alternative. On the far side of the narrowing valley of Crowden Great Brook are some distinctive rock outcrops known as the Castles. Heading downhill to converge with the brook, a significant amount of height is lost. Fording a couple of side streams, then crossing and re-crossing the brook itself, the flagged path heads gently up a broad ridge (Grain Moss) towards the OS pillar marking the summit of Black Hill (4 = SE 078 047).

Hey Moss

The first part of the return route follows the original line of the Pennine Way down a broad ridge towards Crowden, a total of 4 miles (6½ kilometres). The initial bearing is 155 degrees, with extreme caution required as an area of treacherous bog is traversed. Crossing a fence stile, follow a cairned route across stony ground until the path enters a grough, threading its way through the heather-crowned peat hags of Tooleyshaw Moss. Dropping to a boggy saddle, to the right is the deepening valley of Crowden Little Brook. Turning south-west, a couple of poles act as guides as the faint path runs over White Low and Westend Moss. Passing a cairn, the route heads steeply downhill before levelling out at Hey Moss (5 = SE 079 013).

The official route from here to the foot of Loftend Quarry has been diverted, and now continues along the ridge to Hey Edge before turning steeply downhill, keeping to the right of the quarry and its dangerous cliffs. The original (and better) route veers south-west, tipping off the ridge to join a stony track heading towards the spoil heaps at the foot of the quarry. This place is known locally as 'Moses Quarry', and once employed around a hundred people producing paving stones for the streets of Manchester. Continuing along the track, at a sign marking the boundary of open country, turn over a fence stile on the right. Heading down the steep, bracken-covered valley side towards Crowden, a farm track is joined. Arriving at a crossroads of routes, the track straight ahead runs past a campsite towards some public toilets. However, we turn left and follow an access road past the youth hostel towards the junction with the A628 (6 = SK 073 993).

> **Crowden**
> Crowden was once a busy little settlement, complete with shops and pubs. When the valley was flooded, a few isolated buildings was all that survived. Crowden Hall was built in 1692 by the Hatfield family, who by the early eighteenth century had become the squires of Upper Longdendale. It was demolished by the Manchester Waterworks Company in 1937, and is now the location of a campsite. The railway station on the south side of the valley closed in 1957. Crowden is notable for its youth hostel, which opened in 1965 to provide accommodation for long-distance walkers, being the first habitation on the Pennine Way heading north out of Edale.

The Longdendale Trail

The final part of the route runs around the head of Torside Reservoir to rejoin the Longdendale Trail. Crossing over the busy main road, head along a permissive path until a finger sign marks a left turn through a gate, following a drain towards Woodhead Dam. Off to the right are the reedy wetlands around the head of Torside Reservoir. Arriving at a weir, climb up some steps leading to a lagoon, beyond which is the dam. Crossing the weir by a metal bridge, an access road heads up through a larch wood to arrive at the B6105, where a gravel path connects to the Longdendale Trail (7 = SK 080 992).

This is followed back to the starting point, providing a pleasant end to the walk. The tree-lined route runs along the valley side,

Woodhead Reservoir

Work began on Woodhead Reservoir in 1848, although problems with water seepage meant that it was not finally completed until 1877. The dam was raised in 1990 to help prevent flooding. Perched above the reservoir is St James' Chapel, which was founded in 1487 by Sir Edward Shaa, later Lord Mayor London. An unmarked grave in the churchyard holds the remains of 28 navvies who died as a result of a cholera outbreak in 1849, during construction of the second Woodhead Tunnel.

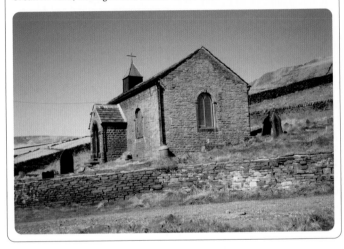

offering fine views over the chain of reservoirs. To the left is the steep, boulder-strewn scarp of the Bleaklow plateau, cut by deep cloughs and delicately wooded in places. After around 1 mile (1½ kilometres), a sign marks a right turn onto a path heading down to the car park.

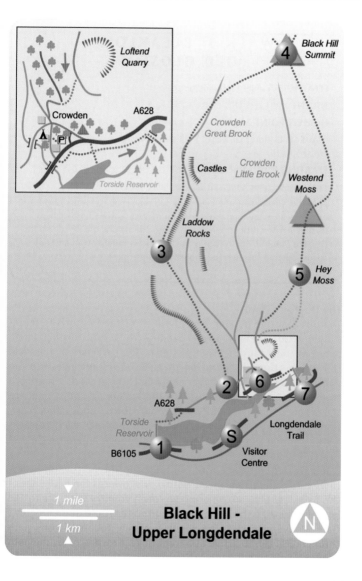

**Black Hill -
Upper Longdendale**

1 mile

1 km

WALK 3: BLEAKLOW – OLD GLOSSOP

LENGTH 13¾ miles (22¼ kilometres)

ASCENT 2,297 feet (700 metres)

HIGHEST POINT 2,077 feet (633 metres)

MAPS OS Explorer OL Map 1 ('The Peak District – Dark Peak')
(West Sheet)

STARTING POINT Doctor's Gate (start), Old Glossop (SK 045 948)

FACILITIES Public toilets at Manor Park. Inn at Old Glossop.

FEATURES Following the course of a Roman road (Doctor's Gate) up
onto the Bleaklow plateau, the Pennine Way is joined as it makes
its way across difficult moorland terrain and along a cliff-edge path
(Torside Clough). The return route includes a railway trail and quiet
roads, passing through the suburbs of Glossop.

The Doctor's Gate

There is roadside parking near the start of the Doctor's Gate, on
a side road (Shepley Street) leading to a bus turning circle
between some factories and a stream. The first part of the walk
follows the Doctor's Gate for 3¼ miles (5½ kilometres) up the
valley of Shelf Brook. A finger sign marks the start of a hardcore
track, which is followed east. On the far side of the stream are
the wooded slopes of Shire Hill, while dotted about the valley
floor are mature oaks and sycamores. As the track veers towards
a stone bridge leading to a farm, turn through a gate on the left
(1 = SK 060 947).

Joining a stony track as it continues up the narrowing valley,
there is rugged terrain ahead, with views towards the hard edge of
the Bleaklow plateau. Ignoring an 'open country' sign off to the
left, another sign straight ahead confirms the route of the Doctor's
Gate. Converging with the winding stream, follow a stony path
through bracken to arrive at a footbridge. Crossing over, the path
heads steeply uphill, with little to suggest that this was ever the

The Doctor's Gate

To the west of Glossop is the Roman fort of Ardotalia, known popularly as Melandra Castle. This was built around AD 75 on high ground above the confluence of Glossop Brook and the River Etherow, at the western end of a route running over the Pennines from Navio (Brough-on-Noe). This route is known as the Doctor's Gate, after Dr John Talbot, vicar of Glossop (1494–1550), who often travelled it on horseback. It was eventually superseded by the A57 Snake Pass, and although a section of medieval blockwork remains, it is hard to imagine that it was once an important thoroughfare.

course of a Roman road. Climbing out of the valley and heading across open moorland, at last there are visible remains of the old road. A short way to the south, traffic can be seen moving on the A57 Snake Pass. Eventually a marker post indicates a left turn onto the Pennine Way (2 = SK 090 933).

The beautiful valley of Shelf Brook, beneath the wooded slopes of Shire Hill.

Bleaklow

The next part of the walk follows the Pennine Way for 2 miles (3½ kilometres) to Bleaklow Head. A gravel path heads north-east along a deep channel cutting through an expanse of bilberry-crowned peat hags. This is the Devil's Dike, and is probably an Anglo-Saxon boundary. As the channel branches, marker stones confirm the route. Turning down a flagged section of path, drop into a gully (Hern Clough), which is followed upstream (north-north-west). Marker stones once again provide a degree of guidance as the

---

Bleaklow

Bleaklow is an appropriate name for such a forbidding place. The plateau is overlain with blanket bog and scattered with Millstone Grit boulders. The 'summit' – at 2,077 feet (633 metres) – is marked by a cairn surmounted by a pole. However, it is the nearby Wain Stones that attract most attention. These look like a pair of heads, and when viewed from the right angle seem to be kissing. The plateau is home to cottongrass, mosses and sedges, as well as patches of heather, bilberry, crowberry and cloudberry. The rare black grouse can still be seen here. Unfortunately, the plateau is also littered with the remains of air crashes.

route weaves around a bewildering maze of groughs, flanked by towering walls of peat. Clambering up onto open moorland, Bleaklow Head lies to the north. However, if visibility is good it is worth visiting the Wain Stones before continuing on towards the summit (3 = SK 092 959).

Torside Clough

From here the Pennine Way continues across the Bleaklow plateau, then along the edge of Torside Clough, a total of 3¼ miles (5¼ kilometres). Heading off from the summit cairn at 340 degrees, the route passes a marker stone and continues between the peat hags of Far Moss. Converging with a fence line, this is followed for a short way before turning onto a path heading west along the edge of a gully. In the distance is Torside Castle, a grassy mound among a sea of heather, thought to be an ancient burial site. Arriving at a confluence of streams, turn right and head down to a good crossing point (4 = SK 081 965).

From here a narrow path runs above Torside Clough, passing towering Millstone Grit buttresses. As heather is replaced by bilberry as the dominant vegetation, the valley deepens dramatically and the path becomes increasingly exposed, running above terraced outcrops (as with the route above Laddow Rocks, the rough moorland to the left offers a poor alternative). Eventually the path heads down towards Reaps Farm, where an access track is joined. Arriving at the B6105, cross straight over to join the Longdendale Trail (5 = SK 057 981).

The Longdendale Trail

The return route initially follows the Longdendale Trail for about 1¼ miles (2 kilometres) along the valley side above Rhodeswood Reservoirs. Arriving at a finger sign indicating a route to Deepclough, as the railway trail continues on towards Hadfield (where the line from Manchester now terminates), we turn through a gate on the left (6 = SK 041 975). Passing through a tunnel under the embankment, an access road is joined. This follows a lane running above the wooded banks of Valehouse Reservoir before crossing back over the Longdendale Trail by a stone bridge and

Glossop

The industrial revolution brought about a dramatic change in Glossop. As the cotton industry expanded during the late eighteenth and early nineteenth centuries, the population of the town grew six-fold and the centre moved from Old Glossop to the area around the turnpike cross-roads at Norfolk Square. The new settlement was originally known as Howardtown, after the Howard family, the Dukes of Norfolk, who had inhabited Glossop Hall since 1606. The town hall was built in 1837, with the market hall and railway station following in 1844 and 1847 respectively. The town received its Royal Charter in 1866, creating the Borough of Glossop. At one point there were fifty-six cotton mills operating within the area, although today there are none. Instead the town serves as a gateway to the Peak District National Park.

heading south towards a junction beside a water treatment works (7 = SK 036 966).

Turning right, follow a quiet road as it heads into the attractive village of Padfield with its Millstone Grit cottages. Taking the first turning on the left, head south along Temple Street, passing the Peel's Arms pub. This joins Platt Street before heading up Redgate. Arriving at a staggered crossroads, cross over to join North Road. A short way along the pavement, turn onto a stony lane heading towards Castle Hill (8 = SK 030 957).

The track runs around the east side of the hill, which as well as sporting a prominent radio mast is home to an old motte known as Mouselow Castle (a beaten path runs up through oak trees towards the grassy remains on the hilltop). From the hillside there are good views over the industrial town of Glossop and its older neighbour, looking towards the surrounding hills. Joining an access road (Hilltop

Old Glossop

In contrast to its industrial neighbour, Old Glossop is a pictur-esque village of Millstone Grit cottages, built around a square that is home to a twelfth-century stone cross. The name is Anglo-Saxon, from 'Glott's hop' ('Glott's valley'), and seems to refer to a local farmer. The village grew steadily during the sixteenth and seventeenth centuries, with wool then cotton being woven on domestic hand looms.

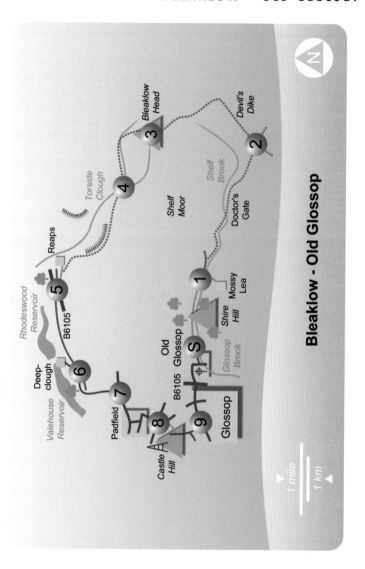

Bleaklow - Old Glossop

Road), head downhill, passing a couple of farms before arriving at the junction with Dinting Road (9 = SK 030 947).

From here it is just 1¼ miles (2 kilometres) through the suburbs of Glossop back to the starting point. Turning left, follow the pavement as it passes the entrance to Howard Park. This was gifted to the townsfolk by the Wood family, owners of the largest mill in Glossop. Crossing straight over North Road, join Talbot Road. Crossing the B6105, note the nearby rotunda. Following the route signed for Old Glossop, head along Hall Meadow Road and Church Street. Passing the stone cross at the village centre, turn onto Shepley Street and continue back to the starting point.

WALK 4: BLACK ASHOP MOOR

LENGTH 8¾ miles (14 kilometres)

ASCENT 919 feet (280 metres)

HIGHEST POINT 1,785 feet (544 metres)

MAPS OS Explorer OL Map 1 ('The Peak District – Dark Peak') (West Sheet)

STARTING POINT A57 Snake Pass, summit lay-by (SK 088 929)

FACILITIES Inn nearby.

FEATURES A simple route encompassing a short section of Roman road, a forest trail and a rough path running up a moorland clough. The flagged route of the Pennine Way is followed along a broad ridge, with fine views of the neighbouring Kinder and Bleaklow plateaux.

Lady Clough

Starting at the lay-by at the summit of the A57 Snake Pass, cross over the road and join the Pennine Way as it heads north-east along a gravel path. Arriving at a crossroads of routes, turn onto the Doctor's Gate (1 = SK 090 933). The course of the Roman road is followed south-east, with the medieval blockwork poking through the grass in places. Converging with the road as it passes the head of Lady Clough, head down some rough steps and cross a small stream before continuing towards a parking area (2 = SK 096 929).

Crossing back over the busy main road, this must be followed for a short way. Whilst there is no pavement or grass verge, a broad curb provides a safe footway. When the curb gives out, hop over a crash barrier and follow a steep path heading down into Lady Clough (this is not an official right of way, but it runs over access land). Crossing a couple of side streams below culverts, the first by an old stone bridge, a fence stile marks the start of a forest trail.

This runs 1¼ mile (2 kilometres) down through Snake Woodland – a conifer plantation climbing the steep slopes on either side of the clough. The forest is pleasant enough by the standards of such

> **The Snake Pass**
>
> The summit of the A57 Snake Pass is 1,680 feet (512 metres) above sea level, making for difficult winter driving conditions. The route was created as a turnpike by Thomas Telford in 1821, bypassing the original Sheffield to Manchester route running through Castleton. Whilst the road certainly snakes about as it climbs over the moors between Kinder Scout and Bleaklow, the name actually recalls the crest of the dukes of Devonshire, who were associated with Buxton. The famous Snake Pass Inn was built in 1821 as a coaching inn, originally known as Lady Clough House.

places, although one day it will inevitably be harvested. Blue-topped marker posts confirm the route, which follows a slippery path running parallel to the stream. Arriving at a forestry road, cross straight over and continue along a path marked by white-topped posts. Eventually the stream is crossed by a footbridge, close to its confluence with the River Ashop (3 = SK 108 908). From here a path heads east towards the Snake Pass Inn, although we turn right, passing a sign confirming the route of the Snake Path (the inn can be visited after completing the walk!).

Snake Path

This is followed west up Ashop Clough for 3¼ miles (5¼ kilometres). The stony path continues through the forest until, crossing a fence stile, it emerges onto Black Ashop Moor. Picking its way awkwardly along heather-clad slopes, the path heads up the side of the deep clough. Passing an old stone ruin, the clough starts to broaden into a boggy plane. The path crosses and re-crosses the infant river, although the route is fairly clear as it runs towards Ashop Head. Eventually a line of flagstones leads to a crossroads of routes, where the Pennine Way is rejoined (4 = SK 064 901).

Featherbed Moss

From here the Pennine Way is followed for 2¾ miles (4½ kilometres) over Featherbed Moss back to the starting point. A marker post confirms the route, which initially heads north-west, climbing towards the top of Mill Hill (5 = SK 061 904). This is marked by a

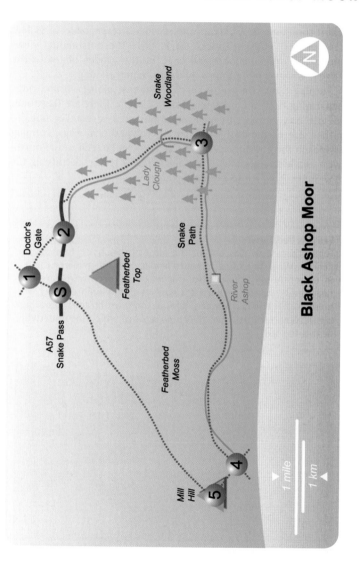

Black Ashop Moor

cairn surmounted by a pole, and reaches a respectable 1,785 feet (544 metres). Pausing to look back, there are outstanding views along the dramatic northern edge of the Kinder plateau ('The Edge'), which is more than 5 miles (8 kilometres) long.

Turning right, the route heads north-east along a broad ridge separating Holden Clough and Ashop Clough. There are flagstones all the way across this once notorious area of blanket bog. To either side of the path are bilberry-crowned peat hags, forming islands in the cottongrass mires. Glossop can be seen to the north-west, while straight ahead, beyond a line of traffic identifying the A57 Snake Pass, is the Bleaklow plateau.

Featherbed Moss

Featherbed Moss was one of the most notorious sections of the Pennine Way. An early attempt to manage erosion involved the use of unsightly plastic webbing. This was subsequently replaced by flagstones, and the path itself is now mercifully uninteresting. The bubbles that rise up between the flagstones testify to the continuing decomposition of the sphagnum moss of which the underlying peat is formed.

WALK 5: KINDER SCOUT – HAYFIELD

LENGTH 9 miles (14½ kilometres)

ASCENT 1,641 feet (500 metres)

HIGHEST POINT 2,077 feet (633 metres)

MAPS OS Explorer OL Map 1 ('The Peak District – Dark Peak') (West Sheet)

STARTING POINT Bowden Bridge car park, near Hayfield (SK 047 868)

FACILITIES Public toilets. Full range of facilities at Hayfield.

FEATURES A splendid hill-walk retracing the route of the famous mass trespass onto Kinder Scout. Heading up William Clough, the Pennine Way is followed along the plateau edge, passing the dramatic Kinder Downfall and visiting Kinder Low before returning by an old pack-horse route.

William Clough

The starting point is reached by following Kinder Road as it heads east from the village centre. As well as the 'pay and display' car park at Bowden Bridge, there is limited roadside parking near The Sportsman pub. There are public toilets opposite the car park, beside the entrance to Hayfield Campsite. The first part of the walk follows the route of the mass trespass, 2¾ miles (4½ kilometres) onto Kinder Scout. From the car park, turn left and continue along Kinder Road, following a leafy lane running parallel to the River Kinder. Crossing the river, a finger sign marks a left turn through a gate.

Following a path above the tree-shaded riverbank, the river is recrossed by a footbridge. Passing the entrance to a water treatment works, head up a steep, cobbled alleyway. As height is gained, Kinder Reservoir comes into view, and beyond it the hard edge of the Kinder plateau. Ignoring a stony track turning uphill, follow a permissive path running along the steep, bracken-covered slopes

Hayfield

Hayfield is an attractive village of narrow streets located on the River Sett. There has been a settlement here since at least Anglo-Saxon times. From the Middle Ages, it served as a stop-over on the pack-horse route carrying salt from Cheshire to Sheffield and wool from Yorkshire to Cheshire. The cotton and paper industries developed here during the nineteenth century. Clough Mill, which opened around 1830, was the home of Hayfield knitting patterns. Arthur Lowe lived here, and his character in *Dad's Army* was inspired by a local bank manager. A country fair is held at the village each September, with runners heading up onto Lantern Pike. The railway link to New Mills was closed in 1970, with the route now serving as a cycleway – the Sett Valley Trail.

above the reservoir until arriving at the foot of William Clough (1 = SK 060 887). This place was named after a miner who operated a smelting works hereabouts, or else a blacksmith whose forge was located in the clough.

From here the Snake Path is followed up the bottom of the clough, which runs north-north-east. Whilst the path is stony, it is initially quite accommodating. However, after crossing and re-crossing the fast-flowing stream a number of times it starts to degenerate. In places there is a choice of routes – that taking to the bracken-covered slopes above invariably proving to be the easier. Eventually rough stone steps and a line of cairns lead to a cross-roads of routes, where the Pennine Way is joined (2 = SK 064 901).

The Mass Trespass

The mass trespass onto Kinder Scout started from Bowden Bridge on 24th April 1932, with 400 walkers heading up William Clough. Scuffles with game keepers at Sandy Heys led to a number of arrests, with five of the walkers being subsequently imprisoned. However, public reaction to their harsh treatment led to the 1939 Access to Mountains Act, and in 1955 the first access agreement was signed for Kinder Scout. The car park – a former quarry – is home to a bronze plaque commemorating the mass trespass. This was unveiled in 1990 by Benny Rothman, one of those imprisoned.

Kinder Reservoir

Kinder Reservoir was built in 1910–11 to provide water for the Stockport area. It occupies the site of a print works that was demolished in 1900. In order to facilitate construction of the reservoir, a railway was driven up the valley from Hayfield. Clay to line the dam was dug out of the area now occupied by the campsite at Bowden Bridge.

Kinder Scout

The next part of the walk follows the Pennine Way for 3½ miles (5¾ kilometres) along the western edge of the Kinder plateau. Turning right, the plateau is reached by a short climb up stone steps. Passing a cairn, an eroded path heads south-east along the edge of the scarp, avoiding the rough moorland of the plateau interior. At Sandy Heys, a promontory edged by massive blocks of Millstone Grit provides a fine viewing point, looking over Kinder Reservoir. Continuing along the rough path, a secluded lake

Kinder Downfall

At Kinder Downfall, the tiny River Kinder falls dramatically over the edge of a Millstone Grit shelf at the head of a steep-sided clough. This recalls the name of the fell – Kinder Scout – which is probably derived from the Old English 'cindwr scwd' ('water over the edge'). When strong winds funnel up the valley, the waterfall actually spurts upwards.

(Mermaid's Pool) can be seen nestling beneath the steep scarp. Arriving at the head of Kinder Downfall, a jumble of boulders provides a ready-made picnic site and an opportunity to stop for lunch (3 = SK 083 889).

Crossing the infant River Kinder, the Pennine Way continues along the edge of the scarp, weaving between boulders as it follows a cairned route heading south-south-west. To the left is an expanse of bilberry-crowned peat hags. Crossing another stream (Red Brook) as it drops over a miniature downfall, ignore a narrow path heading off to the right and continue towards Kinder Low, veering away from the scarp. In poor visibility, navigation could be a problem here, with the route crossing mounds of peat as it heads south towards an OS pillar. This stands atop a boulder, and marks the usual target destination for walkers (although it is not the actual 'summit', which is lost within the inaccessible interior) (4 = SK 079 871).

A number of routes lead away from this point, so a degree of care is required. Heading south, a towering block of Millstone Grit (Edale Rocks) is soon passed. From here the path is flagged for a way as it heads down towards a terrain feature known as the Swine's Back, where we leave the Pennine Way. Following a rough path heading south-west around the bluff, a gate leads to a stony track that was originally part of a pack-horse route connecting Cheshire and Sheffield (5 = SK 077 861).

Kinder Scout

At 2,087 feet (636 metres), Kinder Scout is the highest point in the Peak District. It takes the form of a star-shaped plateau extending to around 6 square miles (9¾ kilometres), surrounded on all sides by steep scarps marked by Millstone Grit outcrops. The plateau is overlain with blanket bog, intersected by a maize of channels that seem to bewitch the careless walker. It is also a place of strange rock formations, created through the weathering of Millstone Grit. These have names such as Noe Stool, Pym Chair and the Wool Packs – although the correct angle and a degree of imagination is required to see the objects they are supposed to resemble.

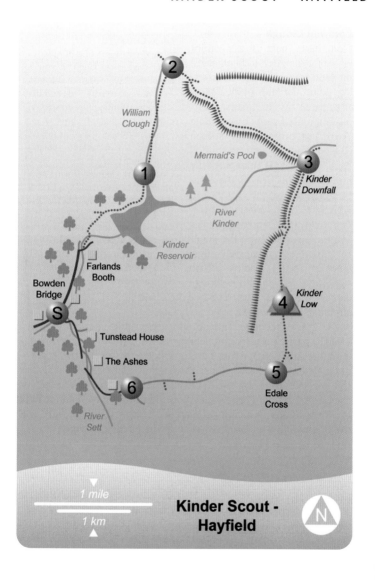

Kinder Scout - Hayfield

351

Coldwell Clough

From here there is a pleasant walk of 2½ miles (4¼ kilometres) on good tracks back to the starting point. Turning right, follow the track as it heads west, passing an old stone cross (Edale Cross) and fording a small stream (Oaken Clough). Pausing to look back, the view is dominated by Kinderlow End. This is the location of a cavern, the entrance to which has been lost since it collapsed in 1843. Looking to the south, the valley of the River Sett is flanked by a shapely ridge. Ignoring routes leading off to right and left, a stone bridge carries the track over another stream (6 = SK 057 858).

Edale Cross

Edale Cross is one of a number of stone crosses marking the boundary of the Royal Forest of the Peak – a 40-square-mile (104-square-kilometre) hunting forest that was gifted to William Peveril by his father, William the Conqueror. Little of the woodland remains today, most of it having been cleared by monks during the Middle Ages to make way for sheep grazing. Edale Cross is also known as the Champion Cross, from 'champayne' – the old name for this part of the Royal Forest. The date carved on the cross, 1810, refers to the year in which it was re-erected.

The track becomes tarmac as it continues beside Coldwell Clough, passing a farm and heading down towards the confluence with the River Sett. From here it follows the river downstream, beneath steep, wooded slopes. Arriving at a choice of ways, take the low-level route on the right, which crosses and re-crosses the river as it runs along the valley floor. Passing the confluence with the River Kinder, a quaint little arched bridge off to the right was the original Bowden Bridge, a relic of the pack-horse route.

WALK 6: KINDER SCOUT – EDALE

LENGTH 10¼ miles (16½ kilometres)

ASCENT 1,837 feet (560 metres)

HIGHEST POINT 2,077 feet (633 metres)

MAPS OS Explorer OL Map 1 ('The Peak District – Dark Peak') (West Sheet)

STARTING POINT Edale village car park, Vale of Edale (SK 125 854)

FACILITIES Full range of facilities.

FEATURES An entertaining hill-walk combining alternative Pennine Way routes. Clambering up a deep clough, the route navigates the maize of peat channels on the Kinder plateau to arrive at Kinder Downfall, before returning via the plateau edge and an old pack-horse route with a stepped path (Jacob's Ladder).

Grinds Brook

Travelling from the east, the starting point is reached by turning off the A625 at Hope village and following an unclassified road running up the Vale of Edale. For those travelling from the west, the Great Ridge is crossed by a difficult zigzag road. There is a 'pay-and-display' car park at the south end of the village, with a train station nearby. From the car park, follow a leafy lane towards the village centre, passing the Rambler Inn, National Park visitor centre and parish church. A walnut tree at the village centre is the traditional starting point for the Pennine Way (1 = SK 123 860). Nearby is the Old Nag's Head, a pack-horse inn dating from the sixteenth century, and a lovely pack-horse bridge spanning Grinds Brook (the latter being worth a short diversion).

A finger sign opposite the inn shows the Pennine Way heading west, although we follow the original route, continuing up the valley of Grinds Brook for 1¾ miles (2¾ kilometres). Heading up a street of stone-built cottages, a finger sign points down into a wooded clough. Joining a flagged path on the far side, the view ahead is already dominated by the hard edge of the Kinder plateau.

> **The Vale of Edale**
> Edale is a picturesque little tourist village of Millstone Grit cottages. The name was originally applied to the valley of the River Noe, which separates Kinder Scout and the Great Ridge, although it is commonly used for the settlement of Grindsbrook Booth. The five booths of the Vale of Edale – Upper, Barber, Grindsbrook, Ollerbrook and Nether – were the locations of temporary shelters used by shepherds during the summer months. The term comes from an old Scandinavian word for a shieling, and is connected with 'bothy'. During the Middle Ages the valley was on the trans-Pennine pack-horse route between Cheshire and Sheffield. The Manchester to Sheffield railway, opened in 1894, runs up the valley before diving into Cowburn Tunnel.

Passing through a belt of trees and crossing a side stream, the path becomes stony as it heads up the narrowing valley. Crossing to the opposite bank, the route picks its way up through boulders, with stepped falls in the course of the brook testifying to the stiffening gradient. Ignoring a side valley heading off to the right, the head of the clough is gained by a steep clamber necessitating a degree of care (2 = SK 105 872).

The Kinder Plateau

From here the original route of the Pennine Way is followed across the plateau, 2½ miles (4 kilometres) to Kinder Downfall. However, before continuing it is worth taking time to enjoy the magnificent views from the edge of the plateau. Initially a flagged path heads west across the neck of a promontory (Grindslow Knoll), avoiding the dreadful blanket bog to the north. Arriving at a small downfall at the head of Crowden Clough, instead of crossing the stream to reach the massive outcrops on the far side (Crowden Tower), turn right and follow the watercourse upstream (3 = SK 095 873).

Initially keeping to the right of the channel, the route soon drops down to follow the bottom of the normally dry watercourse, heading northwards. Climbing out of the channel, ignore a cairn off to the right (which marks the location of Crowden Head) and head north-west across boggy moorland terrain before dropping into one of the groughs that feed the River Kinder. Here the 'trench warfare' takes on a dramatic aspect as the route runs along the bottom of the deep channel. Following the watercourse downstream, the channel broadens as it is joined by others, and at one point is flanked by Millstone Grit outcrops known as Kinder Gates (note that water can pool here after rainfall, making it necessary to take to higher ground). Eventually the stream arrives at the head of Kinder Downfall (4 = SK 083 889).

Kinder Low

From here the Pennine Way is followed south along the edge of the plateau for 2 miles (3¼ kilometres), passing Kinder Low (5 = SK 079 871) before arriving at the Swine's Back. This time, instead of veering towards Edale Cross, follow an eroded path heading south-east to join the old pack-horse route at its summit (6 = SK 081 861).

Kinder Gates – Millstone Grit outcrops near the source of the River Kinder.

Upper Booth

The final part of the walk follows the Pennine Way for 3¾ miles (6 kilometres) down the Vale of Edale. Heading east, a stepped path (Jacob's Ladder) zigzags downhill beside a deep clough nestling the headwaters of the River Noe. Ahead are fine views over the Vale of Edale, looking towards the Great Ridge. Arriving at the foot of the slope, cross over a narrow pack-horse bridge (Youngate) and join a track heading south-east down the valley, which is populated with clumps of broadleaf trees. Passing between the buildings of Lee House Farm, this is run by the National Trust, and a display inside the byre is worth a look. Continuing along an access road, this dips into a dene (Crowden Clough) before reaching Upper Booth Farm at the start of an unclassified road (7 = SK 103 853).

A finger sign shows the Pennine Way turning through the farmyard. From here a waymarked path runs east-north-east across a

Jacob's Ladder

Jacob's Ladder was named after Jacob Marshall, who created the original stepped path on the pack-horse route during the eighteenth century. At the nearby Edale Head House – now a ruin clinging to the hillside – he provided an overnight stopping place for the pack-horse drivers. These were known as 'jaggers', recalling their use of German 'jaegar' ('hunter') ponies originally bred to transport animal carcasses. Today the path is busier than ever, with a seemingly endless procession of walkers ascending and descending.

Mam Tor

Mam Tor ('mother rock') stands astride the Great Ridge, which separates the Vale of Edale from the Hope Valley. It is one of the 'seven wonders' of the Peak, and is known as the 'shivering mountain' due to the frequent land slips that occur on its steep sandstone and shale slopes. The summit plateau – which reaches 1,696 feet (517 metres) – is the location of an Iron Age hill-fort. The caverns around the hill are the only significant source of the semi-precious stone blue john (from the French 'bleu-jaune', 'blue-yellow') – a form of fluorspar. The A625 trans-Pennine route used to wrap around the hill, but was permanently closed in 1979 after a major land slip.

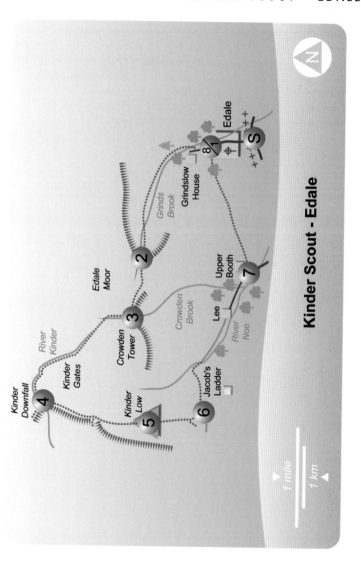

Kinder Scout - Edale

belt of pasture sheltering beneath the Kinder escarpment. Looking across the valley with its patchwork of tree-lined fields, Mam Tor can be seen, dominating the Great Ridge. A flagged section of path runs across some fields, before a finger sign shows the route turning down a tree-shaded path (Peat Lane) beside a small stream. Emerging onto the road near the Old Nag's Head (8 = SK 125 854), there is the opportunity for a well-earned pint.

APPENDIX: HILLS HIGHER THAN 2,000 FEET IN THE PENNINES

Whilst the Pennines can doubtless boast many fine hills below the 2,000 feet threshold used here, this is an established cut-off point among hill-walkers. The issue of what constitutes a separate hill is not as clear-cut as it might seem. This is particularly true with regard to the Pennines, which are generally characterised by moorland fells, rather than by the kind of dramatic peaks found in mountainous areas such as the Lake District. For our purposes, a hill can be defined as an area of high ground with at least 30 metres of all-round ascent (after Alan Dawson, *The Hewitts and Marilyns of England* (TACit Press, 1997), from which the information below is drawn). On this basis, there are fifty-one hills of 2,000 feet and above in the Pennines.

North Pennines (25 hills)

	Feet	Metres	Grid Reference
Cross Fell	2,930	893	NY 687 343
Great Dun Fell	2,782	848	NY 710 321
Little Dun Fell	2,762	842	NY 704 330
Knock Fell	2,605	794	NY 721 302
Mickle Fell	2,585	788	NY 804 243
Meldon Hill	2,516	767	NY 771 290
Little Fell	2,454	748	NY 781 222
Burnhope Seat	2,450	747	NY 785 375
Dead Stones	2,329	710	NY 793 399
Melmerby Fell	2,326	709	NY 652 380
Great Stony Hill	2,323	708	NY 823 359
Chapelfell Top	2,306	703	NY 875 346
Round Hill	2,251	686	NY 744 361
James's Hill	2,215	675	NY 923 325
Murton Fell	2,215	675	NY 753 245
Killhope Law	2,208	673	NY 819 448
Black Fell	2,178	664	NY 648 444
Grey Nag	2,152	656	NY 664 476

	Feet	Metres	Grid Reference
Three Pikes	2,136	651	NY 833 343
Viewing Hill	2,129	649	NY 788 332
Cold Fell	2,037	621	NY 605 556
Bink Moss	2,031	619	NY 875 243
Flinty Fell	2,014	614	NY 770 419
The Dodd	2,014	614	NY 791 457
Burtree Fell	2,008	612	NY 862 432

Central Pennines (24 hills)

	Feet	Metres	Grid Reference
Whernside	2,415	736	SD 738 814
Ingleborough	2,375	724	SD 741 745
Great Shunner Fell	2,349	716	SD 848 972
High Seat	2,326	709	NY 802 012
Wild Boar Fell	2,323	708	SD 758 988
Great Whernside	2,310	704	SE 002 739
Buckden Pike	2,303	702	SD 960 787
Pen-y-ghent	2,277	694	SD 838 733
Great Coum	2,254	687	SD 701 835
Swarth Fell	2,234	681	SD 755 966
Plover Hill	2,231	680	SD 849 752
Baugh Fell	2,224	678	SD 740 916
Lovely Seat	2,215	675	SD 879 950
Great Knoutberry Hill	2,205	672	SD 788 871
Rogan's Seat	2,205	672	NY 919 030
Dodd Fell Hill	2,192	668	SD 840 845
Fountains Fell	2,192	668	SD 864 715
Little Fell	2,188	667	SD 808 971
Nine Standards Rigg	2,172	662	NY 825 061
Simon Fell	2,133	650	SD 754 751
Yockenthwaite Moor	2,110	643	SD 909 810
Gragareth	2,057	627	SD 687 793
Darnbrook Fell	2,047	624	SD 884 728
Drumaldrace	2,014	614	SD 873 867

South Pennines (2 hills)

	Feet	Metres	Grid Reference
Kinder Scout	2,087	636	SK 085 875
Bleaklow Head	2,077	633	SK 092 959

In addition, the Cheviot Hills are on the route of the Pennine Way and the Howgill Fells are normally regarded as part of the Central Pennines – although both areas are in fact geologically distinct from the Pennines:

Cheviot Hills (6 hills)

	Feet	Metres	Grid Reference
The Cheviot	2,674	815	NT 909 205
Hedgehope Hill	2,342	714	NT 943 197
Comb Fell	2,139	652	NT 924 187
Windy Gyle	2,031	619	NT 855 152
Cushat Law	2,018	615	NT 928 137
Bloodybush Edge	2,001	610	NT 902 143

Howgill Fells (5 hills)

	Feet	Metres	Grid Reference
The Calf	2,218	676	SD 667 970
Calders	2,211	674	SD 670 960
Fell Head	2,100	640	SD 649 981
Yarlside	2,096	639	SD 685 985
Randygill Top	2,047	624	NY 687 000

SELECT BIBLIOGRAPHY

Bédoyère, G., *Hadrian's Wall: History and Guide* (Tempus Publishing Ltd, 1998).

Breeze, D.J. & Dobson, B., *Hadrian's Wall* (Penguin Books, 2000).

Countryside Agency, *Countryside Character Initiative*, Volumes 1, 2 & 3 (1998).

Dawson, A., *Hewitts and Marilyns of England* (TACit Press, 1997).

Gillham, J., *Pennine Ways* (Crowood Press Ltd, 1994).

____, *South Pennines* (Dalesman Walking Guides, 1996).

Hall, A., *North Pennines* (Dalesman Walking Guides, 1996).

____, *Border Country: A Walker's Guide* (Cicerone, 1999).

Hannon, P., *Northern Peak* (Hillside Publications, 1997).

Harding, M., *Walking the Dales* (Mermaid Books, 1989).

____, *Walking the Peak and Pennines* (Michael Joseph Ltd, 1992).

Hopkins, A., *Northumberland National Park* (Webb & Bower Ltd, 1987, Pevensey Guides, 2002).

____, *Pennine Way South: Edale to Bowes* (Aurum Press, 1995).

____, *Pennine Way North: Bowes to Kirk Yetholm* (Aurum Press, 2000).

Mitchell, W.R., *High Dale Country* (Futura Publications, 1992).

Nuttall, J. & A., *Great Walks: Peak District* (New Orchard Editions, 1991).

Raistrick, A., *Pennine Dales* (Methuen, 1968).

Spencer, B., *Yorkshire Dales and North Pennines* (Visitors Guides Ltd, 1998).

____, *Peak District* (Visitor's Guides Ltd, 1999).

Talbot, R. & Whiteman, R., *Peak District* (George Weidenfeld & Nicolson Ltd, 1997).

Wainwright, A., *Wainwright on the Pennine Way*, (Michael Joseph, 1985).

Wright, C.J., *Guide to the Pennine Way*, (Constable, 1991).

INDEX

Illustrations are indicated by italics.

Aire Gap 247–8
Airton 257, 259
Alston 82, 117–18, 120, 132
Alwinton 25, 36
Arncliffe 238–9
Ashgill Force 124, *124*

Barnard Castle 168
Bellingham 57, 66–7, 70–1
  Cuddy's Well 67, *70*
  Gingall 72, *72*
Black Dean 295–6, *296*
Black Hill 327, 332
  Holme Moss Transmitter 326–7
Blackstone Edge 308, 315–16, *315*
  Aiggin Stone 307, *307*, 316
Blanket Bog 321–2
Bleaklow 338–9, *338*
Blencarn 139
Border Forest 58–9, 64
Border Reivers 22–3, 57–8, 79, 86
  Bastle Houses 57
  Black Middens *58*, 63
  Centre of Britain Hotel *87*
  Gatehouse 63
  Peel Towers 57
Bowes 182–3, 186, 188
  Bowes Castle 189, *189*
Brontë Sisters 278, 281–2
  Brontë Bridge 288–9
Burtersett 220
Buttertubs 214
Byrness 50–1
  Byrness Chapel 50

Calderdale 278, 294
Cam High Road 218, 221
Canals
  Huddersfield Narrow 277, 325
  Leeds & Liverpool 246, *246*, *249*, 264, *266*
  Rochdale 276, *276*, 300, 301, 304
  Tyne-Solway 87
Cashwell Mine 134
Castleshaw (Rigodunum) Fort 317
Cauldron Snout *17*, 154, 159–60
Causeys (Pack-Horse Routes) 275, 323
  Long Causeway 303
Central Pennine Fells 196
  Three Peaks 222, 227, 229, 233
Cheviot Adder 44, 59
Cheviot Hills 21, *42*
Cheviot Sheep 23–4
Cheviot, The 25, 32–4, *33*
  Hanging Stone 34
  Hen Hole 32
Cloth Manufacturing (South Pennines) 273–5, *283*
  Gibson Mill *274*, 297
Corpse Road (Garrigill – Knock) 133, 140–2
Cottonshopeburnfoot 53
Cowling 268
Crag Lough 90
Cragg Vale Coiners 310
Cross Fell 8, 135, 140
  Greg's Hut 134
Crowden 333
Crowden Great Brook (Laddow Rocks) *9*, 321, 332

INDEX

Denshaw 317

Dere Street 45–6
  Brownhart Law Signal Station 47
  Chew Green 46

Doctor's Gate 336–7, *337*, 343

Dodd Fell Hill 217

Droveways 23
  Clennell Street *23*, 34, 38–9
  Green Trod 173–4
  Street 37, 44

Dufton 143–4, 148

Dufton Pike 144–6

Earl Crag Monuments 284

East Gill Force 200, *201*

East Marton 263–4

Edale 11, 353–4, 358

Edale Cross 352

Falcon Clints *13*, 154, 159

Featherbed Moss 345–6, *346*

Featherstone Castle 110

Force Garth Quarry 173

Fountains Fell 240–1

Gargrave 256–7, *257*, 262

Garrigill 122–3, 133

Gearstones 228

Glossop 340

God's Bridge 185–6

Goldsborough 183–4, *184*

Gordale Scar 254

Great Dun Fell 135–6, *136*

Great Shunner Fell *198*, 211

Great Whin Sill 82–3, 96, 101, 129, 150, 160, 163, 171–2, 174

Greenlee Lough 79, 94

Hadrian's Wall 83–6, *84*
  Antonine Wall 86
  Carvoran (Magnis) Fort 110
  Cawfields Quarry 95–6, *96*
  Great Chesters (Aesica) Fort 101–2, *102*
  Housesteads (Vercovicium) Fort *85*, 91–2
  Knag Burn Gateway 92
  Milecastle 37 91, *91*
  Milecastle 42 (Cawfields) *16*, 95
  Sycamore Gap 89–90
  Walltown Quarry 100–1

Haltwhistle 8, 82, 88, 103

Haltwhistle Burn 103

Hardraw 212

Hardraw Force 212, *212*

Hareshaw Head Colliery 68

Hareshaw Iron Company 68

Hareshaw Linn 59, *59*

Hawes 197, 213, 216–7, *217*

Hayfield 347–8

Hebden Bridge 278, 298, 304

Hebden Dale *14*, 297

Heptonstall 292

High Clint *194*, 213

High Cup Nick *12*, *129*, 149, 150, *150*, 152

High Fells (North Pennines) 128, *128*

High Force 172, *172*

High Roads (Durham Dales) 169

Hill Farming *18*, 23–4, *28*, 48, 166–7, *167*, 195–6, 202, 278–9, 323

Hitching Stone 286

Holwick 174

Holywell Cottage 74, *76*

Horton-in-Ribblesdale 226–7, 232

Ickornshaw 267, 280

Jacob's Ladder 356
Janet's Foss 254

Keld 200
Kinder Scout *322*, 349–52, 353–5
    Kinder Downfall 349, *349*
    Kinder Gates 355, *355*
    Mass Trespass 348
Kirk Yetholm 11, 25, 26
    Little Egypt 27
    Town Yetholm 26, 30
Kirkby Malham 258–9
Kirkcarrion 178
Kirkland 142, *142*
Kisdon Hill *197*, 206–8
Knock 145
Knock Fell 144, *146*

Lambley 106–7, 114
Lambley Viaduct 107, *116*
Landscape Designation
    North Pennines AONB 132
    Northumberland National Park 24
    Peak District National Park 324
    South Pennines Heritage Area 279
    Yorkshire Dales National Park 199
Langstrothdale Chase 223–4
Lead Mining 128–32, *130*
    Allenheads Heritage Centre 131
    Killhope Lead-mining Centre 130
    Nenthead Mines 130
Levy Pool 183
Lime Kilns 63
Limestone Features 193–5, 226–7,
    230, 233, 236, 244, 251, 254
    Hull Pot 233
    Hunt Pot 236
Ling Gill 222–3, *222*
Little Dun Fell 135

Littondale 233, 239, 242
Longdendale 331
Longdendale Trail 333–4, 339
Lothersdale 268, *272*
Low Force *164*, 171
Lumbutts Mill 303

M62 (Trans-Pennine Motorway)
    314–5
Maiden Way 107, 110, 114, 119
    Whitley Castle 119, *119*
Maize Beck Gorge 155, *156*
Malham 244, 250, 258
Malham Cove 251, *251*
Malham Tarn 239, 252
Malham Tarn House 239–40
Mam Tor 356–8
Mastiles Lane 253
Methodism 165–6
Middleton-in-Teesdale 132, 168–9,
    170–1, 178
Millstone Grit 273, 320–2
Monasteries (Yorkshire Dales) 195,
    228, 233, 241, 253
Moorland Management 190
Muker-in-Swaledale 205–6, *206*

Old Glossop 336, 340
Otterburn Training Area 25, 45,
    52–3
Oughtershaw 224

Padfield 340
Padon Hill 62
Pendle Hill 248, 251, 269
Pennine Ridge (South Tynedale) 88
Pen-y-ghent 235–6, *235*, 242
Ponden Hall 282, *282*
Prince Bishops (County Durham) 165

INDEX

Raby Estate 167

Ravens Knowe 51

Reservoirs
  Baitings 306
  Balderhead 177
  Blackton *168*, 176–7
  Catcleugh 52, *52*
  Chew 332
  Cow Green 154, 156, *162*
  Derwent Valley 323
  Grassholme 177–8
  Hebden Water 288
  Hollingworth Lake 316
  Hury 176–7, 180, *180*
  Kielder 59
  Kinder 349
  Ponden 281
  Ryburn 306
  Selset 177–8
  Summit (Rochdale Canal) 309
  Torside 330–1, 333
  Upper Longdendale 331
  Walshaw Dean *278*, 287
  Wessenden *326*
  Withens Clough 310
  Woodhead 334, *334*

Ribblesdale 229

Rivers
  Aire 193, 244, *244*, 247, 257–8
  Calder 294, 300, 301
  Coquet 48, 53
  Greta 185–6, 188
  North Tyne 56, 70
  Rede 50, 56
  Ribble 193, 226, 228–9
  South Tyne 82, 87, 120, 122, 126, 138
  Swale *7*, 193, 200, 204, 207
  Tees 135, 159, 163, 170–3

  Ure 193, 212–13, 218
  Wharfe 193, 218, 223, 239

Saddleworth Moor 328

Schil, The 27, 31–2

Sedbusk 213

Semer Water 220

Settle and Carlisle Railway 198

Skipton Castle 247

Slaggyford 112–13

Snake Pass 344

Sourhope 31, *31*

South Pennine Fells 321

South Tynedale Railway 113

South Tyne Trail 106, 112, 116, 120, 126

Stainmore Pass 185

Stanbury 282–3

Standedge 314

Stanegate 83
  Chesterholm (Vindolanda) Fort 97

Stonehaugh 73–4, 77, *78*

Stoodley Pike 293, 302, *302*

Sugar Limestone 129

Swaledale 207

Swaledale Sheep 196

Tan Hill Inn 190, 192, 210

Tees Valley Railway 179

Teesdale 163

Thirlwall Castle 109, *109*

Thornton-in-Craven 263, 269

Thwaite 205–6, 210–11

Top Withins 288, *289*

Tyne Gap 86–7

Vale of Edale 354, 356

Warcop Training Area 154–5
Wensleydale 218
Widdy Bank Farm 159
Windy Gyle *37, 38*
Wolf Stones 281
Worth Valley Railway 248
Wynch Bridge 171

Yearning Hall 47